Paradox

Christ versus Marx

The China Paradox

Christ versus Marx

by

George N. Patterson

WORD PUBLISHING

WORD (UK) Ltd
Milton Keynes, England

WORD AUSTRALIA
Heathmont, Victoria, Australia

STRUIK CHRISTIAN BOOKS (PTY) LTD
Maitland, South Africa

ALBY COMMERCIAL ENTERPRISES PTE LTD
Balmoral Road, Singapore

CHRISTIAN MARKETING NEW ZEALAND LTD
Havelock North, New Zealand

JENSCO LTD
Hong Kong

SALVATION BOOK CENTRE
Malaysia

THE CHINA PARADOX: Christ Versus Marx

ISBN 0-85009-320-1 (Australia 1-86258-083- 9)

Typesetting by Suripace Ltd, Milton Keynes.
Reproduced, printed and bound in Great Britain for Word (UK) Ltd, by Richard Clay Ltd, Bungay.

"The Christian church must be guided by the Word of God and by it alone. It must not forget for an instant that all political systems, right and left alike, are the work of men. It must hold itself free to carry out its own mission, and to work out a possibly new form of obedience or resistance. It must not sell its birthright for any conservative or revolutionary mess of pottage".

Karl Barth

CONTENTS

AUTHOR'S PREFACE

I first went to China in 1946 as a missionary on my way to the forbidden land of Tibet. I was pursuing a vision of knowing God and the possibility of knowing His purposes in the world in the twentieth century, and my possible place and function in that purpose.

I found China confused, chaotic, exploited, starved and ravaged, disintegrating from within. The Chinese Communist Army had conquered the territory north of the River Yangtze, but had not yet brought it under control; and south of the Yangtze the Kuomintang, or "Nationalist" Government of Generalissimo Chiang Kai Shek was but a name, no longer interested in control but in ways of escape from the catastrophe they had so foolishly precipitated.

Millions of homeless, foodless and moneyless refugees poured into Shanghai and other major cities looking for food and shelter, only to add to the confusion, starvation and misery which already existed there. Trucks plied the streets of the cities every night loading up with the dead bodies lying on the open pavements and ditches. Millions of defeated, leaderless soldiers roamed the countryside, plundering, raping and robbing. All central control was breaking down; all trade was grinding to a halt; mails were delivered with difficulty; all transport was uncertain, perilous and extortionate. In, over and through the chaos, making everything worse confounded, was the searing, uncontrolled, fantastic inflation.

It was the death throes of a nation, the end of an epoch. Or it was the shrugging off of a useless chrysalis, the beginning of a new era. It depended on whether one was north or south of the River Yangtze, east or west in one's ideological loyalties, left or right in one's political bias. For to the north of the Yangtze a new force in China's affairs was gathering, a new ideology was taking shape, a new China was emerging, the creation of persons and policies of China's first Communist, or Marxist, Government.

It was not only a new government which was emerging in China, but a new era which was about to begin. A new creed, a new spirit, a new orthodoxy, new alignments, new methods, a new vision of Chinese world empire, were the themes of all political conversations in the universities and homes I visited, and they caught the imagination of the long-tormented and frustrated Chinese people with their magic and promise.

This was my first confrontation with a dynamic Marxism and a dying Christianity. I saw Mao Zedung, as earlier I had seen Karl Marx, in highly personal terms: namely, if he with materialistic vision and human passion could revolutionise his country – almost a third of the world's population – I thought, why should not I be able to do the same or more with a spiritual vision and divinely inspired passion?

I, too, was sick of the way my country and the world was going: the stench of the hypocrisy, the sterility of the disillusion, the cheapness of the gaity, the ruthlessness of the expediency, the acridity of the defeatism, the debasing of the values, the scorning of the virtues, the destruction of the beauties.

I, too, was tired of the way governments were run: the cynical disregard of priorities, the abuses of power, the shameless acceptance of lying statements, the tolerance of corruption, the excusing of tyranny, the undermining of justice, the heartlessness of the bureaucracy, the public posturing and private cowardice, the empty ambition and emptier hearts.

I, too, was angered at the way the Christian Church was led: the confusion of its teachings. the inadequacy of its teachers, the weakness of its authority, the decline of its glory, the betrayal of its principles, the dishonouring of its commitments, the impotency of its representatives, the deceptions of its members, the decay of its sympathies, the loss of its compassion.

I, too, was appalled at the way the family was disintegrating: the lack of natural affection, the carelessness of parents, the thoughtlessness of children, the parents' absorption with trivia, the children's absorption with self-indulgence, the disappearance of shared interests, the increase in mutual disrespect, the multiplying of intolerable barriers between each other.

My selection of the theme and material for this book, therefore – particularly the spiritual ideas and emphasis – is both personal and arbitrary. It is based on two important factors: one, my own understanding and analyses of Mao Zedung's unique Marxism in a social and political revolutionary situation acquired in over thirty years' observation and experience as a journalist and practising Christian in Asia; and, two, the significance to me of the spiritual nature of Mao's revolutionary ideas for the committed Christian who, like Mao and myself, in his or her own lifetime wants to change the world.

It was left to Mao Zedung of China to meet the challenge of launching Marxist revolution based on love; or, in the traditional phraseology of the Utopian socialist, on "cooperation and friendship", epitomised in Mao's greatest slogan, "Fight Self, Serve the People". Some nineteen hundred years before Mao Jesus Christ had launched an even greater revolution with the command, "Thou shalt love thy neighbour as thyself". But in pursuit of His goal of creating a perfect society He forbad the use of force with the dictum: "If my kingdom were of this world then would my disciples fight". So the means to the end were diametrically opposed in more ways than one.

Both Jesus Christ and Mao Zedung wanted to bring

"light" into the world, and to change it. Jesus was one of God's "chosen people", the Jews, of whom God had said they were destined "to be a holy nation ... a nation of priests, ... to enlighten the nations of the world". Jesus was declared to be "the Messiah", the Anointed Servant of God, "the Light to enlighten all men and women", the God-appointed founder of the Spiritual Body known as "the Church of Jesus Christ".

Mao Zedung's declared purpose for the Communist Party of China in his lifetime was:

"In the present epoch of the development of society, the responsibility of correctly knowing and changing the world has been placed by history on the shoulders of the proletariat and its party. This process, the practice of changing the world, which is determined according to scientific knowledge, has already reached a historic moment in the world and in China, a great moment unprecedented in human history; that is, the moment for completely banishing darkness from the world and for changing the world into a world of light such as never existed before ..."

Whatever the ultimate evaluation of Mao's methods in seeking to realise his Marx-inspired vision, in his lifetime he raised unquestionably the social and political – and, yes, the *spiritual* – consciousness of his own Chinese people. Unfortunately, the true meaning of the word "spiritual" – the early Greeks had twelve words where modern English only has one – has been restricted to a rigid, out-dated, other-wordly, effeminate pietism. The Oxford Dictionary gives its meaning as: "of spirit as opposed to matter; regenerate man (opp. to natural, carnal); concerned with sacred or religious things; having the higher qualities of the mind".

Mao was not the only Marxist in modern times to accept the spiritual dimension to a socialist society. The Communist Party leader in Italy, Palmiro Togliatti, in a speech in 1954 declared:

"... We have to understand that the aspiration for a

socialist society can not only find a place among men who have a religious faith, but that it can also find a stimulus in the religious conscience itself confronted with the dramatic problems of the contemporary world . . ."

But Mao was the only Marxist leader to think and *attempt* the unthinkable: that the "subjective creates the objective", that mind might act directly upon matter, that a spiritual or non-physical reality might break through and change something held fixed for millenia instead of being a passive prisoner of an irrevocably historic process. Mao elevated spiritual ideas to a primary place in the Chinese Communist Party programme, and made them the core of his challenge to China and the world.

It was this revolutionary process which fascinated me during my thirty years in Asia as a "China-watcher" based in India and Hong Kong. Before going to China I had become interested in Marxism, rejecting it in favour of a dynamic Christianity; but, as I watched Mao's struggles to transform a nation with an atheistic philosophy, while I was involved with Christian leaders in India and China and other countries in Asia seeking to do the same with a Christ-centred gospel, inevitably I was drawn into the confrontation. This book is the story of the struggle as I experienced it in China.

Marxism will pass, is already passing, although it is only just over one hundred years old. Christianity has been in existence for two thousand years, derived from a Judaism that was in existence for another two thousand years before Christ, and it is once again gathering itself for one of its historical revolutionary forward surges. But twentieth century Christians can learn important lessons from Marxism, especially the form of Marxism which Mao developed and practised in China, despite its many weaknesses, in the same way that Jesus told His disciples they could learn valuable lessons from the Pharisees. The message of this book, therefore, is not so much the high-lighting of the failures of the institutional Christianity in China, great though these were, as demonstrating the superiority of a Scriptural and indigenous Christianity over any secularised imitation religion such as Marxism and Maoism.

Until Mao Zedung is exceeded by some Christian leader with similar commitment to a revolutionary vision – in unswerving application of fundamental principles passionately believed, in singleness of purpose attempting to fulfil an impossible dream, in holding responsibly the uneasy balance between freedom and force – the true Christian vision will never be realised: to create a perfect, holy people as the Spiritual Bride of Christ on earth. For, without this divinely destined vision the New Covenant people of God will fail as inevitably and as catastrophically as the Old Covenant people of God, Israel. Without faith it is impossible to please God.

The conflict in China between Marxism and Christianity inevitably reached the critical flashpoint: Which founder's teachings were more truly believed *and practised* by their respective followers? For some forty years in China the obvious answer was "Mao Zedung". His followers believed and practised daily "the Thoughts of Chairman Mao" on a scale only rarely attained by a very few dedicated Chinese Christians. The majority of Chinese Christians, when their churches were closed by an atheistic Communist regime, found the ritualised traditionalisms of Western Christianity were incapable of meeting the challenge of a dynamic Marxism, and they disappeared into unbelieving oblivion.

Except for a few who had taken the time and trouble to learn the challenging and revolutionary teachings of their Lord, Jesus Christ. They reeled under the onslaught against their faith; they were imprisoned; they were tortured; they were socially disgraced; they died. All the things that happened to their Master on earth. Only a handful remained to fight back, believing the words of their Lord, "greater is he that is in you than he that is in them". Their numbers now exceed the numbers of Marxist faithful in China, and they are thrusting in their sickles to reap a ripening harvest – with valuable lessons for the world.

This book is their story, and it is dedicated to them.

George N. Patterson
London, 1990

PROLOGUE

Marxist and Christian Revolutions in the 20th Century

On 22 January, 1905, tens of thousands of unarmed protesters marched on the great square of Moscow in Russia. They sang Christian hymns as they marched, and the only banners they carried articulating their protests were religious and not political in content. Those peaceful protestors were mown down by merciless rifle-fire from their own nation's soldiers. It was the spark which fanned the flames of the Russian Revolution which followed.

Over eighty years later, during a visit to China by Russia's Marxist leader, Mikhail Gorbachev, marching protesters, who eventually numbered over a million students and workers, demonstrated against the oppressive and corrupt Marxist Government of China. The People's Liberation Army was called in, and after a "Bloody Sunday" of massacre they imposed a rigid Marxist orthodoxy on a nation that had become tired of Marxist rule.

It was obvious to the informed "China-watchers" who observed the unfolding drama either on the spot or on television that China was on the brink of yet another revolution. Henry Kissinger, who, with President Nixon, had been responsible for restoring China's re-entry into the community of nations, wrote that there were three possible options for China following the nationwide protest demonstrations: one, there could be a descent into civil war, or chaos; two, there could be a measure of stability at the cost of continuing oppression; or, three, there could be a resumption of the policy of economic reform with some modest political concessions. Kissinger concluded that the third option was the least likely.

The main student demands were for "more democracy" and "less corruption". Unfortunately, they had no clear idea of what kind of "democracy" they wanted. Unlike Dr. Sun Yat Sen, the earlier revolutionary hero of both Nationalists and Communists who wrote the definitive Chinese political book, *San Min Chu-I,* ("Three Principles Of The People"), they had no strong Christian values on which to construct an adequate alternative political and social policy to oppose the failing Marxist theories. If Marxism failed to produce an appropriate political theory, as they were claiming so vociferously, then there was nothing in Chinese history to provide them with a satisfactory alternative.

China, historically, had been divided into seven realms, each with its own identity, each struggling to occupy the dominating position of "the Mandate of heaven". Encircled by deserts and mountains and oceans, the Chinese people had excluded all forcign ideas and directed their awesome energies inwardly. Every Chinese family compound reflected this inwardness of vision as high walls shut off outside views and internalised all the inmates' culture and thinking. Confucianism and Taoism and Buddhism taught the people compromise and detachment from circumstances.

The Chinese novelist Ya Ding, who participated in an earlier student protest movement in China, and who started the first Beijing University student magazine, has written:

"The West believes in God, but the East in heaven. But, whilst God has a name, an image, and leaves concrete messages (like the Testaments) heaven in China has neither an image nor a concrete message. Remaining vague always, this powerful divinity can only reveal itself through the agency of a man: the Son of heaven. Judeo-Christian civilisation has only two sides – God and man. Once God was out of the equation the spirit of equality and democracy among men emerged. Whereas in China, despite formal changes in the social system, man has always retained absolute obedience for the emperor – a habit of mind forged over the course of 5,000 years. So, under the title of the popular republic, Mao and Deng became the two Sons of heaven, both demanding complete submission from the population".

The people of China had been taught by its chosen leaders for four decades that Marxism was riven with contradictions. During these forty years since assuming power in Beijing critics of the dominant Communist system had been saying that the Party had no true legitimacy; that for all the apparent passivity of the people most of them were not just unhappy but were deeply resentful and increasingly overt in their acts of defiance.

After five thousand years of imperial tyranny and warlordism China in the twentieth century tried to change the continuing oppressive circumstances – which all their brilliance in arts and science and philosophy could not alleviate – by means of two important Western concepts: institutionalised Christianity and sinocised Marxism. One billion Chinese people were disillusioned first with their Christian Nationalist, and then with their subsequent Marxist, leaders. Now, as the latter arteriosclerotic octogenarians reluctantly cast off their mortal coils, together with their Marxist beliefs, the nation seeks another alternative. The million student and worker protesters in Tienanmen Square declared to the watching millions across the world that they wanted China to be "more like Hong Kong – Taiwan – the United States" in materialist possessions. But fifty million Chinese Christians inside China had emerged triumphantly from forty years of persecutions to assert the pre-eminence of spiritual rather than material values for the nation.

Soren Kierkegaard said that there are two kinds of revolution: the really passionate revolution, which tears everything down; and the other, bloodless, kind, which leaves everything standing but "cunningly emptied of significance". But the post-Marxist, twentieth century prophet, Russian exile Alexander Solzhenytsin, has added another, third, kind of revolution:

"...a moral revolution...because of a change to *inward* development..."; and he went on to quote Dostoyevsky in his *Diary of a Writer:* "...when, with the passage of time, a nation's spiritual ideal is sapped, that nation falls, together with all its civil statutes and ideals".

The most significant debate taking place in the world-wide Christian Church in the twentieth century is that between the proponents of Marxist and Christian philosophies of revolution. Although the latter has been most clearly and emphatically articulated by South American Christian leaders as "Liberation Theology" and is now being debated in Asia – especially China and the Philippines – it had its roots in the University of Louvain in Belgium and the Jesuit intellectual community there. The trumpet-call to that revolution was sounded by Pope John XXIII in his famous address, *Peace on Earth,* in 1962, in South America; and followed by the Vatican Council II, from 1962-5, which effectively decentralised the Roman Catholic Church's hitherto oligarchic authority.

Despite the many irreconcilables between the two philosophies of Christianity and Marxism the point at which they become most similar is in the concept of *praxis,* the important emphasis on practical activity over theoretical abstraction; or, better still, the uniquely dynamic inter-relationship of the two aspects. In *praxis,* experience is the source of the theory which informs the action; and the ideas which are inseparable from activity have meaning only in relation to each other. What this means in practice is the consequent inevitable change of both individuals and society.

In Christianity, love and righteousness, truth and justice, are things that you *do,* and not just what you believe should be done. This central fact of His gospel was stated explicitly by Jesus when He said:

"Whoever lives by the truth comes into the light, *so that it may be seen plainly that what he has done has been done through God*". (my italics).

And Chairman Mao Zedung, in one of his essays, *On Practice*, said:

"Whoever wants to know a thing has no way of doing it except by *coming into contact with it, that is, by living (practising) in its environment*...If you want knowledge, you must take part in the practice of changing reality. If you want to know the taste of a pear, you must change the pear by eating it yourself...If you want to know the theory and methods of revolution, you must take part in revolution..." (my italics).

This necessity to transform men and women *before* changing society has never been lost in theory by Marxists over the years, but it has been certainly ignored or neglected in practice, despite their fine words. In 1961, at the important 22nd Party Congress of the CPUSSR in Moscow, the creation of "the new man" was emphasised as a fundamental priority and categorical necessity in the statement:

"The Party regards the education of the new man as the most difficult task in the communist re-shaping of society. Until we remove bourgeois moral principles, roots and all, train men and women in the spirit of communist morality *and renew them spiritually and morally, it will not be possible to build a communist society."* (my italics)

This necessity for individual transformation is the second, very important, similarity between Marxism and Christianity. But, like the first similarity with *praxis*, it would be a grave error to assume that the superficial similarity in analysis of the individual and social conditions means that the respective solutions to the world's problems are equally similar. Unfortunately for "Liberation Theologians", they are diametrically opposed.

The idealistic youthful Marx tried to find a means of changing human nature. He failed, and became simply a social revolutionary. But, in the process of changing social and political structures, his "communist" methodology became a pseudo-religion requiring total belief and obedience and performance. The imperative transformation of the individual expressed in theory took second place to the transformation of society.

Like Christianity, Marxism is a philosophy of life for transforming the world. Marx's *Weltanschuung der Welveranderung* means literally "world outlook", or "philosophy of life", and "world change" or "transforming the world". Marx developed the theory originated by Bacon and Descartes, that it is possible to know nature and to use this knowledge in such a way as to master and change nature. To postulate that human history is not a meaningless and accidental sequence of events, but that there were laws of social development which could be discovered, accelerated and realised on the basis of that knowledge. But neither Marx, nor his disciples, have been able to solve the inherent problem of this postulation: how is it possible to transfer a thesis appropriate to the natural sciences and apply it to men and women endowed with consciousness and will?

Marx's early vision was to turn men and women, reduced to empty self-centred individuality, away from their personal selfish interests and preoccupations and to unite them with a community based on freedom and compassion rather than the exclusively self-indulgent dominance of an elite few. The new Marxist individual would not be self-centred but humanity-centred in all personal and social relationships through rational scientific logic.

Men and women, he affirmed, were imperfect, fragmented, disfigured, and incapable of transforming themselves. But the more they were able to appropriate "human reality" in all its forms, through the spirit as well as the senses and the intelligence, the greater was the possibility of being "whole".

The early Marx was passionately concerned with men

and women *loving* rather than *having,* with *caring* rather than *getting.* Speaking of "the whole man...the man endowed with all the senses", and the realising of his place in society by "appropriation", he saw love as an essential form of such appropriation. But in a world given over to the possession of things, to commerce and profit, this creative human act has shrivelled into becoming the mere act of "having". He denounced the mentality of "having", which saw immediate physical possession as "the unique goal of life and existence". This mentality had infected the concept of love itself, twisting the relationship between men and women into one of ownership and domination, debasing it into a "thing". Love was something to be made – "to make love" – and the lover someone to be "possessed".

In 1856, thirteen years after his marriage to Jenny von Westphalen, Marx wrote to her:

"The complexities in which study and modern education involve us, the scepticism we must necessarily bring to bear on all subjective and objective impressions, are perfectly designed to make all of us small and weak and petulant and undecided. But love, not the love of Feuerbach's Man, nor Meleschett's metabolism, nor again the love of the proletariat, but the love of the beloved, and more particularly of you, makes a man a man again..."

Yet love – or one of its predominant characteristics, compassion – is now a forbidden word as well as concept in the Marxism-Leninism of the Soviet Union. An American medical colleague of my wife, who has visited the Soviet Union on several occasions, wrote to her of his surprise when the subject of compassion was discussed on one occasion:

"During my stay I talked with many serious scholars who have concerned themselves with the goals and developments of the medical profession. The problems of teaching and learning ethics, the conceptualisation of the doctor-patient relationship, the complexities of inter-personal relationships, were dealt with directly and in depth...Strangely, it was compassion which raised a discordant note...

"The mere mention of *stradanya*, literally co-suffering, set Russian physicians on edge. Their pupils widened, bodies grew tense and voices sharpened. The most frequent immediate response was to label compassion a religious idea belonging to a dishonoured past. In tones of disdain and repugnance they explained that though there was nothing illicit or illegal about the word, it was not acceptable, simply that the concept had withered. Compassion has been replaced by something better, a national striving for the highest Communist ethic..."

What, it may be asked, had happened to change Karl Marx for the worse instead of the better in the search for "the new man and woman"? Where had his idealistic philosophy of improving change in the individual gone wrong?

Marx was born into a world seething with revolutionary changes. Following on the French revolution of 1789 there were the revolutions of 1830, 1848 and 1871, passing from the spiritual to the political to the social, and then to the industrial and socialist. Neither institutional religion nor secular philosophies could meet the proliferating changes and challenges as Western society staggered from one crisis to another.

Marx was born on 5 May, 1818, the offspring of a long line of Rabbis and son of a solicitor who had adopted Christianity the year before Karl was born. He attended a Jesuit school at Trier in Germany for five years, and went on to read philosophy, history and jurisprudence at Bonn and Berlin Universities. His personal search was directed towards finding a moral solution to the immoral society around him.

The young Marx was concerned with values, with high ideals, rather than the historical necessity and inflexible economic laws of his later years. He criticised the French Revolution for having produced only political emancipation and not "a human emancipation". The Revolution had provided political freedom to the individual, but had not made him a true human being who would live as a brother with his fellow men. It had created liberty, but not fraternity. (This is still a problem of modern Marxists whose atheism prefers the term "comrade" above "brother", and "solidarity" above "brotherhood". Men and women can only be "brothers and sisters" in a relationship where God is recognised as "Father".) The inherent problem was shelved by declaring that man still had to be freed from the bondage of his own inhumanity, delivered from his innate egotism; and Marx even quoted Rousseau in saying that the goal was nothing less than the changing of human nature. Later, in *Das Kapital*, he said, "Original sin is everywhere at work". But neither then nor later did Marx or his followers ever demonstrate how original sinners were to be made whole.

In Marx's thinking at that time the "new man" would have to put his inherent selfishness aside, and put the interests of others before his own, without specifying the mechanisms for change. In his "Eleventh Thesis on Feuerbach" he laid down his famous axiom on revolution: "The philosophers have only interpreted the world; the point, however, is to change it". He found it easier to provide axioms for revolution than to provide solutions for changing human nature, like so many revolutionaries before and since.

Marx knew of the love of Christ before he developed his own theories of the love of Communism. His first youthful composition had been entitled, "The Union of the Faithful with Christ", and in it he wrote: "...through the love of Christ we turn our hearts to our brethren for whom He gave Himself as a sacrifice". This theme was to recur several times in his later writings as a young man.

Significantly, it was not rationalism, nor humanism, nor materialism, which precipitated Marx's sudden departure from Christ-centred belief, but *occultism*. He became fascinated with Satanism, and his poems reflected this obsession; for instance, with "Oulanem", the name used in Satanic hymns and black masses to denote the Devil. In "Oulanem" he wrote:

"Till I go mad and my heart is utterly changed
See this sword, the Prince of Darkness sold it to me".

With his friends Bakunin and Proudhon he became a member of the *Dokter-Klub*, with its notorious occult ceremonies. His prowess indicated a perverse delight in the theme of destruction of men and women, and a favourite quotation of his was that of Mephistopheles in Goethe's *Faust:* "Everything in existence is worth being destroyed". It might well be asked, Sold in exchange for what?*

The point of this anecdotal digression is to suggest a significant change of emphasis in Marx's philosophy of change: from love as a constructive instrument in changing human nature to less idealistic and more ultimately destructive weapons of coercion. By the twentieth century Marxism was concerned primarily with changing social and political structures, and only incidentally with changing people – and that by official *diktat*.

As a consequence, the glaring weaknesses of nineteenth and twentieth century institutional religion, combined with Marx's own inability to devise a means to transform selfish into unselfish individuals, led him and his followers into ferocious attacks on the evils of "religion" – although Marx himself theoretically was not against religion *per se*. After Marx, Lenin was faced with the same dilemma – which has not been solved by any Marxist group in any Marxist country, but was attempted in China by Mao Zedung.

* Later, Joseph Stalin's first chosen pseudonym was said to be "Demonoshile", the demoniacal. It would be a fascinating study to investigate the actual part Satanism played in the lives and theories of the first Marxist leaders.

It has been clear to every Marxist leader since Marx that external social conditions are not sufficient to usher in the new world order they covet. *Individual transformation is essential*, not just in theory, but in practice, and it just is not there in classical Marxism-Leninism. Lenin thought it could be done through education, through relationship with nature, and through scientific knowledge, and he emphasised an investigation of "man's centre of motivation".

But seventy years after Marxist Revolution in Russia, the Marxist-Leninist leaders are still trying to cope with a dying atheism and an increasingly selfish and corrupt Marxist society, while a dynamic Christianity spreads throughout the Soviet Union and the Soviet Bloc and China. All the educational directives and official declarations of "State atheism" have produced only more destructive government policies imposed on an increasingly disillusioned people, and more overt and covert interest in religion in all the Marxist regions.

In June 1976, in a letter addressed to the Supreme Soviet of the USSR by 28 Soviet Christian signatories, they appealed for a change of policy towards religion because of the manifest failure of official atheism:

"...The aims on which the present attitude of the state to religion is based were developed more than a century ago, when the total destruction of faith in God was produced as a realistic goal that could be attained in the near future. But life has demonstrated the illusory nature of these hopes. The influence of religion is spreading, young people are being drawn to it. In these new circumstances we must not cling to points of view which life has totally refuted. The attempt to ignore reality is always dangerous in the life of a nation.

"We are not the first to make an appeal of this kind, and we are not so naive as to hope that it will be met with instant understanding. But our feeling of responsibility before our country and before history moves us to express our views in the hope that our word will be heard – if not now, then at least before it is too late".

Thus, the failure of the greatest Marxist Revolution of the twentieth century as the Soviet Union grapples unsuccessfully with the vital problems of human nature – corruption, selfishness, alcoholism – without an adequate spiritual philosophy.

Paradoxically, the weapons which Marx chose to effect his world-wide anti-religion revolutionary changes were "spiritual" – but not Christian, nor any other religion. They were satanic, in the full sense of that term (which means "Adversary"). Instead of salvation and reconciliation for the individual, as his solution he chose destruction and alienation for his main philosophical themes. And, final irony, he ended up with a religion anyway!

Marxism has its Bible: *Das Kapital.*

Marxism has its *Twelve Apostles:* Engels, Bernstein, Kautsky, Bakunin, Luxemburg, Plekhanov, Lenin, Trotsky, Zinoviev, Bukharin, Stalin and Gramsky.

Marxism has its *Ten Beatitudes:*

(i) Expropriation of landed property, and the use of land rents to defray state expenditure.

(ii) A vigorously graduated income tax.

(iii) Abolition of the right of inheritance.

(iv) Confiscation of the property of all emigrées and rebels.

(v) Centralisation of credit in the hands of the state, by means of a national bank with state capital and an exclusive monopoly.

(vi) Centralisation of the means of transport in the hands of the state.

(vii) Increase of national factories and means of production, cultivation of uncultivated land, and improvement of cultivated land in accordance with a general plan.

(viii) Universal and equal obligation to work; organisation of industrial armies, especially for agriculture.

(ix) Agriculture and industry to work hand-in-hand, in such a way as by degrees to obliterate the distinction between town and country.

(x) Public and free education for all children. Abolition of factory work for children in its present form. Education and material production to be combined.

By means of these *Ten Beatitudes*, every Marxist is convinced, all class distinctions will be swept away, all poverty abolished, all social, economic and political differences will be eliminated, all state apparatus and religious institutions will wither, and the kingdom of Utopia will be ushered in. Truth, honesty and integrity will guarantee it. From these will spring the appropriate rituals, customs, doctrines, ideas, beliefs, books, etc., from which all other external practices of an enlightened society will be sustained, the existential and experiential factors so fundamental to the believers of all religions.

In pursuit of this utopian goal its empassioned evangelists launch strikes, boycotts, gather petitions, organise private and public meetings, demonstrations, days of protest, pamphleteering, campaigns on popular issues of discontent and refusal to pay taxes.

Further, just as a sacrament is a religious ceremony or act regarded as the outward and visible sign of an inward and spiritual grace, so the Marxists' externalised rituals – from the most jejune sloganeering, jeans and jargon, to the most complex social analysis – become justified and sanctified by reference to the mysterious and sacred significance and influence of the "laws of Marx". By means of arcane knowledge communicated by these "laws" it is possible for all Marxist elites to predict accurately and dogmatically the truths regarding revelation, redemption, salvation, assurance, death to self and new life experience, penance for sins committed, forgiveness when penance is observed, and guaranteed entrance into the future utopian Marxist kingdom.

But all this – in the words of the ex-Marxist Arthur Koestler – to many millions, billions, across the world is already seen to be "the god that failed".

Of the seven original "Politburo" members in that "glorious October of 1917", Lenin died, Zinoviev and Kamenov were executed, Sokolnikov was in prison, Bubnov had "disappeared", and Trotsky was exiled in 1929 and later assassinated. By March, 1938, of the 24 members of the Central Committee of the Party in 1917, seven had died natural deaths, six had been executed, six had "disappeared", one had committed suicide, one was in prison, and one was "retired". Of both groups, only Stalin remained.

The greatest tragedy for orthodox Marxism, however, was its failure in the field of dealing with human nature, of which avarice was the most conspicuous vice. Greed, national and personal, for power; greed, national and personal, for status; greed, national and personal, for wealth; greed for personal advancement and national expansion; they were all indulged with a ruthless and unprincipled brutality by almost all Marxist leaders in the name of Marx. This was as true of the Marxist East European satellites as of the Soviet Union.

Classical revolutionary Marxism of the high ideals for a just and moral society failed because the followers of Marx betrayed those ideals in their neglect of the spiritual nature of men and women and the damaging hungers to be fulfilled.

Only Mao Zedung in China was prepared to address himself to this central problem of changing men and women in order to change society. In arriving at his unique Maoist-Marxist solution, however, it involved a traumatic break with classical Marxism – which still exists between the two Marxist empires. For a time, in terms of both numbers and extent, Mao was more successful in solving this problem than any other Marxist leader.

According to other Chinese Marxist leaders, Marx had gone well beyond all other social scientists in that, while the latter studied small-scale milieus, Marx did the same but within the structures of a total society. Other social scientists altered their societies with only potentially acceptable reforms; Marx condemned the societies totally, and demanded the sort of revolution that China needed. Significantly, it was the *material,* and not the *spiritual,* aspects of Marxism which first attracted the early Chinese revolutionaries. Writing in his major theoretical study, *On Practice,* in 1937, Mao declared categorically:

"It was not until Marx and Engels, the great men of action of the proletarian movement, made a synthesis of the positive achievements in the history of human knowledge and, in particular, critically absorbed the rational elements of Hegelian dialectics and created the great theory of dialectical materialism and historical materialism, that a great, unprecedented revolution took place in the history of human knowledge. Later, Lenin and Stalin have further developed this great theory. Introduced into China, this theory immediately brought about tremendous changes in the world of Chinese thought."

But Marxism was not equipped to solve China's problems, and Mao departed from it in several fundamental aspects. At first he patterned his thinking more on Lenin than on Marx, and then he developed his own unique synthesis. He stated this explicitly in a lecture delivered at the opening of the Chinese Communist Party School on 1 February, 1942:

"Theory and practice can be combined only if men of the CCP take the standpoints, concepts and methods of Marxism-Leninism, apply them to China, and create a theory from conscientious research on the realities of the Chinese revolution and Chinese history".

In his book, *Communist China Today,* Peter Tang confirmed this significant departure from classical Marxism-

Leninism by Mao Zedung:

"It should therefore come as no surprise that the Chinese Communists have assiduously neglected and even rigorously suppressed Marx's 'classical Asiatic conception' of Chinese society. Lenin, with his determination to exploit the revolutionary potentialities of China and other backward countries, completely abandoned Marx's classical view of a static Oriental society. Both he and Stalin rejected the view that such societies followed a line of development of their own, outside the dialectic course which had characterised the societies of the Western world ..."

Ironically, the only alternative to Marxism for the disillusioned and impatient Chinese revolutionaries at the turn of the century was Christianity – and that had been in China for many centuries in one form or another, and was seen by them to be part of the problem and not part of the solution. Christianity in China in the twentieth century was Westernised, institutionalised, organised, sanitised, secularised, compromised and paralysed. It was certainly not a revolutionary instrument for personal, social and political change.

The Christianity of China, like that of Asia generally, was either rejected or neglected because of its institutional-imperial-paternal character; it reflected the culture from which its missionaries came, rather that the teachings of its founders, Jesus and Paul. Historical Christianity separated from its indigenous Scriptural sources always compromised with the existing secular authorities to its spiritual detriment; whereas Scriptural Christianity was inherently divinely principled, dynamic and revolutionary, usually overthrowing or contributing to the overthrow of corrupt and oppressive regimes.

In his book, *The Gods of Revolution*, writing on the subject of the English, French and American Revolutions, the author Christopher Dawson has a chapter entitled, "The Birth of Democracy". In it he says:

"...this (European Enlightment) movement was not originally a democratic one and it was only in the second half of the eighteenth century that the democratic ideal was clearly formulated".

Then, going on to speak of Jean Jacques Rosseau as the real force behind the French Revolution, and not the usually accepted Voltaire or Dideret, he declared:

"It was he who first fired men's minds with the ideal of democracy not as a mere system of government but as a new way of life, a vision of social justice and fraternity which is nothing else than the kingdom of God on earth. It is true that Rousseau himself was not a revolutionary in the ordinary sense. The revolution that he preached was not a political or an economic one *but a spiritual one...*" (my italics).

But the historical institutional Christian Church at that time, both Catholic and Protestant, was in no spiritual state to deal with the variety of social and political issues being raised, and it was left to the Jacobin Society, led by the notorious Robespierre, to emerge as the "spiritual" voice of France following on the revolution. At first, even Robespierre – unlike Miraneau, Marat or Danton – regarded the Revolution as essentially a moral and religious reformation. Launching the new radical religious movement, "The Worship of the Supreme Being", at Paris, on 8 June, 1794, before a huge audience it was said that Robespierre himself "officiated as a kind of priest" and said:

"Is it not He who from the beginning of time had decreed the Republic, and has ordained for all ages for all peoples, liberty, good faith and justice? He has not created kings to devour the human race; He has not created priests to harness us to the chariot of kings and to give the world an example of baseness and perfidy and falsehood. But He has created the universe to manifest His power; He has created men to help one another, to love one another and to attain happiness by the way of virtue..."

Yet in time Robespierre himself became the embodiment of despotism and terrorism which destroyed the ideals of the Revolution.

Meanwhile, the Christian churches were in disarray, and "popular religion" discredited, and so the developing Secular Democracy of the Western nations became less and less interested in spiritual content and practices, principles and possible solutions, and eventually only used Christian religious representatives at ceremonial occasions. Just as modern Democracy was being born, historical institutional Christianity was entering its terminal stage.

Writing of this period in his book, *Evolution and Revolution*, W.F. Wertheim said:

"Evidently, in order to attract broad masses, a revolution needed elements of popular cultism that had been hitherto associated with religion. In later revolutions there were similar experiences. One could quote in this connection the Lenin cult in the Mausoleum on the Red Square in Moscow, or certain facets of the Mao cult in China...

"Evidently, the kind of fervour associated with religious movements seeks expression in familiar forms even though the prevalent revolutionary ideology is a- religious or anti-religious, as, for example, the branding of religion by classical Marxism as "opiate of the people". Each revolutionary movement, though rational in its means and immediate political aims, represents, at the same time, the dream of a fully renewed social order, and this dream may find expression in quasi-religious forms..."

It was this spiritually-motivated revolutionary ferment among the Christians of Latin America which caught the attention of the Marxists and led them to invite Christians to join in the struggle to transform the variously oppressed and exploited societies there in the 1960s. In his book, *Christians and Marxists*, the Latin American writer Jose Miguel Bonino wrote:

"Juan Rosales, an Argentine Marxist author who has given careful attention – and much incisive criticism – to the role of religion in our society, makes this rather startling assertion:

'...the bringing about of true revolutionary transformation in our country...is for us (communists) *inconceivable* without the participation of a renewed and engaged Christianity, which is equipped to make its specific contribution to the revolutionary baggage'.

"But right and left, ecclesiastical hierarchies and the common man in the street, the social analyst and the journalist, Latin Americans and foreign observers, are equally arrested by this new phenomenon: not a Christian-Marxist dialogue but a growing and overt participation in a revolutionary project, the basic lines of which are undoubtedly based on a Marxist analysis..."

According to W.P. Wertheim, already quoted, what distinguishes revolution from evolution is the cataclysmic character of the social change brought about. And Hannah Arendt has argued that there seems to be a special additional quality in the concept of revolution which places it in a different category from revolt, or rebellion, or mutiny. That difference seems to lie in the criterion that a revolutionary always aims at the overthrow of an existing social order and of the prevalent power structure; whereas all other types of protest, whatever they may be called, simply aim to deal a selected blow at those in authority and lack this vital aspiration to fundamental change of existing society. Chairman Mao Zedung of China summed up Marxism by declaring: "Marxism consists of a thousand truths but they all boil down to one sentence: It is right to rebel".

At the "First Latin American Encounter of Christians for Socialism", which met in Santiago de Chile on 23-30 April, 1972, under a banner displaying a man freeing himself from chains, were the words of the Cuban revolutionary leader, Che Guevara: "When the Christians dare to give an integral revolutionary testimony, the Latin American revolution will be invincible".

Another Latin American revolutionary, the Christian Paul Freire of Brazil, in one of his books, declared:

"I am more and more convinced that true revolutionaries must perceive the revolution, because of its creative and liberating nature, as an act of love. For me the revolution, which is not possible without a theory of revolution – and therefore science – is not irreconcilable with love. On the contrary: the revolution is made by men to achieve their humanisation. What, indeed, is the deeper motive which moves men to become revolutionaries, but the dehumanisation of man? The distortion imposed on the word 'Love' by the capitalist world cannot prevent the revolution from being essentially loving in character, nor can it prevent the revolutionaries from affirming their love of life. Guevara (while admitting 'the risk of seeming ridiculous') was not afraid to affirm it. He is quoted in *Venceremos:* 'Let me say, with the risk of appearing ridiculous, that the true revolutionary is guided by strong feelings of love'. It is impossible to think of an authentic revolutionary without this quality".

The hero-martyr of Latin American revolutionaries is Camilo Torres, a Roman Catholic priest who stated passionately: "I took off my cassock to be more truly a priest. The duty of every Catholic is to be a revolutionary, is to make revolution. The Catholic who is not making revolution is living in mortal sin".

Six months after Torres' death, in September 1966, the journal *Christianismo y Revolucion* was launched "to reflect the meaning, the urgency, the means, the movements of Christians in the revolution...because only revolution can feed the hungry, house the homeless, care for the sick, bring dignity to the dispossessed, freedom to the exploited, life to the drowning, calm to the frightened, happiness to the miserable, the earth to the meek..."

One year later the Latin American "Encounter Camilo Torres" was established to get all Christians of Latin America to work together, those "who feel that our duty as

Christians is to be revolutionaries and know that the duty of all revolutionaries is to make revolution". At its first general meeting on 15 February, 1968, in Montevideo, they issued a four-page newspaper, pre-dated 1 November, 1967, which included a Manifesto signed by seventeen bishops, entitled, "Gospel and Revolution: Pastoral Letter from the Third World", under the direction of Archbishop Helder Camara of Brazil. This Manifesto sparked revolutionary movements in Africa and Asia, the repercussions of which are still spreading.

China, under its Marxist Government from 1949 onwards, was isolated from all contact with this kind of revolutionary Christianity, but behind the "bamboo curtain" Christians and Marxists battled passionately and often bloodily for the revolutionary philosophies they espoused.

The greatest challenge to both of them was that China had a long history of ignoring religion as a means for transforming people. From its earliest records it was evident that they had never been a "religious" people. In over five thousand years they had produced many philosophers and poets, sages and artists, but few memorable priests and fewer religious leaders. Even the few recognised leaders of Confucianism or Taoism or Buddhism had more to say about the conduct of life in the material world than revealing insights of truth from the spiritual world.

China was always happier with superstition rather than religion; with responsibility to family and earthly authority rather than obedience to divine revelation. Both the parents in the household, and the local and national leaders, conciliated the spirits of the mountains and rivers and streams with sacrifices of food and other things. The five elements – minerals, wood, water, fire and soil – were associated with the body's organs, the primary colours and individual characters. The ruler of the country was "the Son of Heaven, the parent of the people, ruling over all under the heavens".

When the early animism of the Chinese was followed by Taoism, Confucianism and Buddhism they were all evolutions out of the lives of the people. Chinese religion had no "Messiah", no "saviour". It was an amalgam of sacrificial rites, magic, charms, alchemy, ancestral and other spirits. Ninety per cent or more of China's masses in recent history worshipped thousands of idols and material objects of historical, Buddhist, Taoist or other origins; and the remaining percentage of the intelligentsia gave recognition, respect and obedience to heaven, ancestors, Confucius, Lao Tzu, Buddha and a few other sages.

There was no belief in heaven or hell until Buddhism introduced it into China, and among those Chinese who might subscribe to the belief it was never allowed to affect their personal conduct in any way. Most Chinese believed in some form of astrology, almanacs, dream interpretation, charms, magic, horoscopes, and various other forms of superficial occultic superstitions.

Over the centuries "religious societies" emerged in different parts of China, based on sectarian "principles" devised by their respective founders. These drew their followers from artisan and labouring classes, or farmers and merchants, and occasionally intellectuals, and they usually ended up as "secret societies" with restricted membership committed to furthering their special interests by questionable practices. Several of these societies in the twentieth century provided the means for modern revolutionaries in China to overthrow existing governments – Sun Yat Sen, Chiang Kai Shek and Mao Zedung all came to power with the help of these religion-based secret societies.

A people conditioned by five thousand years of mainly religious superstitious practices, therefore, presented a formidable challenge to the two greatest revolutionary movements of the twentieth century seeking to win "the hearts and minds of the people". The Christians had greater experience, but many more failures. The Marxists had newer theories, but a poor track record.

The challenge to Marxism in China was that, in the century since Marx started propogating his teachings, no advanced capitalist society had responded successfully to a proletarian or Bolshevik revolution based on historical and dialectical materialism such as he had proposed; they had only succeeded by imposition in backward peasant societies with autocratic governments. How, then, would China with its backward and materialistic peasant society, but its long and respected cultural history and demanding intellectuals, respond to the ruthless twentieth pseudo-religion of Marxism derived from a Soviet Union which had already avariciously plundered China of some million square miles of her territory by means of nineteenth century imperialist expansion?

And what would happen to an effete and compromised Christianity in China which, in its modern guise, had entered the country in opium ships and enforced treaties from commercially unprincipled colonising nations, and which was publicly and universally identified with the corrupt and hated Nationalist regime of "Christian" Chiang Kai Shek?

That was the intriguing China paradox.

PART ONE

HOW CHRIST CAME TO CHINA

CHAPTER 1

HOW CHRIST CAME TO CHINA

Through Imperial Policies: The 7th to 19th Centuries

The exact time when Christianity entered China is not known. It is tempting to accept the legend that one of the apostles, Thomas, was the first to bring the teachings of Jesus Christ to such an influential people and country. But there seems to be little doubt among modern scholars that this is merely legend.

Another well-known legend is that Emperor Ming of the later Han Dynasty (A.D.67, the same year in which the Apostle Paul was martyred in Rome) had a dream in which he was led to send messengers to the West in search of a new religion. It was supposed to be in response to this search that, instead of Christians, it was two Buddhists who were found to be willing to go to China. This legend originated in the latter part of the second century.

The first certain date concerning the entry of Christianity into China is connected with the work of the Nestorian Church – "the Church of the East" – during the T'ang Dynasty (A.D.618-907). The historical record is taken from the Nestorian Monument erected at Hsianfu in A.D. 781, giving the date of arrival of Nestorian missionaries there, the then capital of China, as A.D.635.

The Nestorian Monument was discovered in 1625 when some workmen uncovered a great slab of stone buried several feet under the ground near the district city of Chou-chih, thirty or forty miles south-west of Hsianfu in Shensi Province. Professor K.S. Latourette, the historian, says that no ancient inscription is better known in the West, rubbings and models of the stone having been taken to many places in Europe and America for further studies. Although at first suspected as a pious fraud it is now accepted as genuine.

According to the text on the Monument, Christianity was introduced into China by a Nestorian missionary called Alopen. The record begins with a statement of Christian doctrine, followed by an account of the Apostolic period, the arrival of the first Christians in China, the fortunes of the infant Christian church there up to the erection of the stone, and finally a kind of eulogy or recapitulation of the history in verse.

The history may be summarised as follows: In the year 635 Alopen, coming overland from a country in the West named Tachin (suggested as "Syria"), arrived in the capital of China. The Emperor, T'ai Tsung, paid him great honour, sending one of his chief ministers to meet him. Alopen was brought to the palace, and there the Christian books were translated. After reading them Emperor T'ai Tsung promulgated a decree in 638 commanding a church and a monastery to be built in the capital. He also gave to Alopen and his followers the right to propagate their faith.

During the next two centuries the Christians experienced mixed fortunes. Under the energetic but infamous Empress Dowager Wu, in 698-99, Christians were persecuted at the instigation of Buddhists. Then there was a favourable period. But in 845 the Emperor Wu Tsung, who was an ardent Taoist, issued an edict proscribing Buddhism, condemned 4,600 monasteries to be destroyed and ordered 300 foreign priests "to return to secular life, to the end that the customs of the empire may be uniform".

The Prophet Mohammed died in 632, and the first impact of his terrifying proselytising followers was on the Syrian region from which Alopen had come. As the followers of

Mohammed spread rapidly through three continents the Nestorian Church, which had begun as "a church on fire" but which had lost most of its early impetus in the intervening centuries, crumpled before the onslaught of the rival religion and, in China, was finally overrun.

By the end of the tenth century Nestorian Christianity had disappeared from China. A combination of militant Mohammedan expansion and absorption by a tolerant Buddhism contributed to the disappearance of that early Christianity. The absorption of Christianity by Buddhism was the most interesting, and still presents an intriguing problem to scholars: Did early Nestorian Christianity influence Buddhism, or was it Buddhism which influenced Christianity?

Christianity had several things in common with the early religions of China. Like Buddhism and Confucianism, it put great emphasis on ethics. Confucianism preached obedience to the ideal of a distant past. Buddhism promised Nirvana to the individual believer, but saw the world as "illusory" or evil. Many of the virtues held important by the Buddha and Confucius were also stressed by Christians, and all worked for a perfect individual. Confucian concern for an ideal social order and Jesus' teaching about the Kingdom of God had many similarities. The idea of vicarious suffering and of salvation by faith in the one who has so suffered is to be found in Mahayana Buddhism as well as Christianity. The ritual of Mahayana Buddhism as practised in Tibet is strikingly similar to traditional Christian ecclesiastical practices. Professor K.S. Latourette has written regarding this:

"Much that is distinctive of the Nestorian, Russian Orthodox, and Roman Catholic Churches bears a striking resemblance to Mahayana Buddhism. All have monastic communities with attendant ascetic ideals. All have elaborate rituals. Christian saints have a likeness to Bodhisattvas. To the Chinese these three Churches do not come, then, as entirely strange. There is even the danger that because of the resemblance the Chinese may identify the ideas derived from Buddhism with the apparently similar but really different teachings of the Church".

Some of these practices may have been inherited from the later Genghiz Khan period when he encouraged several religions to send missionaries to his court. In 1245, after the Council of Lyons, Pope Innocent IV sent John de Plane Carpini and other monks to intercede with Genghiz Khan's son, the new Khan Ogdai. When they arrived two years later they found Greek Christians and a chapel already in existence. In 1262 Kublai Khan made provision for Christians in a decree, as well as for followers of other religions. Marco Polo found Christians at Baghdad, Kashgar, Yarkhand, Samarkhand and several other places in his travels.

In the early fourteenth century the celebrated Franciscan Friar Oderic visited China with other monks and founded Christian communities. Following on his death Archbishop Nicholas went to China and reached Peking in 1342. Soon afterwards the whole Mongol empire in China began to crumble, and for the next three centuries no mention of Christians appears in any Chinese annals.

In 1517 the first Western ships appeared in Canton in South China. These were Portuguese vessels who had just established their presence in Malacca and had discovered for the first time that the fabled Cathay of Marco Polo was the land of China, now open to their adventurous ships from the sea.

Strictly speaking, although there had been several missionary attempts by Roman Catholics to "evangelise" China in the intervening centuries, it was not until the sixteenth century and the arrival of the Roman Catholic Francis Xavier that Christianity began once again to make any impression on China. This period of Roman Catholic effort synchronized with the Renaissance and Reformation movements in Europe, and the great exploratory ventures that were to influence profoundly the whole world.

When Ignatius, the Founder-General of the new order called "Society of Jesus", or Jesuits, commanded one of the founder-members, Francis Xavier, to set sail for the conversion of India, they had to seek material aid from Portugal. The only way to reach India in 1541 was by Portuguese ship because only the Portuguese had knowledge of routes, winds, currents, etcetera, and they kept their knowledge a closely guarded secret to safeguard Portugal's imperial commercial interests. As a consequence, the Church's missions in the East were linked with the power and politics of Portugal. For example, its rulers claimed the right to appoint bishops, a claim which in later years seriously affected the progress of the Church in Asia. The story of Francis Xavier's labour in India, his mission to Japan, and his death off the coast of China, is a fascinating dichotomous record of inspiring spiritual zeal and depressing human failings.

In 1560 the Portuguese took Macao, the small peninsula jutting into the China Sea off the south coast of China; and in 1574 Father Alexander Valignane, Superintendent of the Jesuits' mission to the East, settled there. The words regarding China so frequently ascribed to Francis Xavier – "O rock, rock, rock, when wilt thou open to my Lord?" – were really spoken by Valignane. He was the one who selected and sent Fathers Michele Ruggieri and Matthew Ricci in a "new approach" to introduce Christianity into China once again. He wrote to the General of the Society of Jesus: "The only possible way to penetration will be completely different from that which has been adopted up to now in all the other missions in these countries".

This "new approach" was to influence the whole Christian commitment, both Roman Catholic and Protestant, for the next four centuries. Father Valignane maintained that the Chinese respect for learning, and their readiness to listen to anything that was put to them in an intelligent way rather than as the religion of a civilisation which claimed superiority to their own, would more readily open their minds to the acceptance of Christianity. Therefore, he gave instructions that all who were assigned to missionary work in China must as a necessary preliminary learn to read, write, and speak Chinese and acquaint themselves thoroughly with Chinese literature and Chinese manners and customs.

In 1582 Father Ricci succeeded in entering China, via Canton, and began his work in the city of Chao-ch'ing. In the hall of the household they hung up a map of the whole world, with the names in Arabic characters. The Chinese visitors were so interested they asked for it to be copied, but with Chinese characters superimposed. This created great excitement and discussion, for the Chinese maps of the "whole world" at that time showed China dominating all with its fifteen provinces and a few islands scattered around its perimeters. All of these islands put together did not add up in size to the smallest of one of China's provinces, so the Jesuit maps with their diminished importance shocked the country's scholars. Eventually, so many copies were printed that they were distributed all over China and, according to Father Ricci, "it was the best and most useful work that could be done at that time to dispose the Chinese to give credit to the things of the Faith".

In addition to the map they brought and built clocks of all kinds, fine oil paintings, and other prints, mathematical instruments and many manufactured items from European craftsmen. They also brought books and illuminated manuscripts covering a variety of subjects, pictures and diagrams; musical instruments of different kinds which greatly amused the Chinese but also gave them a greater appreciation of the culture of those they had always considered "barbarians".

This was the manner in which Christianity came to China in the sixteenth century, and it became the standard approach. Christianity became identified with the secular learning, techniques and material benefits of the West, at the expense of the revolutionary, individual-transforming, spiritual teachings of Jesus Christ.

Father Ricci soon decided that the only way in which the whole Christian missionary venture to China could be placed on a secure base was to obtain the formal recognition of the Emperor; otherwise the project could be endangered at any moment if some antagonistic minor Chinese official reported adversely the presence of strangers in the country. To obtain this recognition he had to get to Peking. In order to make themselves acceptable to the Chinese scholars on the way, he and his missionary companions grew long beards and long hair (to distinguish them from the poorly regarded Chinese monks, or bonzes), and wore the distinctive dress of Chinese scholars.

Ricci arrived in Peking in 1601, just twenty-one years after landing in Macao. Since that time missions had been set up in several places between Macao and Canton. When Ricci died in 1610, an imperial edict ordered a monument to be erected to his memory. His greatest monument, however, consisted of about 340 works on religion, philosophy and mathematics which he and his colleagues had published in support of the second stage of their work; namely, showing the Chinese how wrong they were in purely material matters, which they hoped would persuade them to see how equally wrong they could be in religious practices. By 1627 there were thirteen thousand Christians in seven Chinese provinces and by 1670 there were approximately one hundred thousand Christians in China. Among them were imperial princes, high officials and even palace eunuchs.

About this time other groups of Catholics, Dominicans and Franciscans, had begun to arrive in China and they were not welcomed by the Jesuits, and a bitter controversy arose among them.

Under the Manchu Emperor Kang-hsi (1669-1722) the Jesuits enjoyed unparalleled imperial favour. He appointed three Jesuits as his close advisers, primarily to devise a new "Calendar" to replace the ancient one produced by earlier Muslim astronomers, who had also used their position to influence the previous Emperors against Christianity. With these Jesuits able to bring new scientific discoveries to China – such as casting brass guns for the Tartar Wars – they were able to persuade the Emperor to conclude his celebrated peace with Russia in 1689, which brought the patronage of the Czar. The Emperor even gave them permission for a magnificent cathedral to be built in their palace grounds, and contribute towards its costs.

Unfortunately for their hopes a dispute broke out between the Jesuits and the Dominicans and Franciscans over "rites" in discussing the anticipatory question: "Shall China become officially Christian?". In 1698 the Jesuits requested the Apostolic See to permit the traditional ancestral rites used by the Chinese into the Catholic liturgy, and also to permit the use of the Chinese language. Both requests were refused. The Jesuits themselves were split over the question, but the Dominicans and the Franciscans were uncompromisingly opposed and they unanimously condemned the proposal. In 1699 it was agreed by Pope Clement IX that both proposals had merit and should be adapted to circumstances. The Emperor became exasperated and felt personally slighted by the on-going controversy and he expelled the Papal Legate, Bishop Tournou, from Peking in 1704. The Legate, in response, ordered the universal obedience of all missionaries and Christians under pain of excommunication, and their submission to Pope Clement XI. The Emperor then commanded that no-one in future would preach the Christian doctrine in China without his licence, which would not be given to anyone who should either disapprove of the ancestral rites or ever contemplate leaving China for Europe. The Jesuits applied for licences, and at the same time accepted the full submission to the Apostolic See decrees of 1710.

The Emperor, angered that any foreigner should dare to express an opinion on Chinese practices, issued an imperial decree: "Henceforth no European missionary will be permitted to spread religion in China. Thus we shall avoid further trouble".

With Emperor Kang-hsi's death in 1772 there began the decline of the great Christian experiment, which was to last until the opening years of the nineteenth century. A combination of factors – persecution in China, the overbearing attitude of the Portuguese traders in Macao, the haughty conduct of the East India Company in Canton, and the overthrow of the Papacy by Napoleon Bonaparte in 1809 – combined to accelerate the decline of the Christian witness in and missions to China.

The first series of wars in Europe between Catholics and Protestants had ended in 1555 with the interim treaty of Augsburg, which established the legal basis of Protestants for the first time. It also undermined the hitherto unique supremacy of Roman Catholicism, and removed religion as a justification for war. The Treaty of Westphalia in 1648 completed the process, in which Catholics and Protestants were given equal rights. By the end of the seventeenth century there were already at least a dozen different Christian denominations, with many others in prospect.

Roman Catholicism was not only in retreat, it seemed to be on the edge of self-destruction. There had been six Popes from Clement IX in 1667 to Clement XI in 1700. The twenty Popes in the seventeenth and eighteenth centuries were known as liars, murderers, adulterers, incestuous, hypocrites, in bewildering succession until 1788 when the 251st Pope Pius VI was deprived of all papal power. The French only recognised Pius VI as "Citizen Pope", addressed him as "Citizen", arrested him in 1798, and imprisoned him in France. Napoleon administered the *coup de grace* by overthrowing the papacy in 1809. The powers of the papacy were confiscated by the French – palace, Naples, Catholic nations and powers – followed by other nations. The repercussions of all this were felt in China.

At the end of the eighteenth century Christianity was forbidden in China, churches were closed, and Christians practised their religion in secret. When Robert Morrison arrived in Hong Kong in 1807 as a member of the Protestant London Missionary Society he had to earn his living as a secretary to the East India Company, and he was not permitted to preach the Christian Gospel. He devoted himself to learning the Chinese language, compiling a Chinese dictionary and translating the Bible into Chinese. When he died in 1834 there were three Protestant missionaries in China.

Meanwhile, the rise of French power in Europe, and the joint Franco-British War against China, gave Catholic missionaries fresh impetus to try to open the way into China once more. They did this by influencing the terms of the Whampea Treaty drawn up between France and China, the 22nd Article of which declared:

"...The French may also in the same manner set up churches, hospitals, hospices, schools and cemeteries. For this purpose, the local authority, after having agreed with the consul, shall designate the districts which are most suitable for the French residence and the places where the aforesaid building operations may be constructed...

"If any Chinese violate or destroy churches or French cemeteries those responsible should be punished according to the severest laws of the country."

The second war with China ended in 1858 with the signing of the Treaty of Tientsin, the 13th Article of which read:

"The Christian religion having as its essential purpose the leading of men to virtue, the members of all the Christian communions shall enjoy entire security in regard to their persons, their property and the free exercise of their religious practices, and an effective protection shall be granted to the missionaries who go peacefully through the interior of the country, provided with regular passports...

"No hindrance shall be put in the way, by the authorities of the Chinese Empire, of the acknowledged right of any person in China to embrace Christianity if he wishes to practise its tenets, without being liable to any penalty imposed for so doing.

"Everything which has been previously written, proclaimed or published in China by order of the Government against the Christian religion is completely abrogated and is a dead letter in all the provinces of China..."

Following the capture of Peking in 1860 a Convention was signed in which the 6th Article stated:

"In conformity with the imperial decree by the Emperor, Tae-kuang, on 20 March, 1846, religious and charitable institutions which have been confiscated from the Christians during the persecutions of which they have been victims shall be restored to their owners through the mediation of His Excellency the Minister of France in China, to whom the Imperial Government will hand them over, together with the cemeteries and other buildings which depend upon them."

Through these provisions, and others in a later treaty, only missionaries (and mostly Roman Catholics because of their earlier missionary efforts) of all foreigners were able to own land in the interior of China outside the Treaty Ports. With the 1860 treaty and the opening of the Five Treaty Ports missionaries were no longer restricted to the Treaty Ports but could go beyond them, in the words of the treaty:

"It is in addition permitted to French missionaries to rent and purchase land in all the provinces, and to erect buildings thereon at pleasure." Subsequent treaties, especially those with the United States, regularised the status of missionaries in this respect of "most favoured nation" treatment.

Dr Robert Morrison of the London Missionary society died in 1834 with ten converts to show for his arduous work. But the London Missionary Society was soon joined by the American Board of Commissioners for Foreign Missions, followed by the American Presbyterians, the Protestant Episcopal Church of the United States, the American Baptists, the American Methodists and others.

Just as in the Middle Ages, by an ironic parallel, the Christian Church was involved with the production and distribution of drugs and alcohol, so in regard to China were the early missionaries with opium. The first missionaries, in the nineteenth century, arrived in Macau and Hong Kong in opium-smuggling ships – but that was not the limit of their involvement. In his book *Prelude to Hong Kong*, Austin Coates wrote:

"In 1830 one of the most extraordinary figures of the period arrived, the indefatigable Prussian, Charles Gutsloff, of the Netherlands Missionary Society, who developed an amazing command of the Chinese language, and with his vehement manner of speech and curiously Chinese appearance could always count on an audience in the mission field...

"In 1832, Jardine (of Jardine, Matheson and Company) invited Gutzloff to take the post of interpreter in one of his ships...Jardine's letter was cautious, worded with delicacy and care. Without precisely mentioning opium he made it plain that Gutsloff if he accepted would be expected to interpret illicit opium deals...

"Gutsloff accepted and was thereafter seen in many an unexpected spot on the China coast, preaching rigorously to wandering Chinese crowds; handing round pamphlets, and then hastening back to assure some merchant that the opium supplied by Jardine, Matheson and Company was guaranteed the very highest quality...In the crucial years that followed, Elijah Bridgman and Wells Whitman performed, apart from their religious work, tasks of the greatest political importance..."

In 1865 James Hudson Taylor of the Chinese Evangelisation Society arrived in China, became sick, went home, finished his study of medicine, and returned to China to found the China Inland Mission in 1865. He issued a call for twenty-four workers, two for each of China's twelve inland provinces and, despite warnings that it was premature to go inland at the time, he went ahead. Three years later the China Inland Mission station at Yangchow was attacked and destroyed.

His example was soon followed by others, and when he died in 1905 there were almost a thousand missionaries in the China Inland Mission alone. In 1800 there had not been a single Protestant Christian living in China; and by the time of his death there were almost a million Christians, Catholic and Protestant.

CHAPTER 2

HOW CHRIST CAME TO CHINA

Through Commercial Developments: The 17th to 19th Centuries

The contact between China and Britain began about the middle of the eighteenth century. Prior to this time the Chinese empire consolidated under the Mongols paid little or no attention to the foreign "barbarians" beyond her established frontiers except for the vassal states immediately contiguous to her sprawling boundaries.

During what were known as the Middle Ages in Europe, and the Mongol and Ming empires in China, there had been considerable expansion by the Chinese, involving them in guerilla battles along the length of their frontiers. By the early eighteenth century two major areas of fighting were in the north-west and south-west of China; and the cost of these campaigns, plus the earlier colossal investment and lack of real enterprise involved in what was known as the Ming "maritime experiment", – of building ships but doing little trade – had bankrupted the nation. These border wars brought them into conflict with the European colonial powers: to the north, with Russia; and to the south, with Britain.

In 1757 the English occupied Calcutta, and in 1766 the province of Bengal, in India. From China a Manchu General, Ming Jui, who had been victorious in the fighting for eastern Turkestan, marched south-westwards against Burma. and in 1790-91 a Chinese army conquered Nepal, to the south-west of Tibet, on the Indian border. This expansion of China's frontiers created new opportunities for commercial activities.

In south-west China, the newly occupied areas of Kwangtung and Kwangsi caught the attention of the wealthy – and the impoverished, but formerly wealthy – Chinese trading and official families as a place to send sons or relatives who were unable or unwilling to enter the ranks of the preferred civil service. In these recently settled areas they sold Chinese products to the native peoples or to the new settlers for high prices. Some introduced new manufacturing techniques and craft industries into the new cities and towns in the south.

But the greatest stimulus to these commercial activities came from foreign, European, trade in the coastal areas; especially American silver, which had flooded Europe in the sixteenth century and which now began to flow towards China in the seventeenth century in exchange for silk and tea and other Oriental goods.

For centuries the economic structure of China had been based on the ideals of Mencius and Confucius. They had predicated their philosophies on the principle that good government was reflected in the economic happiness of the people; and this, in turn, depended on harnessing nature to the industry of the people. For example, the Confucian principle was: "To centralise wealth means the destruction of national unity; to distribute and equalise wealth makes for political unity".

In China it was the family, and not the individual, which was the political and social unit. In reality the family clan was seen as a miniature State, a complete entity executing quasi-civil and judicial functions. Theoretically, supreme power was vested in the father as head of the family; but, in practice, this often became collective and was exercised as a family council, with the father as executive officer. The link between generations was sustained by means of ancestral worship. The ancestral hall in the home was both the "capital" of the family-State unit, and its "temple".

When there were several families these formed the village; with the family elders the village "gentry", or rulers, exercising criminal and civil judicial authority. The town dwellers did not differ in essence from the village, simply extending the same principle into the various trades and guilds and other organisations. The leading members of the guilds, societies and other organisations formed the city "gentry", or rulers. This was further extended through the cities, towns and villages of the provinces.

In the Central Government there were six divisions of government, each presided over by a Minister. The highest of these departments was "the Office of Heaven", which became the Board of Civil Office, and this was supreme over all other departments and officials. The Chief of this department was the Prime Minister, next in rank to the Emperor.

In the fifteenth century China was the lure that attracted Columbus to begin his western voyages of exploration in 1492. When he reached America he thought it was the south coast of China. He was followed by John Cabot, Vasco da Gama, Magellan, and others, all seeking the tempting riches said to be waiting in the fabled land of Cathay.

The British East India Company reached the Portuguese settlement of Macao in 1638 and, despite Portuguese resistance by sea and land, managed to establish a base for trade in Canton in South China in 1684. But this position was not secured until 1713, and they were forbidden by China to trade officially elsewhere. Nevertheless adventuring merchantmen were willing to risk their ships and their lives for the sake of the profits to be made.

By the nineteenth century the British Government was faced with the necessity of extending its official responsibilities into Asia and not just leave them to the freebooting merchantmen, like the East India Company. But when they sent high-ranking officials to China to open talks they were treated with arrogant contempt and were refused audience with the Emperor and his advisers.

Meanwhile the economic and political situation inside China had become very sensitive because of the dramatic increase of the opium trade into China through Hong Kong, conducted mostly by Britain's commercial representatives, the East India Company.

These combinations of circumstances precipitated two important developments: for the first time the Chinese, reluctantly but significantly, entered into large-scale trade with European "barbarians"; and, for the first time, large-scale emigration of Chinese nationals was permitted into the surrounding countries of the Nan-yang, or "Southern Sea". The pressure of increased population and potentially lucrative trade in the southern coastal provinces of Kwangtung, Kwangsi and Fukien pushed Chinese into establishing businesses and setting up communities in South-East Asian countries. Hong Kong was a centre for this flood of emigration, and also an important link for them wherever they settled.

This gave Hong Kong greater importance than Macao, the Portuguese colony which throughout the previous two centuries had been the chief port for Western trade with China. Macao had been useful when the shallow-draft vessels were plying their trade, but with the coming of the steamship and larger vessels Hong Kong's huge natural harbours became increasingly attractive – for both legal and illegal trade.

The East India Company had enjoyed a monopoly of trade with China through Canton until 1833. It then licensed private traders to handle the "country trade" between India and China but it denied the right to reside in Canton to these traders. They, in turn, got around this obstacle by becoming consuls for foreign states. With the circumvention, and then abolition, of the Company's control there was rapid expansion of trade, and by 1837 there was an enterprising foreign community of 308 persons, mostly British, almost all of them employed by the 57 foreign firms or agency houses.

There was a similar monopoly on the Chinese side, held by a group of merchants called *Co-hong*, the official Chinese trading representatives. The Co-hong members, who had paid for the privilege, traded as individuals but were corporately responsible for the behaviour of all Western "barbarians" and acted as official go-betweens.

Before the large-scale introduction of opium into China the normal trade of tea and silks left China with a trade balance in its favour, mostly realised in silver. With the huge sale of opium the silver in China had to be exported and China was faced with a large and worrying imbalance. This was a prime factor in China's official banning of the opium trade.

Opium had been used in China as a drug for over a thousand years. But the smoking of opium as a drug-abuse vice was only about three centuries old. The first edict against smoking opium was issued in 1729 when only some 200 chests a year were imported. By the end of the eighteenth century the import by all nations had reached some 4,000 chests. Two other edicts were issued, one in 1796 and one in 1800, prohibiting both importing and native cultivation.

But the East India Company had the monopoly of both the cultivation and sale of opium in India, and with the willing cooperation of the corrupt *Co-hong* monopoly in China the Company – supported by American, Danish, Dutch, Portuguese, Spanish and other ships – brought the drug from Persia, Turkey and other places.

The *Co-hong* worked out an elaborate and extremely profitable system of bribes and extortions in addition to their regular profits and as these became unbearable to the increasingly frustrated and infuriated foreign merchant community, with little hope of redress, they put pressure on the British Government "to do something". They found the Government unsympathetic because, although the Government liked the profits from the trade, the freebooting merchantmen were notorious for their aggression, their impatience with legal restraints, and their resentment at any form of official interference with their profiteering. But the foreign merchants needed something to counter the unscrupulous *Co-hong's* official backing by the Chinese Government.

The British Government finally decided to make a serious attempt to get China's cooperation in securing ordered trade, free from exorbitant charges and arbitrary arrangement and free from official interference, and for agreement on law and order of a general kind in which such trade could flourish. There were examples of this in Bombay and Singapore, and some adaptation of this system was envisaged for China. But in order to safeguard Britain's interests it was necessary to have a base which could be defended by naval power, be policed by British guardians of the law and administered by British courts and civil services – so Hong Kong was given official approval to develop into such a base. But because of the slowness of travel, and the even greater delays in communications between the officials of both countries, by the time official propositions were received the local situations had already surpassed what was being officially debated for consideration.

Meanwhile the trading situation in Canton reached a crisis. The Emperor, tired of the controversy over corruption by the *Co-hong*, removed his Viceroy and appointed a representative with integrity, Commissioner Lin. When the corrupt Viceroy was removed the Emperor relieved him of 425,000 acres of land, 13,500 ounces of gold, six million pounds sterling worth (at the then rate of exchange) of silver, 11 boxes of jewels, and shares in over eighty banks and money establishments which he had acquired during his term of office.

Commissioner Lin Tse-hau began his official operations on 10 March, 1839, with a demand that all opium be destroyed and/or turned over to him for destruction – about 20,000 chests, at about £2.5 million sterling valued at the time. He demanded a bond that the foreigners must leave immediately, and promise never to return. To enforce his orders he surrounded the foreign settlement with troops and vessels, and cut off all supplies of food and water. He also demanded that sixteen British merchants be handed over as hostages. Eventually, he agreed to let the British leave Canton on 24 May for Macao, on condition that the sixteen merchants sign a bond never to return. Others could return to Canton later for legitimate trade, but all trading in opium was to cease forthwith.

In the official correspondence between the two countries' representatives Commissioner Lin stated his position with honesty and dignity:

"In all my service I have never treated a man contrary to propriety. Far less will I maltreat those who have braved the perils of a myriad leagues of sea in the hope of making here a little money. But there are limits; a nation's dignity cannot be sacrificed; there are eternal principles; there is right and wrong. The said Barbarian is of reasonable intelligence; his speech, it is said, is placid and slow. If he applies himself with perseverance, he might yet distinguish right from wrong. Let him not be led by those about him; there are men among them who would delude him...He must rouse from those deceptions and repent his errors, obey the Edicts, answer through the Hong, abandon obstinacy and reverentially submit..."

If this generously utopian offer was ever likely to be considered by British officials in London it was rendered obsolete by local events in Hong Kong. The British representative from Canton, Captain Elliott, had arrived there with the fleeing British merchant community, and a local incident occurred in which a Chinese subject was killed in a brawl with drunken English seamen. Captain Elliott offered to pay a sum in compensation, but the angry Commissioner Lin sent troops and armed vessels to bombard Kowloon and Hong Kong.

Several months later a fleet of British gunboats arrived to relieve the small foreign community, defended only by the merchant freebooters and adventuring pirates seeking spoils. The Chinese – ill-equipped, arrogant in their contempt of the "barbarians'" potential, their army as well as their officials riddled with corruption – were no match for the British expeditionary force, and were defeated. The British fleet sailed on into Nanking where on 29 August, 1842, the "Opium War" officially ended and a Treaty was signed. The Treaty of Nanking permitted Britain to establish what was to become the greatest port of the Far East, Hong Kong, and secured the indemnity of six million dollars for the destroyed opium. Opium importing, which had caused the war, was not restricted in any way, the Treaty merely expressing the pious hope that "smuggling would cease".

In a Supplementary Treaty of the Bogue, in October 1843, Article XIII permitted the Chinese to ship goods from any of her Treaty Ports to Hong Kong to purchase goods; but if they required a Chinese vessel to ship their goods they had to obtain "a pass or port clearance...of the port whence the vessel may sail for Hong Kong". This implied, among other things, that Hong Kong was one of the Treaty Ports, and also omitted any provision for Hong Kong junks. Between this, and other equally confusing Articles XIV and XVI, both Chinese and British smuggling practices increased enormously.

With corrupt Chinese operating as official merchants, and with their main interest being the opium trade with its vast profits, the many Chinese who flocked into Hong Kong looking to make their fortunes were drawn from the worst elements. The framework of British law which had been set up was difficult to apply to the aggressive British and other foreign entrepreneurs, and next to impossible to apply to the Chinese emigrants. It was really only "a rule of action and a measure of right", and the Chinese were left alone mostly to their own customs and usages consistent with the needs of law and order.

The European community developed a strong social life, but their activities were confined to the comparatively few wealthy foreigners by whom the rumbustiously growing colony was dominated. There was little attempt to build a community. There were, in fact, many communities of regional Chinese and foreign nationals having nothing in common except sharing the small island and making as much money as possible.

Writing of this period in his book, *Borrowed Time, Borrowed Place,* Richard Hughes said:

"William Jardine and James Mathieson were the most successful opium runners and accordingly the most successful traders on the China coast. They were both Scottish, both religious in the stiff Calvinist way, both scrupulous in financial and personal matters, both indifferent to materialistic reflections on contraband and drugs...

"Mathieson could write a dry criticism of a ship-master in the Company's employ:

" 'The *Gazelle* was unnecessarily delayed at Hong Kong on consequence of Captain Crocker's repugnance to receiving opium on the Sabbath. We have every respect for persons entertaining strict religious principles, but we fear that very godly people are not suited for the drug trade. Perhaps it would be better that the Captain should resign'..."

In less than ten years from the signing of the Treaty of Nanking it was estimated that 54 per cent of the total British imports to China was opium, worth a phenomenal £700 million sterling, or four thousand million taels of silver in the currency of the period. In the English Parliament there were protests from high officials, such as Sir William Gladstone, who said: "I am not competent to judge how long this war may last, but this I can say, that a war more unjust in its origin, a war more calculated in its programme to cover this country with permanent disgrace, I do not know, and I have not read of...". But another M.P., Sir George Campbell, declared: "If the Chinese must be poisoned by opium, I would rather they were poisoned for the benefit of our Indian subjects than any other exchequer."

In his book, *The Imperial Drug Traffic*, Joshua Rowntree declared:

"Never has a great trade sprung up in more extraordinary circumstances. A government pushed to the utmost the growth of the poppy, and the manufacture and sale of the drug, for the sake of revenue. It licensed the ships that carried the drug, with their captains and crews. It provided that they should be absolutely controlled by its officers in China. It affixed its own stamp to the drug and took pains that it should be manufactured to the taste of the Chinese. Yet because the trade was illegal, it disclaimed, and instructed its officers at the receiving port to disclaim, all knowledge of the trade...The Government receiving its income from such a source ostentatiously washed its hands in innocence, and forbade its officials to engage in the later stages of the trade!".

In the first year of official British administration the Chinese population in Hong Kong increased from 5,000 to about 15,000. While many of them were wealthy family traders or small merchants, others were fishermen or labourers or clerks seeking work in the rapidly expanding island colony. Coming from different coastal provinces they became increasingly dependent on their regional guilds and associations and societies rather than the traditional family and community structures with which they were familiar in China. These traditional organisations – craft guilds, such as peasants or fishermen, and political associations – had developed into powerful representative movements inside China as "secret societies" able to challenge and overthrow national as well as provincial authorities. Inside China they were the only true, and feared, "voice of the people" with effective political leverage; but, also, they were feared as ruthless Mafia organisations associated with all forms of criminal activities.

The rise of the powerful secret societies in China is still difficult to trace – for obvious reasons. But what is known is that they emerged from a surprising source – "religious" societies. They were China's equivalent to the Freemasons. The well-known Tsa Li Society, or "Abiding Principle" society, founded sometime between the Ming and Ch'ing dynasties, emphasised "spiritual awakening", "escape suffering", "obtain happiness", "discipline body and mind" in a combination of Taoism and Buddhism. The "White Lotus Society", founded about the eleventh century in Soochow, was organised as a Buddhist sect, emphasising prayers and incantations before going into martial arts. It then split into several other secret societies covering the whole country, including one that became the notorious "Boxers". Another, in South China, in the seventeenth century became the infamous "Triad Society". From the Triad Society sprang the "Elders Society" in Central China, to which many political leaders belonged.

The main religious and secret societies all began in protests in one form or another against invaders and their foreign influences. First, against the Chin, then the Mongols and Manchus; and, when the Western countries turned their imperial interests to China in the nineteenth century, the societies proliferated in response to the Western invasions.

In 1796 the White Lotus Society began a revolution against the ruling Manchu dynasty which lasted for ten years, then petered out unsuccessfully. In 1786 the Heaven and Earth Society launched a bloody revolution in Taiwan, also against the Manchu garrisons. On the Chinese mainland the Heaven and Earth Society joined with the White Lotus Society in a number of anti-Manchu revolutions in various provinces in the first decades of the nineteenth century. By 1850 the Government in Peking was forced to outlaw the secret societies because of their large-scale military activities throughout the nation.

One of the most powerful secret societies emerging at this time was a hitherto little-known one called Pai Shang-ti-hui, or "Society of God-worshippers", with strong Christian connection. It was founded by a remarkable propagandist, Feng Yun-shan, soon joined by a charismatic leader, Hung Hsu- ch'uan. Both of these men were itinerant Christian preachers who fearlessly denounced idolatry, taught worship of the only true God, belief in Jesus Christ and eternal happiness in heaven. Hung's greater authority as leader derived from the vision he claimed to receive from God. He led the increasing number of followers from denouncing idolatry to the physical destruction of images and temples and shrines. He also denounced adultery, seduction, disobedience to parents, theft and robbery and gambling.

The Province of Kwangsi, where the God-Worshipping Society operated, was far away from Peking and was one of the poorest and most corrupt provinces in the country. Imperial officials sent there preyed upon the people, and it was a haven for outlaws of all kinds. The few official militia and police could not protect the people from the roving bandits, and they even added to the widespread oppression and tyranny. On the coasts pirates and bandits controlled the sea approaches and the inland road transport.

In 1849 a great famine precipitated a series of riots throughout many provinces, and in the general linking-up of mutual interests of regional secret societies against the corrupt authorities the God-Worshipping Society associated with the powerful political Heaven and Earth Society, now commonly known as "the Triad", despite the religious and political differences.

Thus began a rebel movement which the London *Times* reported as "one of the most important and remarkable movements of mass protest in modern history", the Taiping Rebellion. "Tai-p'ing" was the new name given to the God-Worshipping Society after prayer when 20,000 of them defeated a Government army on 1 January, 1851. The name, *T'ai-p'ing T'ien-kua*, or "Heavenly Kingdom of Great Peace", was chosen to celebrate the newly established Biblical era of anticipated "Great Peace" when all men would live together in harmony as brothers. 1851 was also the beginning of the great *Taiping* revolt of the masses to bring in that kingdom, and banish all political corruption and economic exploitation in China.

From 1851-56 the *Taiping* swept forward nationally with a radical economic, social and cultural policy, accompanied by an equally radical religious revolution of extreme iconoclasm. Its leaders abolished social evils, slavery and prostitution, and raised moral standards by forbidding the endemic gambling, opium-smoking and adultery. But internal dissension broke out among the leaders in 1856 which erupted into violent opposition and eventually to murders, rapidly declining personal morality and ultimate betrayal of the revolution.

The Taiping Rebellion precipitated other revolutions inside China and set the example for revolutions elsewhere. The Sepoy Mutiny in India in 1857 was said to be influenced by the Taipings, threatening British domination there. Incidents in Korea, Hong Kong, and Singapore, with repercussions in western countries, were also influenced by the Taiping "religious-political movement". Karl Marx, in his essay, "Revolution in China and Europe" published in the *New York Daily Tribune* on 14 June, 1853, wrote of it enthusiastically as an influential example of a proletarian revolution. But Western missionaries, like the Western diplomatic and commercial representatives, resisted associating themselves with the Taiping movement, seeing it as a threat to their own respective religious and political interests.

The same treaties which had legalised the opium trade for Western traders gave privileges to Christians in China to spread the Gospel of Jesus Christ. The introduction of opium on a vast scale was viewed by the Western nations as providing an important means by which to undermine and destroy China's archaic and corrupted administrative system which so frustrated and obstructed their political and commercial ambitions. At the same time, the respective Western Governments encouraged the Christian missionaries under the same treaties to efforts which they saw would undermine and eventually destroy, culturally and socially, a society which made them feel inferior and guilty. The Chinese historian, T'ang Leang-li, writing of this period has stated:

"Socially, missionary activities in attempting to substitute an alien civilisation and, to the Chinese mind, an unreal and impracticable system of religious morality in place of the national system of civilisation and ethics, have resulted in the creation of a schism in the solidarity of the Chinese people. The Christians in China were always apt to form a community of their own, in separation from the rest of their fellow-citizens, under the protection of their missionaries, and ultimately, under the protection of the missionaries' respective governments. Religion became a means of wholesale denationalisation, and of acquiring a privileged social and political status. The tradition has further been allowed to grow and even encouraged that acceptance of the Christian creed makes the Chinese Christian somehow a superior being, and the absence of a historical sense in a majority of the converts has led to the uncritical and unqualified contempt for the native institutions which cannot fail to be associated with the dark ages of paganism."

Thus the common Chinese view emerged of the tragic

error of the Western missionaries' association with traditional Christian institutional alignments with their governments' policies, and their own uncritical social and cultural prejudices and practices. A more objective and Scriptural stance might have led them to a closer association with the Taiping leaders in their early and formative stage which might have transformed the movement and the whole of China. The leader of the Taiping Rebellion, Hung Hsu-ch'uan, was said to "maintain a blameless deportment...gentlemanly in manners" by the first missionary he approached for baptism and spiritual teaching yet he was rejected by that missionary for "financial reasons". Ironically, that same western missionary a few years later had to leave his mission because of inability to get on with his colleagues, and his "great interest in financial matters". When the Taipings entered Nanking successfully, the Christian community there were ecstatic with the policies and practices. Dr. W.H. Medhurst of the London Missionary Society wrote two letters to the *North China Herald*, on 26 November and 17 December 1853, which declared:

"What a moral revolution! To introduce 100,000 Chinamen, for months and years together...to live without dollars, and all share and share alike...it is the wonder of the age!"

At that time, despite being there for many years, the Western missionaries had been unable to win a single convert.

With the collapse of the Taiping Rebellion, and its religion-orientated policies, the secret societies became dominated by political and commercial interests; and, eventually, many of them by criminal elements. With the opening of the Treaty Ports the Triad Society, which inherited a large part of the disintegrated Taipings, captured Amoy in 18 May, 1853, and Shanghai in September. They then spread out into the surrounding cities and towns. The Western business communities were happy to enter into trading arrangements with the Triads, and they covertly helped them in their expansion into other areas and other commercial operations for profit – especially the lucrative opium trade. The Peking government knew of these arrangements but was helpless to stop them.

By the middle of 1854 Canton was suffering from secret society activities; and, in the fighting, over a million lives were lost in the province of Kwangtung. To provide a measure of protection for their ships and subjects, and to prevent a total severance of communications between Canton and Hong Kong trade, the British and American authorities agreed to grant permission for the British and American flags to be flown aboard Chinese boats.

In Hong Kong itself, the secret societies had infiltrated from the first year of its inception, and within a few years it was found necessary to institute an "Ordinance for the Suppression of the Triad and other Secret Societies". Two years later it was officially recorded:

"Here (in Hong Kong) it was that the Triad Secret Society flourished unchecked, Hong Kong having become its headquarters for the south of China, and three-fourths of the Chinese population were believed to be enrolled as members. With such a society flourishing, and with the police ignorant not only of the habits and haunts of the most active and dangerous of its members, but unable to converse with those who did know them, it was not at all wonderful that crime should have been on the increase and its detection became every day more difficult..."

It was the secret societies who organised the peasant drift to the increasingly affluent Chinese cities, as commercial opportunities increased. It was the secret societies who organised the peasants and the new industrial workers in these cities. It was the secret societies who were strong enough, working behind or with the benevolent associations as fronts when necessary, to impose conditions on foreign *Taipans* and Chinese officials alike. It was the secret societies who encouraged and even "shanghai'd" the poor

Chinese to emigrate, to Hong Kong, South East Asia, and elsewhere. It was the secret societies who went with them and organised fares, employment, protection, donations, graft, vice and crime in the overseas communities. Above all, it was the secret societies who were behind the organisation of the lucrative and influential opium trade from the beginning. They had the official connections inside China, they were the recognised distributors, they had the outlets – smoking dens, brothels, gambling houses, village and town and city connections. With the increasing demand for cheap labour in the rapidly expanding Western capitalist societies they organised the "pig trade" – the equivalent of the overcrowded African slave-ships. Inside China, Shanghai was the centre of Triad activities, while Hong Kong was the centre of its international operations.

But despite its many criminal activities the Triad Society was essentially a political organisation, using its illicit wealth to influence official decisions affecting its organisational, national and international interests. In addition to Hong Kong, there were local lodges in Indochina, Indonesia and especially Malaysia. In Malaysia, the Triad had its own police force, imposing its authority on non-members as well as members of the Society. In Hawaii and California they were particularly strong. Through these networks of lodges, either willingly or by coercion, the immigrant Chinese paid large financial contributions to the political causes as well as criminal activities in China. So that whoever wanted to rise to influence in Chinese affairs had to have the support of one of the powerful secret societies.

In Hong Kong, because of the hidden power of the Triads, combined with the persuasive corruption of the Chinese merchants and the unscrupulous Western traders, the experiment of having dual Chinese and British law was found to be unworkable in practice. It was therefore decided in Britain that "native interests would be better served by the policy of non-discrimination", and that the

Chinese were to be brought increasingly within the scope of the British administration.

With this firm imposition of a central, non-discriminating, stable official administration in the Colony, the hitherto free-wheeling, commercially incestuous and restricted trading pattern was abandoned, and a new era of commercial development was initiated. In addition to Europe and America trade was now developed with more distant nations – Australia, South America, West Indies, and others. Linking Chinese communities sprang up in these countries, all retaining their national and commercial connections with China. Hong Kong, with Shanghai, became the entrance and exit to new worlds for both Chinese and Westerners.

CHAPTER 3

HOW CHRIST CAME TO CHINA

Through Missionary Practices: The 19th and 20th Centuries

When Robert Morrison of the London Missionary Society died in 1834 there were only three Protestant missionaries in China, two British and one American. In 1834 a Dr Peter Parker from the United States began medical work in Canton with a small dispensary. In 1861 Dr William Lockhart of the London Missionary Society went to Peking to set up medical work, but with permission as a Legation doctor and not as a missionary.

In the middle of the nineteenth century the Western powers were occupied with the Crimean War in Europe, but not too busy to extract considerable advantages to themselves from the Chinese with the Treaties of Nanking, Tientsin and Peking in 1842, 1858 and 1860 respectively. These opened all doors into China through the Five Treaty Ports.

By 1870 there were 254 European and about 150 native Catholic priests, with some 404,530 converts. Catholic influence in China was mostly synonymous with French missionary activity, and this diminished almost to zero with the Franco-China war of 1884. But by the turn of the century there were 38 Vicarials-Apostolic, 21 Bishops, 42 mutually independent Catholic missions, with 1063 Europeans and 493 native priests, 4961 places of worship and 803,000 converts.

Regarding the Protestants, by 1877 the number of missionaries at 113 principal mission stations in China had reached 305, of which 109 were British, 90 American and 17 German. Including independent preachers, colporteurs and other associated Christian activists there were 417 missionaries in all. By the turn of the century there were over 300 mission hospitals treating two million patients and 2,500 Protestant missionaries, from almost 100 societies, distributed over 18 provinces. Of these societies only about a dozen were represented in China at the date of the Peking Treaty of 1858.

The London *Times*, reporting an address by Bishop Cassels of West China to the Church Missionary Society in England, said:

"A few years ago China was said to be dying, and the European Powers, like harpies, were already beginning to divide the spoil. These pangs, however, had been not a sign of approaching death, but the birth-pangs of a new life. With a Literary Chancellor, exhorting students to read Christian books and distinguish between Protestants and Roman Catholics; with the spread of a purely native movement against foot-binding; with the rise of colleges and universities, mints and arsenals, post offices and publishing establishments; and with a new attitude to Western ideas in general, there was abundant proof of an awakening which gave glorious opportunities for Christianity..."

One of these missionaries contributing to the Christian vision in China was Dr Timothy Richard. He had been converted at a Welsh revival meeting, and had gone to China with the English Baptist Missionary Society in 1870. The great famine of 1877-79 made an unforgettable impression on him. He saw that Western knowledge was required, as well as the gospel, in order to deal with the chronic social conditions. In his diary he noted:

"Heard stories at the inn that night of parents exchanging their children as they could not eat their own; that one dared not go to the pits for coal as mules, donkeys and their owners were liable to be killed and eaten...I heard from other eye-witnesses that they had seen 270 dead on the roadside in three days...Small wonder that I began to doubt my sanity or my senses amid such scenes of horror. Was I among the living or the tormented dead?"

Richard was one of the few who made the attempt to cross the great gulf which separated Protestants and Roman Catholics in China. He gave his own account of an incident provoked by the governor of Shansi Province:

"The Governor's brother Tseng Kwoh Fan, the most eminent statesman in China during the Taiping Rebellion, had already presented his views on Roman Catholicism and Protestantism to the Government to the effect that these two parties hated each other so much that they would counteract each other's influence and thus save the Chinese Government any aggressive action against either. When I asked the Governor's advice as to how I should best dispose of the sums I might in future receive for famine relief, he replied, with a twinkle in his eye: 'There is a Roman Catholic missionary in this city who applied a few days ago for some grain for an Orphanage in his charge. You had better hand over your two thousand taels to him'. I thanked him for his suggestion, and replied that I would call on the Bishop to discuss the matter with him...The Bishop, however, would not agree to my proposal...'"

Richard became secretary of the Society for the Diffusion of Christian and General Knowledge in 1891; he founded the first public school for Chinese in Shanghai, and helped to found the university at T'aiyuanfu in Shansi. He was then asked by the Government to establish similar universities in each province. He also urged the introduction of railways.

At the beginning of the twentieth century modern universities began to be introduced into China and the young

Chinese intellectuals went on to studies in Hong Kong, Japan, Europe and the United States. These young intellectuals were deeply offended and ashamed by the humiliations heaped upon them by the Treaties imposed on them by the Western nations, contemptuous of their traditional leaders and corrupt officials who had betrayed their country, and aflame with the ferment of the new political ideas reaching them from the West. When they reached the West where the revolutionary political ideas were involved with equality, liberty and fraternity, with nationalism and socialism and communism, with lower-class freedom against upper-class privilege, they concluded rapidly that the only road to revolution in China lay through the existing network of the nationalistic Triads, both overseas and inside China.

In 1894 Japan had defeated the Chinese over a Korean dispute and through this had obtained Formosa, the Pescadores, and other advantages. In 1897 the murder of two Catholic missionaries by bandits was used by Germany to extract a harbour in Shantung in compensation. Russia moved into Manchuria, arousing the suspicion and enmity of Japan, and this led to the Russo-Japanese War in 1904. France acquired additional rights and territory; and England, attempting to head off Russian and German interest, agreed to lease Wei-hai-wei. At the same time they increased the security of Hong Kong by leasing the area around it.

It was these events which forced the Chinese youth to go overseas in pursuit of solutions to save their disintegrating country. Inside China the pressures generated by the imposed Treaties created great animosity against all foreigners, and with the foreign missionaries being the most visible and accessible they became the targets for increasingly murderous attacks. These local insurrections rapidly developed into civil wars as the secret societies mobilised their members in pursuit of their particular goals. The former White

Lotus Society had broken up into several sects, the most powerful of which was the predominantly political Big Sword Society, which in turn became the Eight Trigram Society, from which sprang the notorious "Boxer Movement" uprising in 1900. Reports of the horrors of Chinese persecutions against the Christians poured into the Legations, and the multifarious provincial civil wars degenerated into anarchy.

It was out of this civil chaos that China's "intellectual revolution" began. The "father of Chinese republicanism", Sun Yat-sen, fled from China to Hong Kong as a consequence of his political activities. He had tried to form his section of the Triad Society into a political party, and was still doing this when he was banished from Hong Kong for "engaging in plots and dangerous conspiracies" in 1896. He went to Honolulu in Hawaii where he organised the *Kwek On Hui*, or "National Stability Society", a later branch of which became the forerunner of the *Kuomintang*, or "Nationalist Party". He was also responsible for the creation of what was probably the first purely Hong Kong secret society during his stay there, the *Chung We Teng*, whose purpose was to co-ordinate the support of all local Triad members for the Republican Party.

Sun Yat-sen was not the only leading political figure, or his group the only secret society, developing their tremendous political potential during their self-enforced exile. Wu Yu-chang, who was later to be one of the doyens of the Central Committee of the Communist Party, together with Chu Teh, future Commander-in-Chief of the Communist People's Liberation Army, was a "Great Elder" in Szechuan's secret society, and joined with Sun Yat-sen and others to form the *Tung Meng Hui* which was the basis of the *Kuomintang*, or Nationalist Party.

The forging of the Triads into a political network of revolution in China was described in a remarkable document, "Supplement on the Chinese Revolution", published in 1908 in France by *La Guerre Social*, the organ of the Parisian Socialist Revolutionaries, and signed by a pseudonymous Chinese student, "Keningtang": "They (Chinese group associations) are of all kinds: religious fraternities, family groups, mutual or corporate aid societies, amongst which the strongest are those of the beggars and bandits; they are infinite in number, have the most diverse aims, and encompass all interests. But alongside these more-or-less recognised or tolerated associations, there exist secret revolutionary associations whose importance in the history of China has been great and whose activity in the contemporary movement is considerable...

"These societies keep alive...a revolutionary tradition which the present revolutionaries have been able to put to good use; but, by themselves, they would not have been able to determine the course of this movement which is so new in every way and which is turning contemporary China upside down...It was necessary for today's revolutionaries to penetrate this army which was all prepared for revolt and inculcate it with their propaganda and ideas to give it a new life and a new programme of action..."

The first decade of the twentieth century was a disaster for China. Politically disintegrated, economically impoverished, socially annihilated, her intellectual leaders were still unable to prove themselves equal to the task of national reconstruction. Then in 1911 Sun Yat-sen launched his revolution, and established the Republic under his leadership in 1912. The immediate success of the revolution restored to the Chinese people the sense of self-confidence lost by so many years of national humiliation. This was helped by the ready recognition of the Republic.

But internally the archaic infrastructure, eroded by centuries of maladministration and corruption, was not in a fit state to be a vehicle of transforming revolution. The new Republican government of Sun Yat-sen and his associates, indebted to the Triads, did not help matters by appointing leading members of the Triads to influential positions. They were thus in a position to form a powerful pressure group in the political and civil affairs of the country, dominated by a vested interest in reactionary practices. They were given monopolies in civic, military and commercial spheres and, by extension, this meant that they had a stranglehold on vice, extortion and corruption. Certain of them were given monopolies in opium-growing, especially in the productive western provinces of China, so that from being an importer of opium in the nineteenth century China now became an exporter in the twentieth century.

Meanwhile Christians in China were concentrating on pouring the benefits of Western education into China, even those with an evangelistic emphasis. The Chinese government had abolished the civil service examination in 1905 because they did not equip students enough to meet the new challenges. The Catholics stressed elementary education, and Protestants higher education in secondary schools and colleges. Protestants also concentrated on introducing medical knowledge into China, with many mission stations having at least a dispensary attached. By 1914 there were several medical schools established.

Professor K.S. Latourette, in his *Christianity in a Revolutionary Age,* has listed some of the additional benefits brought to China by Protestants in response to needs: "Units of the Red Cross, public playgrounds, social service clubs, labour-saving machinery in the spinning of cotton, and methods for improving the quality of silk-worm eggs. They fought the age-old custom of binding the feet of women, combatted the production, sale and use of opium...sought to ameliorate the lot of the blind, the deaf and the dumb, founded orphanages, gave famine relief, encouraged sports and physical education."

But, unfortunately, the proliferation of sectarian denominations, both outside and inside the missionary societies, created dissensions and problems. In addition to combined educational and medical work, other forms of cooperation were tried, such as the Christian Endeavour Movement and the Young Men's and Young Women's Christian Association, or even unions of branches of the same denomination from different countries. The arrangement which had the most significant effect, however, was the "comity agreements". These perpetuated the divisions of denominationalism by dividing the country into areas where each denomination could carry out its particular practices without interference from others.

By the second decade of the twentieth century Christianity – at least in its educational, medical and institutional aspects – had made a formidable impact on China. But this tremendous expansion of Western education, medicine and literature also met with resistance and antagonism, riots and persecutions. These arose principally from the popular resentment, reinforced by the objections of the scholar class, who had been reared on Confucianism, against the growing threat of the spreading Christianity; and by the growing number of powerful Chinese intelligentsia who were opposed to the debilitated traditions and ineffective policies of China's post-Manchu, 1911-Republican, revolution. The latter were becoming convinced that Sun Yat-sen's National Socialism was not likely to solve China's problems and it was the revolutionary theories of Karl Marx which attracted them.

Meanwhile, Christianity was weaving itself into the fabric of China, from peasant to President. Professor Latourette recorded: "Although in 1914 its adherents numbered only about one in two hundred of the population – a much smaller percentage than in India – Christianity was having a pronounced effect upon the revolution which, arising from the impact of the Occident, in that year was still in its early stages".

From the late nineteenth century China had drawn some of the finest representatives of Western Christianity. Notable converts in Britain, such as C.T. Studd, the brilliant cricketer, and the famous "Cambridge Seven", in their new-found consecration thought first of China. They were later followed by the Olympic athlete, Eric Liddell. The same was true of the flower of American youth. Three of the student leaders at Yale University – Horace Pitkin, Sherwood Eddy and Henry Luce – went to Union Theological Seminary to prepare for the China mission field. Eddy later recalled:

"When I would box every afternoon with Pitkin and when we would run our daily mile in the gym or the open air, we would say, 'This will carry us another mile in China'".

John R. Mott, organiser of the Student Volunteers at Cornell University, declared that his field would be "the world", but China was the focal point. Eddy declared: "China was the goal, the Lodestar, the great magnet that drew us all in these days". And the same happened in Germany, France, Italy and other countries.

But the unity of that blazing Christian vision deserted them when they arrived in China, for in the first half of the twentieth century Protestant missionaries were divided into three distinct categories: the conservatives, the liberals, and the fundamentalists. Conservatives and fundamentalists agreed that the missionaries' task was to lead individuals to conversion and salvation through Christ. The conservatives did not agree with the liberals but did not spend time or energy in fighting with them, which the fundamentalists did with considerable passion. The liberals de-mythologised Jesus and the Bible, and concentrated mainly on social work.

In 1920 the China Bible Society was organised by fundamentalist missionaries from every denomination in order to defend the doctrines "held by the great body of Evangelicals". By 1921 the China Bible Union had 1,700 members among the missionaries, and by 1923 there were 2,000.

The Union campaigned in the various denominations to have the financial support of the liberals cut off, and to have their mission boards accept as future missionaries only those who subscribed to the statement of faith.

This was the period when the infant Chinese Communist Party was being founded with sixty to seventy members.

There was also controversy over the China Sunday School Union, which was doctrinally conservative and published a great deal of the literature used by missionaries in their work. The liberals wanted to block the influence of the fundamentalists, and asked the World Sunday School Union to do something about it (the China Sunday School Union was largely supported by the WSSU). There was, naturally, opposition to this move, especially from the China Inland Mission. Eventually, however, the World Sunday School Union did withdraw its financial support.

The bitterest attacks on both sides were carried on by only a few diehards. Charles Clayton Morrison, editor of the *Christian Century,* published an editorial in the 12 March, 1930 issue, insisting that the only way Chinese could be saved was for Christianity to identify itself with revolutionary social forces. He considered the fundamentalists the main obstacle in bringing about this identification.

But both the conservatives and the fundamentalists were basically non-political, and they paid little attention to the economic problems of the peasants or industrial workers. They could sympathise with the poverty, and help to alleviate it with food or financial relief, but they identified the causes unsympathetically as "too much land given over to growing opium" or "money wasted on gambling".

The liberals, on the other hand, took little interest in theology; they saw humanitarianism as the heart of the Christian gospel. They were impressed by the teachings of Confucius, by the long history and culture of China, by the desperate conditions of the peasants and the low state into which the country had fallen. They took less interest in "converting the heathen" than in emphasising the social aspects of Christian teachings and "Christianising" Chinese society. The liberals tended to concentrate on cities, as centres of influence, while the others were found mostly in towns and villages – again, with certain exceptions.

As a result of denominational differences, sectarian prejudices, and doctrinal emphasis, therefore, there were isolated pockets of varied Christian witness across the country, little islands of Western culture and Western denominational practice in the surrounding ocean of Chinese animism, Confucianism and ancestral worship. This was a cause of considerable concern to several Christian leaders in the 1930s, but with the spread of the Nationalist-Communist civil war in the country and the menacing threat of the Japanese military intervention in Manchuria, there was little they could do other than express their concern.

In contrast to the poor state of rural Christianity, there were more than 100,000 student applications for ten thousand openings in the Christian universities and colleges, which had more than 70,000 students. But outside of this intellectual elite the country pastors were mostly poor, ignorant and dependent on the foreign missionary. And both the missionary and the pastor ignored the real problems of the community – landlordism, tenancy, money-lending at usurious rates – the very problems being debated by the two forces fighting for China, the Nationalists and the Communists.

The Republic of Sun Yat-sen had been followed by the dictatorship of Yuan Shih-k'ai, and this in turn succeeded by ambitious and divisive war-lords selling their regional influence to whichever national leader, Nationalist or Communist, served their selfish interests. The body of China having been picked apart by foreign vultures was now being ripped to destruction by its own.

Out of all the Christian universities and colleges and

schools no dynamic Christian leader emerged to deliver his tormented fellow-citizens with a Christian-based philosophy. The clever Christian graduates used their Christian education as a stepping-stone to personal advancement in commerce or some profession. Only about 20 per cent showed interest in campus religious life, and even these tended to remain in the cities on graduation and enjoy Western-style comforts.

With the formation of the National Christian Council in China in 1922 the centre of influence moved significantly from the clergy to the lay Christian believers. This lay movement, non-Western rather than anti-Western in emphasis, was to play an important part in its impact on China and in its distinctive Christian witness to the rest of the world.

Meanwhile, a major split took place in the Nationalist Party of Sun Yat-sen when he decided on a policy of admitting, in their individual capacity, members of the recently formed Communist Party, and to alter their foreign policy stance to favour Russia. When he died in 1925 one section of the Party established its headquarters in Shanghai, while the other, left-wing orientation, remained in Canton. The left-wing was composed mostly of the radical intelligentsia, while the moderates were composed mostly of the professional politicians, the wealthy merchants and industrialists. The conflict between the two groups became acute in March, 1926 and ended in the victory of the military Commander-in-Chief, Chiang Kai Shek.

When the Nationalist armies under Chiang Kai Shek in 1926 successfully united the country south of the Yangtze River and arrived on the outskirts of Shanghai, Chiang was faced with the possibility of a war with the West who controlled vast interests in and through Shanghai. It was also a time of crisis for Chiang with the Communist elements in the Nationalist Party, who were strongly entrenched in the unions and other organisations in Shanghai. Chiang finally resolved the crisis by deciding that he would league with the Shanghai bankers and also attempt an alliance with the Western powers at the expense of the Communists. He struck quickly, expelled the Communists from the Nationalist Party and ordered the Communist leaders to be shot. But enough of them escaped and they were eventually to regroup, together with units of the Nationalist Army who mutinied and fled to the mountains. When Chiang Kai Shek entered Peking in 1928 the process of unifying the country, apart from the small Communist group, was virtually complete.

Then in 1931 the Japanese intervened, first by trying to annex Manchuria and a large part of Mongolia as a puppet state then, later, in 1937, with a full-scale invasion of the whole of China. In 1930 Russia invaded North Manchuria to hold the Chinese Eastern Railway and her possessions there. By the end of 1937 the Japanese had captured Shanghai and Nanking. Chiang and his government moved from Nanking to Hankow, then, as the Japanese advanced, fell back on Chungking in Szechuan Province in West China.

The Japanese invasion and the Nationalist defeats produced havoc among the Christian foreign missionaries as they were arrested, murdered and scattered by the advancing or retreating marauding soldiery. Also the breakdown in the already chaotic administrative machinery meant that salaries were not paid, expenses not met, food and transport short or non-existent.

And in Europe there was talk of another war with Germany.

PART TWO

HOW MARX CAME TO CHINA

CHAPTER 4

HOW MARX CAME TO CHINA

Through Armed Uprising: 1919-1935

Despite the feverish intensity of the "intellectual revolution" in China as aspiring political leaders sought Western solutions to their devastated country's horrendous problems it was remarkable how little attention was paid to the ideas of Marx and Lenin. It was the October Revolution in Russia in 1917 which finally caught the interest and then the enthusiasm of some Chinese leaders. Later, the greatest of them, Mao Zedung, was to describe it:

"Before the October Revolution, the Chinese were not only unaware of Lenin and Stalin but did not even know of Marx and Engels. The salvoes of the October Revolution awoke us to Marxism-Leninism. The October Revolution helped the progressives of China and the whole world to adopt the world outlook of the proletariat as the instrument for perceiving the destiny of the country, and for considering anew their own problems".

Even then, Communism in China in its initial stages did not have much popularity, and its miniscule membership was deeply divided over policies and goals. The initial membership of the Chinese Communist Party when it was set up in 1921 was between 60 and 70. At the Third Congress of the CCP in June 1923 there were only 20 delegates representing 300 members. At the Fourth Congress in 1925 there were just over 70 delegates representing 1,500 members. Within a short period of time after the Fourth Congress the membership had reached about 10,000. At the time of the Fifth Congress in May 1927, during the critical struggles with Chiang Kai Shek, there were about 100 delegates representing 58,000 members. By 1947, just prior to success in the civil war, Party membership was about 2.7 million. In 1950, when it set up the first Communist Government, it was 5.8 million, or just under 1 per cent of the population.

When the Chinese Communist Party was inaugurated Mao Zedung was a founder-member, representing his native province of Hunan, where he had personally established one of the six existing branches of the Party. Yet only four years previously, in 1917, when a group of students met together to discuss ways of saving the country, Mao had given as his reasons for not going into politics, as was being suggested to him, "because it needs money and connections". When pressed for his ideal he declared: "Imitate the heroes of Liang Shan-P'o". (Liang Shan-P'o was the name of the mountain fortress on which the bandit heroes of Mao's favourite novel, *Water Margin*, established themselves to fight for justice and order in an unjust and disorderly world).

But between 1917 and 1921 Mao came under the influence of the two men who were to leave a deep impression on him for the rest of his life: Li Ta-chao, his professor at Peking University, and Yang Ch'ang-chi, his ethics teacher, educated in England and Japan, whose daughter he later married. But at this stage, according to his own writings, although he was "more and more radical" he was also "confused and looking for a road". He was 24 years of age. Later he told Edgar Snow:

"At this time my mind was a curious mixture of ideas of liberalism, democratic reformism, and Utopian socialism. I had somewhat vague passions about 'nineteenth century democracy' Utopianism and old fashioned liberalism and I was definitely anti-militarist and anti-imperialist..."

Another influence on him was the *New Youth Review*,

founded in 1915 by a Peking University professor called Ch'en Tu-hsiu, which was one of the leading vehicles of expression of the revolutionary cultural renaissance. Among those who had influenced Ch'en were Rousseau, Adam Smith, John Stuart Mill, Darwin, Spencer and John Dewey. But what was most distinctive about Ch'en's contribution to the revolution was his passionate emphasis on the potential of China's youth to bring about the cultural reawakening of the weak and languishing China. In the first issue of *New Youth Review* he stated passionately:

"Oh, young men of China! Will you be able to understand me? Five out of every ten whom I see are young in age, but old in spirit; nine out of every ten are young in health, but they are also old in spirit... When this happens to a body, the body is dying. When it happens to a society, the society is perishing...We must have youth if we are to survive. We must have youth if we are to get rid of corruption. Here lies the only hope for our society."

China in 1919 was still in a resentful ferment because of the West's signing over to Japan the German concessions in Shan-tung. When the news reached China there was a mass protest on 4 May, 1919, by some five thousand students from the Peking University supported by other institutions. They demanded the rejection of the Treaty, together with others, and punishment for those Chinese who were betraying their country by such agreements. The campaign spread to other parts of China, and the mass movement became known as "the May Fourth Movement" and the birth of the Chinese labour movement. It was also the basis for the founding of the Chinese Communist Party. Within a year after the May Fourth Movement protest Communist groups were formed in the major Chinese cities.

It was at this point that the Communist leaders in Russia, particularly Lenin, saw the potential in the Chinese revolutionary movement. Lenin had been advocating a policy of promoting revolution in colonial and anti-colonial areas and in the spring of 1920 the Comintern sent a mission consisting of a Russian and an overseas Chinese to establish contact with the burgeoning Chinese Communist group. The formal inauguration of the Chinese Communist Party took place at the First Congress held in Shanghai on 1 July, 1921. The twelve or thirteen delegates included Mao Zedung. The First Congress formally and closely associated itself with the Communist International. It also rejected the various "bourgeois reformist ideologies" of the time, mainly because they had failed in their earlier attempts at revolution through identifying themselves with traditional and cultural patterns.

Two of the first Chinese intellectuals to adopt Communism were Li Ta-chao and Ch'en Tu-hsiu. The latter was the real founder and first Secretary General of the Party, though later discredited for "Party deviations"; but it was Li, executed in 1927 as a Communist, who is now regarded as the founder. It was Li, with the active support of Mao, who argued intensely for a different kind of revolution to meet the challenges in China, the concept of revolution through transforming the thought of individuals. What this meant was described later by a Western authority:*

"The strong link between culture and politics in the evolving ideology of the May Fourth generation produced a new concept of revolution. Even as the movement began to interpret politics in the terms of organised popular action based on specific issues as a mechanism for changing society, intellectuals felt that the political action would succeed only if carried out in a larger context of cultural change. *From this aspect of ideological development emerged a concept of revolution which, unlike Leninism, interpreted the essence of revolutionary change as a restructuring of thought*

*Richard H. Solomon: "From Commitment to Cant: The Evolving Functions of Ideology in the Revolutionary Process".

rather than just the capturing of state power and subsequent efforts to transform China's largely agricultural economy". (my italics).

Writing of the young Mao at this time Jerome Ch'en, in his study, *Mao*, says:

"Mao's understanding of human nature is founded upon Mencius' exposition of the goodness of man, Wang's of man's malleability, the dialectics of Marx, and, above all, his own rich experience in handling men; modern studies of human nature have never formed a part of his scheme. At the time when he became acquainted with Wang Fu-chih's theory, he was also interested in questions of morality (his reading of F. Paulsen), philosophy (his avid reading of newspapers)...Within this mixture of revolutionary, utilitarian and voluntaristic thoughts germinating in his mind, he found the *New Youth*, the radical journal edited by Ch'en Tu-hsiu, eminently palatable and he read it regularly..."

It was the 21-year-old visionary Marx – the "world creator", with his *Weltanschauung der Welveranderung*, "world outlook for world change" – who so impressed the young Li Ta-chao in China, and through Li the young Mao, with his declaration:*

"He who no longer finds pleasure in building the whole world with his own forces, in being a world-creator instead of revolving forever inside his own skin, on him the Spirit has spoken its anathema...Least of all are we entitled to assume on the strength of authority and good faith that a philosophy is a philosophy, even if the authority is that of a whole nation and the faith is that of centuries..."

Mao Zedung was born on 26 December, 1893, in the village of Shaoshan in Hunan Province, the son of a poor peasant who became a rich peasant. He had a strict father, a kind mother, two brothers and a sister. Hunan had a strong revolutionary tradition and in 1911, the year of the

***Marx in His Own Words:* Ernst Fischer: Penguin, 1973, p17.

Republican Revolution of Sun Yat-Sen, the seventeen-year-old Mao went to Changsha, the provincial capital, to further his education. His imagination had been fired by the reports reaching Shaoshan regarding the exploits of one Huang Hsing who had escaped from Changsha after the failure of an attempt to assassinate the principal imperial officials gathered there to celebrate the birthday of the Empress Dowager.

In Changsha he was introduced to the writings of the young romantic revolutionary of a generation earlier, T'an Ssu-t'ung. T'an had been beheaded by the reactionary Empress Dowager at the age of 34 for his reformist ideas. But before that he had been able to produce the first modern newspapers in Changsha, the daily *Hunan Journal* and *Hunan Students' Journal*. In these and other writings T'an protested against all the obstacles restricting the old society: the individual selfishness, the hypocrisy of the "Five Cardinal Relationships", and especially the formalism of the prevailing culture. He attacked the Manchu regime virulently, while rejecting empty nationalism, and preached universal love and the abolishing of frontiers. One part of his vision deeply impressed the young Mao:

"...to break out of the entangling net (created by) the pursuit of selfish interests and of official emoluments; to break out of the net of such vulgar teachings as those of the school of textual criticism and of stylistic formalism; to break out of the net of all (conforming) theories and teachings throughout the globe; to break through the trammels imposed by rulers; to break out of the net of the "basic human relationships"; and to break out of the net of 'heaven'..."

Fifteen years later Mao was to articulate his own revolutionary goals in similar terms:

"A man in China is usually subjected to the domination of three systems of authority: (i) the state system (political authority), ranging from the national, provincial and county government down to that of the township; (ii) the ancestral temple and its branch temples down to the head of the household; and (iii) the supernatural system (religious authority), ranging from the King of Hell down to the town and village gods belonging to the nether world, and from the Emperor of Heaven down to all the various gods and spirits 'belonging to the celestial world'. As for women, in addition to being dominated by these three systems of authority, they were also dominated by the men (the authority of the husband). These four authorities – political, clan, religious and masculine – are the embodiment of the whole feudal-patriarchal system and ideology, and are the four thick ropes binding the Chinese people, particularly the peasants..."*

With the arrival in China of the Comintern adviser, Mikhail Borodin, on 6 October, 1923, as Russia's representative, a new and potent factor was introduced into the Chinese revolutionary situation. He quickly gained a great influence over the Chinese Communist leaders in the most formative years of their lives, and this influence was enhanced by the fact that he was a professional revolutionary embodying successful theories. He introduced radical but practicable government based on peasant and labour unions, advocated closed relations with Moscow and subversion from within the Nationalist Party, and ultimately seizure of power. He also emphasised efficient organisation, training and military supplies to the armed groups. In May 1924 he helped set up the famous Whampoa Military Academy, staffed by Russian military advisers, operated by Russian funds, and furnished with Russian equipment and supplies. Its Commandant was the Nationalist leader Chiang Kai Shek, but its political instructor was the Communist Zhou Enlai.

**Report on an Investigation of the Peasant's Movement in Hunan.*

By these means Borodin was able to organise a politically conscious Chinese revolutionary army, instead of the feudal and mercenary forces used so far. The adaptation of Russian tactics in mobilising the workers and peasants of Kwangtung into a revolutionary fighting force was far-reaching in its impact, for within the next few years the Nationalist-Communist joint command had taken over 16 of China's provinces.

In *Bulletin No 3* of the Kuomintang Publicity Department dated 24 September, 1926, it was stated:

"The secret of our successes lies in the fact that the soldiers are true to the *Kuomintang* principles. Ours is an army of Party men. It has received not only a military training, but also political instruction in *Kuomintang* principles. Every soldier is, at the same time, a Party worker. He knows his principles, and he reasons when he has to fire. When he temporarily hides his sword, he clambers on to a tree-trunk or soap-box somewhere near the camp and preaches to the workers and peasants the principles for which he is fighting. For him, firing his rifle is not the simple execution of a duty, but a step towards the final aim. While soldiers of the militarist armies sell their services to a separate personality or a number of personalities, the soldiers of the Revolutionary Army serve only the *Kuomintang* principles...Sometimes the political workers go ahead of the Army in order to tell the people about its aims which will bring them a better future. Under such conditions it is not surprising that the people always welcome the Revolutionary Army and render it innumerable services in time of need, as guides and translators, and by providing food. This is an army of the people, and it fights for the sake of the people. The success of the Army will also be the success of the people..."

But, despite the high hopes expressed, it was the powers of the political commissars in the Army units which precipitated, first, the crisis in relations between the Nationalists and the Communists and then, finally, the defeat of the civilian leader Wang Ching-wei by the Commander-in-Chief, Chiang Kai Shek. The latter, in his *coup d'etat*, expelled the Communists and dismissed Borodin. The Communists responded by adopting a policy of force and direct action against employers and land-owners in the name of the proletarian revolutionary movement, in seizing land in Hunan Province in the months of April-May, 1927. This was the native province of Mao Zedung.

The Moscow-dominated leaders directed their strategy in the Russian emphasis on attacks against cities rather than in the countryside and this resulted in a series of catastrophic defeats. Meanwhile, Mao Zedung, who had argued against this strategy and for the opposite strategy for attacks in the countryside, was in the nearby Kiangsi Province where he had built up an effective operation. His plans were "to encircle and subsequently seize the cities occupied by the counter- revolution, by means of armed, revolutionary districts".

With this in mind in 1925 he had concentrated on peasant organisation rather than on forming trades unions, organising them into "peasant association" and "peasant soviets" out of their basic existing "secret societies" but teaching them by trained Communist cadres with the sole object of "exterminating local tyrants, evil gentry and lawless landlords". 1925 was probably the most critical turning-point in making Mao into a unique voluntaristic Marxist. Out of his experience of working with the peasants Mao experienced what he described as "a fundamental change...in the bourgeois and petty-bourgeois feelings implanted in me by the bourgeois schools". But from the point of view of the classical Marxists he went to the opposite extreme of not basing revolution on urban workers but in agrarian revolution from the peasantry. He argued that:

"All kinds of arguments against the peasant movement must be speedily set right...For the rise of the peasant movement is a colossal event. In a very short time, in China's central, southern and northern provinces, several hundred million peasants will rise like a tornado, or tempest, a force so extraordinarily swift and violent that no power, however great, will be able to suppress it. They will break all trammels that now bind them and rush forward along the road to liberation...All revolutionary comrades will stand before them to be tested and to be accepted as they decide..."

From Li Ta-chao Mao had learned the importance of organising "the great union of the popular masses" in a revolution, and now he had discovered the key in the peasants' revolts he organised. He wrote in one of his earliest published works:*

"Who are our enemies? Who are our friends? This is a question of the first importance for the revolution. The basic reason why all previous revolutionary struggles in China achieved so little was their failure to unite with real friends in order to attack real enemies."

But Mao was still far from being an orthodox Marxist in any sense. If anything, he was a nationalist revolutionary, with support even for Chiang Kai Shek's revolutionary aims. He was even viewed suspiciously by his Communist comrades as the most pro-*Kuomintang* of them all, despite his apparent socialism, and because of his disapproval of the Russian strategy.

On 18 February, 1927, Mao declared his own revolutionary creed:

"...a revolution is not a dinner party, or writing an essay, or painting a picture, or doing embroidery; it cannot be so refined, so leisurely, so gentle, so temperate, kind, courteous, restrained and magnanimous. A revolution is an insurrection, an act of violence by which one class overthrows another. A rural revolution is a revolution by which the

**Analysis of the Classes in Chinese Society*, in 1926.

peasantry overthrows the power of the landlord class...The rural areas need a mighty revolutionary upsurge, for it alone can arouse the people in their millions to become a powerful force...To put it bluntly, it is necessary to create terror for a while in every rural area, or otherwise it would be impossible to suppress the activities of the counter-revolutionaries in the countryside or overthrow the authority of the gentry. Proper limits have to be exceeded in order to right a wrong, or else the wrong cannot be righted..."

But in order to accomplish his singular vision of a rapidly transformed Chinese society from the grass-roots, Mao had to apply other principles learned from Li Ta-chao, and he sought evangelically to make new converts for his revolution – from bandits as well as the secret societies, from the despised and rejected of Chinese society. His passionate conviction that " the subjective creates the objective", that the human mind was infinitely malleable, able to expand spiritually, and that the human will, once rectified, was all-powerful – in other words, that human faith could remove the mountainous obstructions of centuries of exploitation, tradition, avarice, corruption and exploitation – was demonstrated in his campaign classes conducted in his own Hunan Province and in Kiangsi nearby.

Writing of this period in his biography, *Mao Tse-tung*, Dr Stuart Schramm says:

"It reflects the accent on the human will, rather than on objective factors, which still characterises Mao's version of Marxism. A little later, commenting on the presence of an extremely high percentage of *eléments déclassés* in his army, Mao affirmed that the only remedy was to intensify political training 'so as to effect a qualitative change in these elements'. The notion that rural vagabonds can be transformed by suitable training into the vanguard of the proletariat is a striking reflection of that extreme voluntarism which has culminated in the idea that 'the subjective creates the objective' ".

With these "reformed" groups of revolutionaries Mao took land from "the exploiting landlords, evil gentry and local tyrants", and distributed it equally among the peasants in proportion to the number per family. They then lived a communal way of life. This was immensely popular, and Mao was rapidly and widely supported in his small-scale agrarian revolutions – whether his theories on Communism were understood or not – while the pro-Russian Communist Party was being defeated in its strategy of armed uprisings in the cities.

It was only a short step from forming these peasant groups to organise a guerilla force based on recruitment from a satisfied peasantry prepared to defend their new possessions. From his successful experiences Mao produced his *Report on an Investigation of the Peasant Movement in Hunan* in 1927. This was not accepted as an approved Communist policy at the time, but it became Mao's own basic operating principle especially with the failure of the pro-Russian armed activities in the cities.

In his *Report* Mao described exultantly how his unique theories of revolutionary liberation were being successfully carried out in everyday circumstances:

"...The political authority of the landlords is the backbone of all the other systems of authority. With that overturned, the clan authority, the religious authority and the authority of the husband all begin to totter. Where the peasant association is powerful, the clan elders and administrators of temple funds no longer dare oppress those lower in the clan hierarchy or embezzle clan funds. The worst clan elders and administrators, being local tyrants, have been thrown out. No one any longer dares to practice the cruel corporal and capital punishments that used to be inflicted in the ancestral temples, such as flogging, drowning and burying alive...In the places where the power of the peasant is predominant, only the older peasants and the women still believe in the gods, the younger peasants no longer doing so. Since the latter control the associations, the overthrow of the religious authority and the eradication of superstitions are going on everywhere..."

But despite his enthusiasm, Mao's ambitious uprising in Hunan Province failed, and in September 1927 he fled with his remaining forces to the southern part of Kiangsi Province. There he re-grouped his remaining force in the Hunan-Kiangsi border region and, using the same methods as in Hunan for recruiting the social outcasts he established "the First Division of the Chinese Workers and Peasants Red Army". In April of 1928 he was joined by some of the remnant troops from the original Nanchang uprising in Kiangsi, which gave him an army of some 10,000 men, with a total of 2,000 rifles. He was political commissar, and his colleague, Chu Teh, was military commander of what became "the Fourth Army".

Over the next three years similar groups were formed in other parts of Hunan, Hupeh, Kiangsi, Anwei and Shensi, until there were some 26 "Red Armies" under the Communist command. In November 1930 Chiang Kai Shek launched his first "extermination drives" against the so-called "Central Soviet Area" controlled by Mao. It took him five such drives, over the next four years, before he was able finally to break Mao's control of the area.

The total territorial bases of the Chinese Communist Party comprised about 300 counties, scattered through 11 of the 18 provinces of China, comprising roughly one-sixth of the area of China proper. The total population of the soviet areas, according to the Communists, was 60 million. The "Central Soviet Area" controlled by Mao was about one-quarter in size and population. In these areas the Communists maintained their own army, police and administration, with their own currency, post offices and stamps. Their banknotes carried the images of Marx and Lenin.

There was a great deal of tension in the Chinese Communist Party during the years 1930 to 1934 when Li Li-san and Wan-Min, with the support of Stalin and the Comintern, attacked the "peasant narrowness" and "conservatism" of the village strategists" of Mao's individualistic and "new" revolutionary interpretation of Marxism. The official line aimed at developing proletarian uprisings in the cities because, the traditionalists affirmed, the proletariat had to be the leading force in any bourgeois-democratic revolution. But they had to argue from the position of failure, while Mao was winning his battles. But Mao, despite occasional set-backs, was adamant in his peasant-orientated revolution and, with consummate daring, went on to argue that his theories were also applicable world-wide. In his *New Democracy* he said:

"In an era when the world capitalist front has collapsed in one corner of the globe (a corner which forms one-sixth of the world)...in such an era, any revolution that takes place in a colony or semi-colony against imperialism, i.e., against the international bourgeoisie and international capitalism, belongs no longer to the old category of bourgeois democratic world revolutions, but to a new category, and is...part of the new world revolution, the proletariat-socialist world revolution..."*

But Mao was isolated by the pro-Moscow leadership of the Chinese Communist Party, and in Chiang Kai Shek's fifth, and major, drive against his forces Mao faced defeat again. Moscow radioed instructions for Mao to withdraw his army and seek safety elsewhere – Mongolia, if necessary and possible. So, on 15 October, 1934, the main forces of Mao's Fourth Red Army, totalling about 130,000, left Kiangsi Province for an unknown destination in the north-west of China. They followed a notorious route made famous by a revolutionary Taiping general, Shih Ta-k'ai, who had disappeared seventy years before. They were harried con-

*Mao's *Selected Works:* Vol 3, p111.

stantly by the Nationalist armies, and by the mercenary troops of local warlords, until they captured Tsunyi in Kweichow Province on 13 January, 1935.

The Long March, as it came to be called, was a political event with far-reaching repercussions, and not merely an outstanding military achievement of over 100,000 people travelling and fighting over some 8,000 miles. Mao described it:

"The Long March is the first of its kind in the annals of history...a manifesto, a propaganda force, a seeding-machine. Since Pa Ku divided the heavens from the earth and the Three Sovereigns and Five Emperors reigned, has history ever witnessed a Long March such as ours?...It has announced to two million people in eleven provinces that the road of the Red Army is their only road to liberation...In the eleven provinces it has sown many seeds which will sprout, leaf, blossom and will bear fruit, and will yield a harvest for the future."

Or, in poetic phraseology. Mao phrased it:

> "The Red Army fears no hardship on the Long March.
> A thousand mountains, ten thousand rivers are nothing.
> The Five Ranges are like little winding ripples.
> The peaks of Wumeng like clay balls tumbling into the plain.
> Washed by the River of Golden Sand, the cloud-covered cliffs are warm.
> Spanning the River Tatu, the iron chains are cold.
> The far-off snows of Minshan only bring us joy.
> The Army presses through, and we all laugh."

In Tsunyi, before proceeding further, it was decided that they must come to some sort of understanding about their ultimate destination. A special Enlarged Session of the Central Committee Politburo was convened, not only to decide the destination of the Red Army but also to decide who was to be the leader of the Party after the disastrous policy mistakes of the past several years by the pro-Moscow faction. Northern Shensi was selected as the approved end of the Long March, as a place where they could gain wide public acceptance by fighting off the hated Japanese invaders. Mao Zedung was elected leader of the Party, and given approval to continue his emphasis on mobile warfare by guerilla groups.

The Long March ended in Yenan, in north-west Province of Shensi, in late 1935. For the next five years Mao was confronted with the task of starting the revolution from the beginning, ignoring or learning from the mistakes of others and building on his own experiences of the past few years. It was his most fruitful period of intellectual growth, as he defined the requirements of his "New Democracy" in the light of the war with Japanese occupation forces and in anticipation of forming the next government of China when they had defeated the Nationalists.

There was little that China's historical traditions of government could teach them, for it had been based on an antiquated system of unacceptable Confucian ethics. Even as late as the previous century there had been only some 40,000 official positions for the management of the central and local government agencies that ruled over 3,500,000 square miles and an estimated population of 400,000,000. These had depended on the historically developed clan and family system at the lower levels to exercise control, locally, provincially and nationally, in a pyramid structure with the father as head of the unit, the elders as head of the clan, and the Emperor as head of the State.

But the Communist forces were sweeping away these traditional systems and, among other things, this meant a whole new system of administration would have to be developed to control and to re-educate the people. Also, with religion being swept away, a new ethical and moral system to support and uphold Communist Party power was essential. For centuries the theory of the interaction between Heaven and man had been a guiding political concept, enabling rulers to rule in the name of Heaven while justifying their policies and persuading the people to accept that authority. The effective operation of this system had depended on the pseudo-religious influence in China's traditional society. But an atheistic Chinese Communist Party had no such resource and would have to create something to put in its place.

The Communist Party had established itself as the largest single force in China in mobilising, developing and directing a vast section of the Chinese people as instruments for change for better conditions; and had demonstrated indisputably in many areas that they were fitted to do the same with the nascent energies of the new China in a time of peace. Nor were they merely successful exponents of a comparatively new Western ideology in a corrupt and effete Eastern environment tied slavishly to the dogma, dicta and example of the first prototype, Russia. They had hammered out their own creed and policies through years of war, hardship and practical application, in the face of bitter opposition from the classical Marxists in Russia. The policy which had emerged from their pragmatic approach, and which had brought them eventual success in their consolidation in Yenan, even if temporary, would be "the correct line" from which all other policies must flow.

Mao, the peasant's son – admittedly, a fairly rich peasant's son – in Yenan, was already looking beyond the regional problems of interior China, beyond the national problems of the old Chinese Empire restored, to a vision of a Chinese world empire – or, at least, a Chinese-led world empire. Once again, China would have her true place in the world, the "Middle Kingdom" around which all others would revolve. To this Utopia the Communist Party would lead the way, with Mao as the new prophet in his generation. But to accomplish this an instrument greater than the

Party would be required: the whole nation must become aware of a new destiny, its new direction, and become an integrated instrument in the liberating of the world from "the accursed imperialist yoke".

In October, 1937, Mao issued a directive to the political workers of the Eighth Army which declared:

"The Sino-Japanese War affords our policy an excellent opportunity for expansion. Our fixed policy should be 70 per cent expansion, 20 per cent dealing with the *Kuomintang*, and 10 per cent resisting Japan. There are three stages in carrying out this fixed policy. The First is a compromising stage, in which self-sacrifice should be made to show our obedience to the Central Government and adherence to Dr Sun Yat Sen's 'Three Principles of the People', but in reality this will serve as a camouflage for the existence and development of our Party.

"The Second stage is a continuing stage in which two or three years should be spent in laying the foundation of our Party's political and military powers, and developing these until we can match and break the *Kuomintang* and eliminate the latter north of the Yellow River. While waiting for an unusual turn of events, we should give the Japanese invaders certain concessions.

"The Third is an offensive stage, in which our forces should penetrate deep into Central China, sever the communications of the Central Government troops in various sectors, isolate and disperse them until we are ready for the counter-offensive and wrest the leadership from the hands of the *Kuomintang*".

Having from the start committed themselves to a programme of organising the peasant masses, and having been so singularly successful, the Chinese Communist Party extended their activities among the peasants beyond their use as effective weapons of revolt. From their inception in Hunan in 1927, until the completion of the land reform programme in 1952, the whole application of Communist strategy was bound to this formula for mass organisation. The new vision accorded to them, and the dramatic success – even in the face of occasional set-backs – caught the imagination of the peasants as they saw a new social order emerging before their eyes and under their own efforts. A visiting newspaper correspondent who had spent many years in China visited Northern Shensi and wrote enthusiastically:

"I could feel the new joy of the peasant in the little bit of land he possessed, his intense pride, and his faith in the Communist Party which made this change possible. He now walked with his back unbent, and his eyes sparkled as he looked straight at you. His wife and his daughter had shared in the glory. They were no longer shut up in the home, cowering to hide their bodies from the lustful eyes of the village lord. There was no incense burning in the village temples before the inscrutable Buddhas attended by saffron-robed priests. New China had emerged and new men were in charge of her destiny".

In the general enthusiasm it was comparatively easy for the Party cadres to organise self-government, as well as self-defence and partisan guerilla groups. Labour teams, production cooperatives, supply auxiliaries and an intelligence network contributed further to the integration and expanding administration of the Communist areas. For the Army, the Communist leaders did not have to resort to the compulsory methods with no-pay recruits, the chief weakness of the *Kuomintang* and the warlord armies. Consequently, the morale of the Communist armies was higher than any Chinese Army had ever been. There was also a spirit of equality and comradeship in the sense of mission and destiny, and the officers and men shared that sense of equality. In this way it became a formidable fighting force, either in small or large campaigns, leading eventually to the formation of what became Mao's famous strategy of "the war of manoeuvre":

"A quick decision requires thorough preparation, correct timing, concentration of a preponderant force, the tactic of encircling and outflanking, favourable positions...A battle is not basically decisive that ends only in routing the enemy...To wound all ten fingers of a man is not so effective as to chop one of them off; to rout ten of the enemy's divisions is not so effective as to isolate one of them."

Two thousand five hundred years before, the Chinese Sun-tzu had enunciated his classical guerilla philosophy, now effectively copied by Mao:

"Enemy advances: We retreat.
Enemy escapes: We harrass.
Enemy retreats: We pursue.
Enemy tires: We attack".

The same uncompromising attitude was carried into the political and economic fields. All "feudal" and "semi-feudal" elements in Chinese society, by Communist interpretation, were outlawed as enemies of the people, and all programmes were designed not just to isolate them but to eliminate them for good.

While the Marxist ideology and regime was something totally new in Chinese history, the idea of a strong, centralised government had been part of Chinese belief for millenia. Under the Han, T'ang, Ming and Manchu dynasties exercise of the imperial authority was based on the "mystique" of the "Son of Heaven" with a divine mandate to exercise control over China through his self-appointed viceroys – "superior men" educated and trained to govern. It was no concern of the other classes what form the government took, or how it was exercised.

The new leaders of the Communist Party in China were intellectuals steeped in the history and classics of China, and passionately committed to restoring its dignity and place in history. In the peculiar circumstances of the evolution of Marxism in China, therefore, it was inevitable that their background and experience should influence their theories in practice. Thus, the Chinese form of Marxism, apart from its first pro-Moscow faction, was different from the Russian, although in the direct line of descent. It was compounded from a curious amalgam of Chinese religion and culture, imperialism and nationalism, atheism and a debased Christianity. The latter had formed the basis of the religious/nationalist Taiping Revolution, and had been part of the early Christian liberal education of the Chinese leaders of the Marxist Revolution. It was no surprise, therefore, that while the Chinese Communist leaders in Yenan were cool towards Stalin for the lack of help to them, and his overt support for the Nationalists, they did approve of the Stalinist concept of autocratic government.

This curious amalgam provided other peculiar colorations to the Chinese form of Marxism. The former Confucian ideal of totalitarian rule by a sage-king was changed by the nineteenth century Christianity to a forward-looking philosophy of a better future for all the people but by possibly new methods. Confucianism itself preached obedience to the ideal of a distant past. Buddhism promised Nirvana to the individual believer, but saw the world as "illusory" and evil. The Christianity of the educated Chinese taught, and seemed to practise, indifference to the present world, and made an impact with its ideal of a changed world in the future through changes in individuals and forms of government.

So the Marxism, or Mao's "New Democracy", of New China preached the necessity of change with the evangelical fervour of Tolpuddle Martyrs. But because of their imperialistic history they used coercion and not persuasion; and because of their chauvinistic history they had a missionary vision to carry the Chinese dogmas to the furthest bounds of the Celestial Empire – and then to the world beyond. The New Democracy must be transformed into Utopian Socialism immediately, and then into Millenial Communism in what might be the far-off future.

The authority of Heaven which the emperor had claimed, and by which they ruled the people of China, was being replaced by the authority of the people – which justified the retention of power of those who had first claimed it on the people's behalf – the Chinese Communist Party, based in Yenan for the present, but whose ambition was to rule from Peking. It was a Messianic vision which the Communist Party carried to the people of China, and to which the people so enthusiastically responded. It was epitomised in the highly moral, even religious, strain of the propaganda; the certainty of the "correctness" of the Party doctrine; the undeviating attachment to certain dogmas; the unquestioning assumption that virtue was inherent in the workers' and peasants' classes, and in their Marxist representatives; the elitist acceptance of the elect; and the confidence of future reward.

It was indeed a breath-taking vision. The Chinese Marxists would not just be political ideologues or social engineers, but religious evangelists. Led by their inspirational Prophet-Chairman, with the members of the Party as the ordained clergy, the People's Liberation Army was the Marxist Church Militant whose mission was to convert all of China, then all the world, to accept the revelatory doctrines of the Communist Trinity – Marx, Lenin and Mao.

CHAPTER FIVE

HOW MARX CAME TO CHINA

Through Spiritual Transformation: 1935-1950

As has been noted earlier, Mao was deeply influenced by his professor at Peking University, Li Ta-chao, who was one of the first of China's intellectuals to embrace Marxism, the first true leader of the Chinese Communist Party and martyr at 39. Li had been the link between the older generation of democratically-orientated and Western-educated intellectuals in the early phases of the New Culture Movement at the time of the "intellectual revolution" from 1915-19, from which the first Marxists emerged. Li was also the first to undertake the task of adapting Marxism to the Chinese environment, combining both into an explosive ideology of militant nationalism and voluntaristic interpretation of Marxism which strongly appealed to his assistant librarian, Mao Zedung.

Li identified more with the young, strongly idealistic Marx rather than the older, pragmatic social engineer. He objected to the later Marxist belief in the inexorable workings of the economic laws of history, foreseeing in the East's primitive conditions what Marx could not see in the sophisticated West, namely, that China, according to this theory, would be condemned to a long and dreary period of capitalist development. Even before he was won over to the vision of a world-wide revolutionary transformation promised, it seemed, by the Bolshevik victory in Russia, Li

Tao-chao had come to believe profoundly in the ability of the human spirit and human will to change the circumstances under which men and women lived.

"When the young men have seen the light", he declared in 1916, "they should break the meshes of past history, destroy the prison of old ideas, and suffer no corpses to restrict their activity".

Li saw in the Bolshevik revolution in Russia the promise of "the mass movement of the twentieth century".

"The efforts of each individual within this great mass... will be concentrated and become a great irresistible social force...In the course of this world mass movement, all the refuse of history which stands in the path of the new movement – such as emperors, nobles, warlords, bureaucrats, militarism and capitalism – will certainly be destroyed..."

In the conflict between the Determinists and the Activists in 1919, shortly after Mao's arrival in Peking, Li rejected the "social Darwinism" of the sterile Determinists, and argued:

"The roots of all forms of socialism are purely ethical. Co-operation and friendship are the general principles of the social life of man...We ought to recognise that human social life will always be controlled by those general principles, and it can be discovered that they are always hidden in the premises commonly and generally recognised by Socialists at any time and in any place. Not only utopian but also scientific socialism...establish their concepts upon these premises..."

So, when Mao came to re-think and to re-state his unique revolutionary programme after arriving in Yenan in his "New Democracy" he gave high priority to the necessity for re-structuring the historically ingrained thinking of the Chinese people and their indoctrination into his own vision of a Chinese Marxist society.

If the Communist People's Liberation Army, as his combined forces were called, was his strong right arm, the propaganda system which he set up was his left arm. "Who is a propagandist" he asked himself in a speech in 1942. "Not only is the teacher a propagandist, the newspaper reporter a propagandist, the literary writer a propagandist, but all our cadres in all kinds of work are also propagandists". To Mao, propaganda was the communication of Marxist ideas in all its forms – education, journalism and literature. "Any person talking with another person is engaged in propaganda", he stated. Propaganda was the life work of a Chinese Communist in fulfilling the goal of bringing the whole nation and its posterity to belief in Marxism.

With this end in view it became a matter of prime importance to make the whole population of China literate, a gigantic task. While this was being accomplished it was necessary to place a radio "in every village, every street, and eventually beside every bed", through which "collective listening" had to be encouraged. Newspapers were required to "enlighten the people, so they could actively promote New Democracy". The publishing houses, film industry and theatres were also "reformed" to suit the new propaganda purpose. In a speech to the Yenan Forum on Literature and Art, in May, 1942, Mao said:

"Literature and art are subordinate to politics , and in turn exert great influence over politics. Revolutionary literature and art are a part of the entire revolutionary enterprise; they are like screws which, in relation to other parts of the machine, may be classified on a basis of importance, urgency or primacy. But they are the screws essential to the machine, and they are the part essential to the revolutionary enterprise."

Mao's comprehensive Marxist revolutionary education programme was more than an extensive elucidation of ideas so that people could make up their own minds; it was unremitting propaganda which aimed at changing their past ways of thinking and acting, and "persuading" them to a whole new way of thinking and acting – to serve the dictates of the Marxist self-appointed representatives, the Communist Party leaders. The educational institutions had to alter the major curricula for colleges, universities and schools throughout the country by "abolishing the politically reactionary courses, and installing revolutionary courses of New Democracy".

In order to bring about this colossal national programme of total "thought reform", again it was Mao who outlined how this was to be done during the Party Reform Movement in 1942-3 when he stated that it was necessary "to wash the brains" of those whose ways of thinking were judged inimical towards, or unhealthy for, the new regime. His theory was simply that, in order to become citizens in the New Democracy, those whose brains had been adversely afflicted by past poisonous thoughts from earlier regimes and practices would have to have them "cleansed" by a "thorough washing". This transforming process for men and women would be necessary before a new Marxist society could be ushered in.

The "Yenan Syndrome", or the "Yenan Model", as it came to be called, contributed most to what was later known as "The Maoist Vision". This phrase itself is inadequate, in the sense that it can be articulated under any category of "ten headings" or "twelve principles" to provide an operational system. In fact, the China scholar, Dr Benjamin Schwartz, argued that the elements of the vision were not always prominent, or even consistent, and that some were even ambivalent, in a dialectic sense lending themselves to support of quite different policies at times. Schwartz explained:

"Not only has the pursuit of this vision often cut across other goals of the leadership, but has with varying degrees of intensity conditioned the manner in which these other goals have been pursued. Some elements of the vision have had an obvious and unremitting impact on reality. The enormous energies invested since 1949 *in the effort to achieve the spiritual transformation of the entire Chinese people,* whether in the form of 'study' , 'thought reform', ' remoulding', 'education through labour', or 'socialist education', is one of the most obvious instances..." (my italics).

Mao's Marxist vision, however, was inherited from and influenced by Li Ta-chao's socialist values of cooperation and friendship, and upon his confidence in harnessing the powerful forces of latent "surplus energy" which had been accumulating in the exploited, oppressed Chinese masses for centuries. Therefore Mao was determined not to be a prisoner of the inexorable and objective laws of social development of Russian Marxism, but would be the inspirer of the ideas, the will and the "self-consciousness of the Chinese people. So he based his whole super-structure of what was becoming known as "Mao-thought" upon two fundamental ideas developed by Li Ta-chao:

(i) that the human mind is infinitely malleable, and able to expand spiritually; and

(ii) that the human will, once rectified, is all-powerful, to the point that the "subjective creates the objective".

The mechanisms of transformation in "Mao thought" were: (i) *mould* the human mind; (ii) *expand* it spiritually; (iii) *harness* its latent subjective power to create the necessary objective changes. He did this by applying a three-fold process: (i) *struggle* between old practices and new ideas; (ii) *criticism* of ingrained and destructive traditions and superstitions; (iii) *transformation* into new and dynamic men and women.

"Self-interest" was the "original sin" of the Marxist spiritual concepts. He saw it as the centre of the revisionist educational system from which came such revisionist ideas as seeking scholastic recognition, advancement to schools of higher levels, theoretical knowledge, and specialised training and status. In study sessions throughout the areas

DISTINCTIVE STRUCTURE OF "MAO-THOUGHT"

(or "MAO'S REVOLUTIONARY LINE")

Influence Nation Through (i) Family, (ii) Community Solidarity Cells (socialist courtyards), **(iii) Neighbourhood Committees**

↑

Conversion into Maoist "New Man and Woman" through "Struggle - Criticism - Spiritual Transformation"

↑

Elimination of "Self-Interest" by "Self-Criticism"

↑

Thought Reform
(primarily administered to cadres and intellectuals)

(i) **Propaganda** (impersonal)
(ii) **Indoctrination**
(personal and face-to-face)
(iii) **Mass Campaigns**
(e.g. socialist education, etc.)

(i) **Production-Directed Mass Movements with Psychological Appeal**
(e.g. "the Party cares for me")
(ii) **Persuasion**
(e.g. "for the good of the nation")
(iii) **Rational Explanation**
(e.g. "it is good and necessary because...")

↑

Szu-Hsiang (or "Correct Thinking")
e.g. in agriculture if there is inadequate production there is no unproductive land, only unproductive thought, or "incorrect thinking".

Human Mind
(infinitely malleable, able to expand spiritually)

Human Will
(once rectified, is all powerful)

↑

"THE SUBJECTIVE CREATES THE OBJECTIVE"

they controlled, therefore, all students and teachers had first to practise "self-criticism", "confess self-interest", "thoroughly destroy self-interest", in order to uphold the concept of "teaching for revolution and learning for revolution". The usual approach was that the Party-cadre students would direct a criticism against some of the past teachings or practices of a particular teacher or professor. The professor or teacher would then be asked to give his explanation and self- criticism to a student assembly, where he would "confess" all his past sins and pledge to learn anew from "Mao-thought" or he would be subject to severe criticism and humiliation from the "masses". These criticisms and corrections would then be published in the media, and the public reaction extended to include further criticisms and confessions in the homes and street-meetings of the area.

"Self-interest" was held to produce careerism, individualism, professionalism, elitism, profiteering, avarice, selfishness, pursuit of fame and privilege. It only took a few years for the majority of the Chinese people subjected to the process to be convinced that "salvation" through "struggle-criticism-transformation" was readily if laboriously achievable, because they had seen the "conversion" process at work.

The Moaist vision of spiritual transformation was both particular and universal in that the Chinese nation under Marxism was seen as the spiritual centre and source of inspiration and example for people's revolutionary liberation movements everywhere; and universal in that it postulated a giant moral battle on a global scale between the forces of good and the forces of evil, while that same moral struggle took place in the life of each individual. It was also intensely evangelical, and, as a consequence, became messianic and eschatological, deifying Mao in the present age and envisioning a new utopian age through the Maoist vision of world revolution.

The chief characteristics of the Maoist vision were categorised by Donald MacInnis, in his book, *Religious Policy and Practice in Communist China:*

(i) an overriding commitment to a society united by something approaching a total consensus, and a society marked by a radical conservatism;

(ii) a unique emphasis on the individual's total self-abnegation, and total immersion in the collectivity as the ultimate good;

(iii) people are more important than weapons, machines or technology;

(iv) *an enormous emphasis on the power of spiritual transformation* (indoctrination is far too weak a term);

(v) peasants and workers, once liberated, have infinite capacity for creative thought and action, and could be trusted while intellectuals could not;

(vi) self-reliance was essential and a moral virtue, whether in individuals, in national or international policies;

(vii) *struggle, conflict and high tension are positive values and essential elements in the spiritual transformation process.* (my italics).

Mao's spiritually transformed "new man" and "new woman", therefore, was someone devoted to collective life, seeing his or her interest inextricably bound up in the progress of all. His or her vocation was to serve the people, to go where needed, sublimating personal desires for the sake of the collective cause even in such matters as sex, marriage and children. One would not maximise personal income, or advance one's own career, or remain in the city if needed in the country, or withdraw from family or group conflict situations for selfish personal reasons of embarrassment or rejection, or consider one's self as superior by looking down on people from other regions or class backgrounds, or accumulate worldly goods, or fail to help others in need. "Fight Self, and Serve the People", became as fundamental a principle to Maoism as "Die to Self; Love

Others" was to Christianity.

The Maoist vision incorporated the reducing and eventual removal of material incentives for work performed; individual performance and financial reward being offset by the progressive development of non-material and social incentives, when most people would be internally motivated by the spiritual values of Mao's form of Marxism.

Enormous effort on a historically unprecedented scale was harnessed to this important primary task of converting the then 700 million Chinese people to the realisation of this vision. "Study", "thought reform", "confession" and other techniques were applied on various levels of Chinese society, first to prospective Party members then to the people as a whole. The transformation of men and women, from being "self-centred" to being "others-centred", was fundamental to the success of the whole revolution in Mao's view, and in this campaign and conception Mao surpassed the young idealist Marx and other Marxist leaders.

In his book, *Ideology and Practice: The Evolution of Chinese Communism,* James Chieh Hsiung provided a lucid breakdown as to how this spiritual transformation was accomplished:

"The Party believes that the key to China's modernisation lies in instilling correct thinking *(szu-hsiang)* in people's minds. The objective of ideological work is to create uniformity of thought, sentiment, outlook, psychic commitment. Several patterns for achieving that objective have been developed, including (i) thought reform, primarily administered to cadres and intellectuals; (ii) propaganda (impersonal), indoctrination (personal and face-to-face), and such mass campaigns as the socialist education campaigns; and (iii) production-directed mass movements combining psychological appeal ('the Party cares for me'), persuasion ('for the good of the Nation'), and rational explanation (it is good and necessary because...)".

James Chieh Hsiung in his book emphasised two very important and distinctive principles by which the individual and the nation would be transformed by Maoist principles. The first is that "Maoism" is not the same as "Mao-thought" to the Chinese. To the Chinese "thought" is conceived as the determinant of all action; and "ism" is associated with the idea of a "principle" only. The true significance of "Mao-thought", therefore, was that it was not just the very synthesis of theory and practice (such as demonstrated to a degree by Lenin and Trotsky's "Bolshevik"), but was the ultimate force that welded the two together. The only correct way to understanding the force of Mao's thought was not to be found in the simplistic cult of personality, as was often assumed in the West, but in the true Chinese meaning of "thought" – the *szu-hsiang*, or "correct thinking" described by James Chieh Hsiung. Mao's "thought" generated "correct thinking" and, as such, "breathes relevance into the actual practice of Marxism-Leninism, maintains situational flexibility within rigid operational principles and schemes, translates doctrine into reality, and can sustain people's faith in the darkest hours".

The second important point made by James Chieh Hsiung in his book is that *szu-hsiang* was something outside the Marxist concept, that ideology is only a superstructure of the economic base or sub-culture. *Szu-hsiang* existed independently of the theory-practice framework, and was voluntaristic; for example: "Many living examples show that there is only *unproductive thought (szu-hsiang)*, that there are no *unproductive regions*. There are only poor methods for cultivating the land, there is no such thing as poor land. Provided only that people manifest in full measure their subjective *capacities* for action, it is possible to modify natural conditions".

Mao-*thought*, then, was the dynamic spiritual power energising *Maoism*. The deification of Mao began officially at the Seventh Congress in April, 1945, when the new Party

Constitution contained a preamble in which "The Thought of Mao Zedung" was officially enshrined as necessary to "guide the entire work of the Party". At that time Liu Shao-chi, the Party's "Organisation Man", praised Mao as "not only the greatest revolutionary and statesman in Chinese history, but also its greatest theoretician and scientist". Nor was this all, for Liu moved beyond the sphere of pure ideology to assert the claim for Mao's thought, and by association with the Chinese leadership, of a leading place in the world revolutionary movement. "The Thought of Mao Zedung", he declared, "...will make great and useful contributions to the struggle for emancipation of the peoples of all countries in general, and of the peoples of the East in particular". Thus, from 1945 onwards, Maoism was official Party policy for the conquest of the world.

Meanwhile, the civil war with the *Kuomintang*, and the national war with the invading Japanese, kept the Communist Party from expanding as they would have liked. In fact, the increasing encroachments of the Japanese in East and Central China threatened the Communists as much as the Nationalists. Consequently, they called for a National Defence Government and an anti-Japanese allied Army for National Salvation. The terms of the truce as proposed by the Communists were adopted by the *Kuomintang's* Central Executive Committee in February 1937, and agreed to be responsible for allotted War Zones under their own commanding officers.

Both Communist and Nationalist forces were left behind the advancing Japanese lines to conduct partisan and guerilla operations. But the Communists used their own greater experience in guerilla warfare not only to harrass the Japanese but also to overrun areas where the Nationalists were operating, and even on occasions to incorporate and re-train and indoctrinate the Nationalist troops. They increased the use of these tactics outside the fighting areas and extended them to taking over some Nationalist provincial governments. This resulted in a phenomenal increase in Communist-controlled areas during the wartime period. By the end of 1943 it was estimated that the "liberated areas" already included a population of some 80 million. By 1944 the figure had increased to 90 million, with 590 county governments in the "liberated areas". A year later, on the eve of the Japanese surrender, the Communists controlled 19 "liberated areas" scattered over 19 provinces, totalling about 100 million people. The Red Army had also grown from 80,000 in 1937 to a total of over a million by the end of the Japanese war.

While the anti-Japanese fighting was taking place the *Kuomintang* was both retreating and shrinking. Chiang Kai Shek and his Government moved from Nanking to Hankow; as the Japanese continued to advance, fell back on Chungking in the Szechuan Province of West China. When Pearl Harbour brought the United States and Britain into the war against Japan, the latter was in possession of most of the coast of China, had captured Hong Kong on Christmas Day, 1941, Singapore in February 1942, and looked like crushing the *Kuomintang* by the end of 1944. On 8 August, 1945, while the Japanese people were still reeling from the shock of the atom bomb dropped on Hiroshima, Russia formally declared war on Japan, and two days later the Japanese surrendered.

Despite their vastly increased strength and territorial gains the Chinese Communists were still not equipped to control or administer the whole country, and they proposed a United Front with the Nationalists. This was encouraged by the United States, and on 10 October, 1945, an agreement was signed calling for a Political Consultative Conference. But by the end of the year President Truman had to intervene to put a stop to the escalating fighting between the two Parties. The talks dragged on and, finally, on 29 January, 1947, the American delegates were officially withdrawn.

In 1948 the whole of North-East China fell to the Communists; and, when the government forces in Manchuria collapsed in November the Communist Army numbered over 3 million to the Nationalists' 2.5 million, and the writing was on the wall. Soon Tientsin, Peking and all China north of the Yangtse was under the control of the Communists, and on 1 October, 1949, the first Marxist "People's Republic of China" was established.

For the first few months after taking power the new Marxist regime followed a moderate policy towards potential opposition factions, relying on persuasion rather than force. Within less than two years of the new Government, they accomplished a remarkable restoration of the nation's economy from the legacy of *Kuomintang* corruption and inefficiency. They quickly restored the disrupted railway communications and ensured the free movement of food and goods between city and countryside, thereby ending the dislocations and horrendous shortages of the last days of *Kuomintang* rule. They also brought inflation under effective control, thus eliminating one of the basic causes of corruption. The rapid stabilising of prices, plus the ruthless and immediate application of penalties against black-marketeers, discouraged speculation and hoarding. But all these benefits were not accomplished without a considerable amount of suffering, and even terror.

In June, 1950, Mao Zedung, in a report to the Party Central Committee, called upon the Party and the masses to "raise their vigilance against the subversive activities of the counter-revolutionaries". The following month the Supreme People's Court issued a set of joint instructions regarding "the suppression of counter-revolutionary activities", as well as the establishing of "peoples' tribunals". A campaign was launched and pursued with increasing intensity throughout 1951, during which over a million criminal and civil cases were brought against alleged suspects. Huge rallies were held throughout the country in the major cities and large towns, eventually reaching down into the villages. It was the Year of the Reign of Terror.

The Terror began with the usual list of crimes, such as imperialism, and revolt against the fatherland, instigating or inducing revolt, plotting or subversion of the masses, acts of sabotage, etc. But then the Act was broadened to include "all other crimes committed with counter-revolutionary intent but not specified in the law", when mass persecution on the flimsiest pretexts became the everyday experience. The penalties ranged from death and life imprisonment, through lengthy imprisonment, to forced labour on farms or exile frontier communities.

After the heady challenge of "The Maoist Vision" of China's "new society" of "new men and new women" the cost to the country was high. Mao had warned that "a revolution is not a dinner party...a revolution is an act of violence by which one class overthrows another...to put it bluntly, it is necessary to create terror in every rural area...proper limits have to be exceeded in order to right a wrong".

First, the Japanese War, and then World War II, had served to blunt the edges of this aspect of Mao's revolution. But with Japan defeated, the *Kuomintang* defeated, and the Marxist regime installed in Peking with totalitarian power, the physical price to be paid for Mao's "spiritual transformation" of China became harshly evident. With the new Party in power in Peking, Mao called on the peasants everywhere in China to rise up and kill the landlords who had oppressed them – "not merely one or two, but a goodly number" – although he had also warned the supervising cadres against "indiscriminate killing". Mao considered this necessary for at least two reasons: one, it brought the peasants into participation with the new system of justice against those who had arbitrarily beaten, exploited, raped and killed them in the past; and, two, it was a climactic act that enabled them to understand something apparently irrevocable had occurred, and that they were now in control of their destinies.

The number of victims in the first revolutionary upheaval against "the landlord class" was relatively limited; that is, compared with what had happened in the comparable period in Soviet Russia, or what was to follow in China. But even at that, it was a traumatic experience. In Peking alone it was estimated, in the year prior to October 1951, 30,000 mass meetings of varying sizes had been held, with an audience participation of over three million people. At the first meeting alone 199 counter-revolutionaries had been executed, over 200 at the second meeting, and so on.

The casualties arising from this period of "accusation meetings" are still a cause of heated debate, ranging from the figure of 800,000 quoted by the respected scholar, Peter Tang, to the 60 million quoted by suspect Taiwan sources. Dr Stuart Schramm says that a reasonable estimate, in his opinion, would appear to be from one to three million. He continues:

"If we take the middle figure of two million victims, this amounts to about 0.3 per cent of the total population of China (it thus corresponds to about 150,000 executions in a country the size of France or 600,000 in the United States). This", he maintains, "is not an enormously large toll for a social revolution of this magnitude, carried out in the wake of a long and cruel civil war which had taken even more victims on both sides..."

Certainly, the figures appeared to cause greater trauma among the many "China-watchers" outside China than to the Chinese population. In his book, *Revolutionary Immortality*, Robert J. Lifton wrote some years later:

"...What all this suggests, then, is that the essence of the 'power struggle' taking place in China, as of all such 'power struggles', is power over death...

"A cultural revolution anywhere involves a collective shift in the psychic images around which life is organised.

In Maoist China, however, it has meant *nothing less than an all-consuming death-and-rebirth experience, an induced catastrophe together with a prescription for reconstituting the world being destroyed...*

"I would suggest that this new community, in a symbolic sense, is *a community of immortals – of men, women and children entering into a new relationship with the eternal revolutionary process.* An event of this kind is meant to convey a blending of the immortal cultural and racial substance of the Chinese as a people with the equally immortal Communist revolution...

"The Maoist corpus is elevated to an all-consuming prophecy: it nurtures men, predicts their future, and changes the world to accomplish its own prediction; it sets in motion spiritual forces against which nothing can stand..." (my italics).

The unique Maoist concept of Marxism, therefore, was essentially spiritual in every sense of the word. From the necessary rebirth of the individual to the remaking of society it was fundamentally evangelical (salvation by faith) and eschatological ("death, judgement, heaven and hell"). It was a spiritual and ethical corpus designed to transform individuals and nations and to shape world history.

PART THREE

THE CHRISTIAN-MARXIST BATTLE FOR THE SOUL OF CHINA

CHAPTER 6

THE CHRISTIAN-MARXIST BATTLE FOR THE SOUL OF CHINA

The Rise and Spread of China's Indigenous Christianity: 1900-1950

By 1935, when the Chinese Communists under Mao Zedung completed their Long March and Mao had emerged as undisputed leader to articulate his Maoist vision of a New China, there were 481,227 Protestant Christians in 6,310 organised local churches. There were 123 separate missionary organisations, and Chinese religious workers numbered 15,680. By 1950 it was reckoned that there were 3.5 million Roman Catholics, and 1.2 million Protestants, plus an incalculable number of Chinese Christians who for one reason or another refused to be associated with the Western denominations and who neither published nor kept statistics of membership. By 1927 a so-called "indigenous" organisation, comprising the Western denominations, had brought together several of them in "the Church of Christ in China".

By 1937 there had been a sizeable increase in the number of Chinese religious "leaders"; Chinese men who had some representative capacity in the existing Western religious churches and organisations. There were more than two thousand Chinese ordained pastors, and roughly two thousand laymen who were on the staffs of religious organisations. There were also about the same number of women workers. Chinese nationals not only had numerical control of the National Christian Council, but also of Church schools and of medical institutions. They also controlled the Y.M.C.A and the Y.W.C.A.

Commenting on this "sinification process", the Roman Catholic writer, Columba Cary-Elwes said:

'The sinification of the Protestant bodies in China was not in itself a bad thing. It would have been well if the Catholics had advanced along that road much faster also. But in the case of the Protestants there were peculiar dangers. The Protestant Chinese neophytes were undoubtedly zealous, but they were not so well grounded in their religion, so well instructed as the Catholics...Thus, once the American or European direction was relaxed, the dogmatic allegiances relaxed also; and the tendencies were towards Modernism on the one hand, or to social work on the other. This latter tendency was to make it fatally easy for many Christians brought up in a philanthropic Christianity to drift in the direction of Communism, not realising theological implications of this new creed and its incompatibility with the true teachings of Christ..."

But while this rapid sinification of the Protestant, and slower sinification of the Catholic, churches was taking place, a much more significant "grass-roots" movement had begun which was "indigenous" in the true sense. This was a spontaneous native version of Christianity based in Biblical teachings and principles, rather than the sinification version of imported Western ecclesiastical systems in the traditional versions of Roman Catholic and Protestant institutional churches. The latter were attempting to impose, or superimpose, Chinese nationals on the Western-conceived ecclesiastical structures; while the former personified a complete break with the Western traditions, and a return to first century New Testament church principles and practices. Here a digression is necessary to give a brief outline of the historical development of the Western Christian ecclesiastical tradition.

Between the deaths of the Apostles Paul and Peter, the first Apostolic martyrs, in or around A.D. 67, and the establishment of the Christian Church as an institution recognised and formalised by the State in the person of the Roman Emperor Constantine in A.D. 312, there were 31 so-called "Bishops of Rome", predecessors of the later "Popes" – the first eighteen of whom died violent deaths. In the year 322, ten years after he "became a Christian" through a vision, the Emperor Constantine entered into an arrangement with "Pope Sylvester I" to create a religious empire modelled on that of secular Rome; a "universal Church" in which the Empire and Church were allies in world conquest. The "Church of Rome" would be one with the existing temporal power – blatantly ignoring the words of Christ – and would be the primary source of all political, civil, military, economic, cultural and economic power. All the other forms of Christian practices – Eastern orthodox, autonomous and indigenous – would be ignored or forcibly suppressed.

The process which began with the institution of the monarchical episcopate by Ignatius, and the so-called episcopal succession of Irenaeus in the second century A.D. – particularly as it was interpreted to mean the tactual transmission of apostolic authority – reached its logical conclusion in the neo-Catholic Roman idea of tradition when canon law was taken from the care of the professional theologians and handed over to the ecclesiastical lawyers. It was the ecclesiastical lawyer who introduced the entirely new notion that "canon law is made by the bearers of ecclesiastical authority", and thus transformed the "Spiritual Church" taught and initiated by the Apostle Paul into a "corporation" or institution. Christianity was no longer the Church of Christ, ruled by Christ, but simply a corporate institution ruled – often falsely – by contesting disputants of the East and West in the name of Christ, until it came to be accepted eventually that Christ could only work through the medium of this universal but fractured "Churchoid", or churchly organisation resembling a church. It only required the passing of several centuries to develop the notion and give it historical credibility and authority. The Tridentine Council had only to place the *sine scripto traditiones* on the same level as the Holy Scriptures themselves, and the latter, being "completed" by this new source of knowledge, were successfully eliminated as the final court of appeal that they had been in the beginning. Finally, the *codex juris canonici* of 1918, by which all matters of faith and morals were subordinated to the Pope, rounded off the whole oligarchic concept.

From a strictly historical point of view the claim of the Eastern Orthodox Church to be the true Catholic Church of ecclesiastical tradition, following on the first and major cleavage with the Western neo-Catholic Roman tradition, was perfectly legitimate. Eastern Orthodoxy did not arise as a result of a revolutionary movement but, on the contrary, from an undeviating loyalty to ecclesiastical tradition, while the Roman Church had diverged by expedient and unprincipled revolutionary processes.

Then as far as the Western Protestant denominations were concerned, they had all derived from the Roman Church; they were largely the product of some fifteen hundred years of Roman tradition adapted to suit their own idiosyncratic purposes. The Reformation was not so much a totally new beginning as a partial and temporary adjustment of ecclesiastical practices with conveniently descriptive labels given to highlight distinctive emphases – Lutheranism, Methodism, Congregationalism, Baptist, and so on.

The only deviation from this traditional ecclesiastical pattern was the appearance of groups from time to time who protested against the unacceptable disparity between the current religious structure and the ideal described in the

Scriptures. Over the centuries these movements emerged in different forms as respective groups sought an authoritative basis for their particular emphasis from the Scriptures. However, the various Scriptures seemed to give, at different times, authority to episcopalian, presbyterian and congregational church practices, while fundamentally emphasising a less systematic corpus of principles than any of these doctrinal labels. The earliest churches of Jerusalem, Antioch, Corinth and Rome all seemed to follow different practices whatever their agreed doctrinal beliefs.

But, despite the problems and persecutions, these breakaway groups returned to the simplicity of "the apostles' doctrine", and met together in whatever manner they could in the circumstances of the time. They would flourish rapidly in their particular generation until, gradually, the purity of their original stand would be corrupted by permitting some human element to dominate instead of the spiritual. Some powerful personality would exploit some personal opinion or emphasis, and slowly the group would lose power and disappear from the historical scene in vague reports of religious eccentricity. In the nineteenth century two of the most important of these groups to emerge from widespread disillusionment with the ecclesiastical hypocrisies of the mainline denominations were the Plymouth Brethren Movement and the Pentecostal Movement; the former with a strong emphasis on Bible authority and teaching, and the latter with a strong emphasis on "the second blessing", or gifts of the Holy Spirit such as speaking in tongues, healings and other "signs".

In the nineteenth century in the West the Industrial Revolution had provided the sinews – financial capital, industries, transport – from which came the impetus for the following century's distinctive Christian missionary contribution. Church buildings belonging to the rich and proliferating Nonconformists and sects multipled in the cities, towns and villages; from huge neo-Palladian mausoleums to Pentecostal tin chapels. The rapid development of capitalism through the expanding industrialisation led to a growing social consciousness, and it was the Evangelicals who were in the forefront – Wilberforce, Shaftsbury and others in the famous "Clapham Sect", William Booth in the Salvation Army; George Muller with his orphanages. Christian businessmen gave more and more of their time and money and ability, forming themselves into groups on the pattern of the boards of the capitalist companies they ran, in order to bring their "spiritual ideas" before the public, soliciting financial support for their particular religious cause. The support gained in this way would enable another batch of missionaries to be sent out to whatever "foreign mission field" particularly interested the "Board of Directors" of the overseas religious institution designated as a "missionary society".

Later, the poet T.S.Elliot described the process cogently in his "Choruses from 'The Rock' ":

> "When your fathers fixed the place of God,
> And settled all the inconvenient saints,
> Apostles, martyrs, in a kind of Whipsnade,
> Then they could set about imperial expansion
> Accompanied by industrial development.
> Exporting iron, coal and cotton goods
> And intellectual enlightenment
> And everything, including capital
> And several versions of the Word of God:
> The British race assured of a mission
> Performed it, but left much at home unsure..."

It was against this Christian historical and ecclesiastical background that there emerged in China in the early part of the twentieth century, despite the proliferation of Western churches and missionary organisations, the "indigenous" Chinese Christian churches. With unique historical irony these indigenous Chinese Christian groups began coming to the fore in the same critical period, 1911-1930, as did the Chinese Communists. Two of the leaders of such groups – Watchman Nee and Wang Ming-dao – between them would be more successful than Mao Zedung and the Communist Party leaders in transforming the hearts and minds of the Chinese people over the next fifty years. They did this without an army, without organisation, without terror or mass murder – and both of them would spend over twenty years in prison with no contact with the outside world.

The "China Jesus Independent Church" was begun in Shanghai in 1906 by Pastor Yu Kuo-chen. The "China Christian Independent Church" was begun in Shantung in 1912 after the Boxer Rebellion. The "True Jesus Church" was established by Paul Wei in Tientsin and Peking in 1917, spreading into the nearby Shantung Province. The "Jesus Family" was begun by Ching Tien-ying in 1921. The household churches which were to become Wang Ming-dao's "Christian Tabernacle" were started by Wang in Peking in 1924, and his powerful "Spiritual Food Quarterly" which was to influence so many in the universities was begun in 1927. The "Little Flock" (or "Christian Assemblies") was begun by Watchman Nee in Fukien in 1926, to become more numerous than all the others put together.

For some time before and during this period of the emergence of the indigenous Chinese Christian groups, as has been noted, there was a gradual attempt at progressive sinification in the institutional churches, Protestant and Catholic, from a general policy of imperialist "paternalism" to one of Western-dominated "fraternalism". But, at the most, all that this had accomplished was a measure of sinification of the Western denominational system. They were not truly indigenous in the sense of "native", "belonging naturally", growing out of the spiritual soil of China.

Each system , Catholic and Protestant, and each denomination and sect, almost totally reflected its Western origin and practice in ecclesiology, liturgy and idiosyncracies, even where there were Chinese bishops, pastors, priests, superintendents or elders. Further, when Chinese evangelical organisations were formed, such as the "China Evangelistic Band", the "Christian Workers Mission", the "Back to Jerusalem Band", they tended to be modelled on similar Western organisations already in existence in China and were primarily financially dependent on Western church sources.

The truly indigenous Christian churches which sprang to life in the early part of the twentieth century in China owed nothing to western *denominational* influences. Many of the leaders, however, had been *personally* influenced by European individuals; and all owed a debt to Robert Morrison and others who provided the translations of the Bible. But the groups themselves, and their respective emphases, were spontaneous outgrowths of Christian witness derived from their independent study of the Scriptures – sometimes, as with Watchman Nee, after recourse to the original Hebrew and Greek – and, in consequence, the distinctive forms in which they emerged were wholly Chinese in interpretation and practice.

The indigenous churches were *self-governing* through strict conformity to New Testament principles of church gathering, practice and discipline; *self-supporting* through New Testament principles of individual and corporate responsibility of voluntary tithing; and *self-propagating* through New Testament principles of no elitist clergy or ecclesiastical ordination. Such autonomy also meant that every church and every individual had to be dealt with separately. Also, that each local church and individual was without the "guilty associations" of Western parent churches which left the Western church members open to psychological and political pressures from the chauvinistic Nationalist and Communist Parties.

One of the earliest of the influential indigenous churches

was the "True Jesus Church", begun by Paul Wei on 1 May, 1917, after he had given away all that he had possessed and went out to preach the gospel of Jesus Christ. The first church was founded in Tientsin, then others in Peking, Shantung and other Provinces. The churches he founded were "Pentecostalist" in emphasis in tongues-speaking, healings, casting out of demons. Another distinctive feature was the "communal living" which they taught and practised in the early days. By 1950 their churches numbered about a thousand, with a membership of over 120,000 baptised and committed believers. The ecumenical "Church of Christ in China" comprising several institutional denominations numbered 196,000 "nominal" Christians.

One of the most unusual of the indigenous churches was the "Jesus Family", started in Shantung Province by a converted Buddhist, Ching Tien-ying, whose family also practised a strict Confucianism. He was educated at a Methodist missionary school and, in 1920, he and his wife – after experiencing "Holy Spirit Baptism" following repentance for sins and separation – like Paul Wei gave away all their possessions and began the "Jesus Family" in 1921, a communal Christian society in the village of Machuang, in Shantung Province, on a piece of land left to him by his great-grandfather.

A few of his friends joined him, and the community, with the land and agriculture as a base, spontaneously and empirically developed a pattern that was the model for other places. Farming was begun, a cooperative store opened, a silk-weaving industry started, and a chapel built. The structure which emerged was that of a pyramid, with agriculture as the base and the chapel as the apex. On this base was built a variety of enterprises such as carpentry, shoemaking, machine-shop, stone masonry, electrical works, printing, book-binding, smithy, bakery, community relations group, accountancy office – everything, in fact, for making and keeping the community self-sufficient and inter-dependent.

The church as the apex was the point to and from which all activities flowed – literally. The chapel was used as a workshop where weaving, spinning, knitting and similar enterprises were carried on when it was not being used for services.

A free translation of one of their hymns read:

"Love is the organising principle of the House of Jesus.
This is a heavenly conception.
Man had small part in its growth.
Since we are fathers and sons by grace and brothers in Spirit,
Leadership is weak and bodily life is very strong.
All are 'one in Christ', whether old or young, male or female, dull or gifted.
All worldly differences are ignored,
Tribe or nation, rich or poor, honourable or lowly.
Truly our aim is, 'Thy kingdom come, Thy will on earth be done' ",

As the Christian communes spread each leader first had to sell his own land and possessions and give it to the poor as a prerequisite of spiritual leadership; and afterwards he was expected to be "the least" or most humble in the commune. In 1930 the communes began the practice of tithing – giving a tenth portion – of their abundant harvests to the poor; and in 1942 this was increased to 20 per cent during the "Great Famine" of that time. One of the communes, with 43 acres of land, supported 500 people, and gave away 90 per cent of the harvest to the poor. When large sums of money were offered to the communes during and after the Great Famine of 1942 the leaders refused them, Ching explaining: "Those foreign churches would rob us of one of our sheet anchors. It is our financial needs which drive us to our knees and force us to cry to God".

In 1948 a Western missionary, Dr Vaughan Rees, lived for

two years in one of the communes, and described it:

"Foreign pigs and a modern pig-sty, a big Hereford bull and milch cows immediately met my eyes as we wandered through the wall of trees. In Chinese villages glass is a rare curiosity. Here it is used in all the fowl houses. Electricity in China is unknown except in the big towns. Here the rooms have electric light, and over the big central well is an electric pump...

"In Mao-chuang their livestock consisted of horses, mules, one blind donkey, cattle, pigs, geese, fowls, ducks and rabbits. The kitchens were large and well-arranged, and all the utensils were made and cast in the blacksmith's department, even the large steam-pressure cooker...

"One day a typical group of (Communists) came and called out loudly for the pastor...I saw him in the distance. He was pushing the manure cart, and he pushed it right into their midst before someone said 'Here he is'. The Communists had drawn back from the offensive cart. They then wanted to know how he could keep adequate discipline when he did such a menial job.

"Chow Shin-ming, the pastor and official head of the community, explained that since they were all equal, he, the leader, had the privilege of doing the worst jobs. The Communists looked sheepish..."

In 1941 there were 141 different communities in eight provinces, the larger number of them in Shandung with approximately 6,000 members. In the late 1940s, as national political conditions deteriorated, the "Jesus Family" expanded rapidly; but as the Communists took over information about the groups disappeared.

The "Jesus Family" communities had "fly-killing campaigns", with rewards for the greatest number killed, long before the Communist Government in Peking popularised the campaigns and made "people's heroes" out of their champions. One story is told of a Communist group after being shown round the Christian commune asking the

Commune leader, "How do you prevent your people stealing the grapes?". They had just made stealing on their own regulated communal farms "a sin against the people and punishable by death". The "Jesus Family" leader's reply was simple and direct: "If anyone has the love of the Lord Jesus in his heart, he does not steal from others".

Pastor Wang Ming-dao was one of the two most influential Chinese Christians in the indigenous movement, yet he founded very few actual churches. His enormous influence was exercised through his powerful preaching, and through his writings in his publication, "The Spiritual Quarterly", which was read all over China, especially in the universities, throughout this critical period.

Wang Ming-dao was born in the year of the Boxer Uprising, 1900. His father worked in the Tong- Ren Hospital in Peking as an orderly while studying to be a doctor. He married Wang's mother, who was a teacher in the Girls' School run by the London Missionary Society, when he was over thirty, and the first four children died. One sister survived before Wang was born, one month and three days before his father's death on 25 July., 1900. Rather than face the murderous fury of the Christian-hating Boxers, Wang's father killed himself before they reached Peking. This left Wang and his sister to be brought up in extreme poverty, a condition which left him a lifetime legacy of ill-health and which exposed his family of mother and sister to endless humiliations and harrassments.

With a passion for reading and an enquiring mind Wang's earliest memories were of two haunting questions: "What really is the meaning of human life?"; and, "Is there anything beyond death?". He attended the London Missionary Society Primary School, and was first in every examination.

Despite their extreme poverty he and his sister were spoiled by their self-indulgent mother. The surrounding circumstances affected him, too, and he was influenced by the conduct of immoral and unprincipled lodgers and neighbours. This made him a strange mixture of the wicked and chivalrous, conservative and impulsive, bullying and considerate, studious and lazy. On the other hand, as members of the London Missionary Society his parents had regularly attended the church and his mother continued to do this after his father's death, and enforced church attendance on the two children. This meant daily attendance at school chapel services, mid-week prayer-meeting, and three services on a Sunday. There were also extra Bible classes.

Writing of this period in his life Wang said: "...to my 14th year I passed my life chaotically, unintelligibly, confused, without faith, without purpose, without hope and without a clear track". But at 14 years of age a fellow-student led him to a belief in God, and showed him how to study the Bible, pray and examine his life daily in the light of this, which transformed him completely.

It was Wang's ambition to become a politician. He had been greatly influenced through reading about Abraham Lincoln; how he had risen from a poor background to become the President of the United States. Now, following his conversion, he began to have second thoughts and, after a struggle, decided to become a preacher. Up to this time he had very little respect for preachers, most of whom he considered "worthless", and the thought of changing from politician to preacher was in his own words "like descending from a lofty tree into a dark ravine". The preachers he knew had been mostly cooks, cleaners, watchmen or language teachers to missionaries, and through the influence of missionaries and a few years at Bible School went on to find churches as preachers – but always servants to foreign missionaries. So, for three years, from 15-18, he argued stubbornly with God against becoming a preacher.

In the year he was due to go to University, 1918, he was still determined at least to study politics, and he wore on his coat as a slogan a badge with the words, "Human determination will decide destiny". Following a series of progressively more serious illnesses until he almost died, he concluded that God was trying to discipline him for his defiance and he submitted to God's will to become a preacher. From that time he made a remarkable recovery.

He was accepted for University entrance but first his mother, then his sister, fell ill and he had to suspend his studies to look after them. He wrote to the Western Missionary Dean of Studies to explain, and to ask for a meeting to discuss his problems. His letters went unacknowledged, and he was never given an opportunity to meet or renew his studies at University. After a struggle he agreed to take a humble post as a teacher in a Primary School in a small town a hundred miles from home.

Despite his low position, and lower spirits, he threw himself into his work as a teacher, not only providing the standard lessons but also, inside and outside school hours, teaching his pupils moral and Bible principles. These proved to be so popular that he was asked to conduct Bible teaching classes in the evenings. The following year, after an experience "of profound blessing by the Holy Spirit" and baptism by immersion, he was regarded as a "rebel" by the London Missionary Society who ran the Presbyterian school, and he was expelled. He was grudgingly permitted to remain overnight in his room, but was ordered not to talk to any of the students. However, five of the students joined him in accepting expulsion for the same reasons.

For some time Wang Ming-dao was unable to find any kind of employment in that disturbed and critical year of 1920 in Peking. Finally, a well-to-do uncle invited him to come and live with his family in a beautiful mountain village. While there Wang read right through the Bible six times in 62 days. From there he was asked to visit a former teacher in the city of Tsang-Hsien, and to preach in the church there. Four months later the same church asked him to return and conduct a teaching ministry, and he did this for three months. He was 22 years old.

For the next few years Wang preached sporadically, but really spent most of his time helping his mother around the house, restless and disconsolate at the apparent aimlessness of his life. In March, 1924, he went with a group of 30 preachers, Chinese and Western, from various churches in Peking to conduct an evangelistic campaign at an army camp farther south. There were some 3,000 conversions, but he was distressed both by the quality of the preachers and of the converts, neither of whom it seemed to him were worthy of the doctrine they professed. He returned to Peking without even waiting for the baptismal ceremony, sick with the spiritual corruption, emptiness and poverty of Christian denominational witness in China. A few months later, when he went to speak at a meeting for leaders in the Congregational Church and churches of the London Missionary Society, he stood up and publicly denounced their unScriptural practices.

On 18 October, 1924, he began holding house meetings in his own room, with three other people studying the Scriptures with him. He also began to have printed and published the first of his Scriptural teachings – *The Christian's Cross, The Christian and Idols, Trumpet Call in an Evil World, A Most Important Matter.* His outspoken condemnation of the hypocrisies of Chinese Christians and Chinese Christian preachers made him a target of bitter attacks by denominational workers, and also limited his number of engagements to preach. He says that "most of the church leaders in Peking at that time regarded me as mentally unbalanced".

It was during those years that Wang's Scriptural theology was formed. Many years later, he wrote of the influence of the Bible studies:

"It was through this that I had to reject some of the teaching in the church which I had received when I was young. What I found in the Bible I received; what I did not find in the Bible I rejected. The truth of the Bible I believed; doctrines not in the Bible I was not prepared to believe. I had not read Bible commentaries. That kind of literature did not appeal to me. In my preaching and teaching today the Bible is my only standard. Church traditions and man-made regulations were not my authority. Even less would I compromise with anything contrary to the truth...So it was contrary to all expectation that God led me step by step to the position I hold today...God sent me on the one hand to be a trumpet-call to the world; and on the other hand, to be a trumpet-call to the Church. He sent me to expose the darkness, corruption, depravity and unrighteousness both of the world and of the Church..."

Then he was approached by a respected and influential Chinese Christian woman, Mrs Pan Wei-jau, who had known his parents and who had been so impressed by his teaching that she wanted to bring friends along to his group, and also introduce him to other influential Christians in the city. She opened her own large home for house meetings, and also the homes of her friends, and soon Wang was preaching every day to these household and other traditional churches throughout Peking.

In 1925 he began sending articles for publication in the *Spiritual Light Newspaper* in Nanking, and in May 1927 he travelled there to meet with the publishers. Shortly afterwards, in the spring of 1927 – the same year in which Mao Zedung produced his Communist *Report on an Investigation of the Peasant Revolution in Hunan* – he began to publish "The Spiritual Food Quarterly" to oppose the undermining work of liberal theologians; and his growing reputation produced invitations to visit denominational churches in Manchuria and other places. He also visited Canton and Hong Kong.

In the autumn of 1930 the meetings in Peking were placed on a more permanent basis, but were so ordered that Wang was free to visit other provinces for preaching engagements for six months of the year while colleagues took the services in his absence. In the six months he visited some twenty places.

In the spring of 1933 Wang and his colleagues in Peking rented a hall to accommodate the greatly increased numbers attending his services. Three years later there were so many converts that this, too, was too small for their purpose. This time they had enough money from voluntary contributions to buy property instead of rent, and since it was required by law that they had to register the name of the church Wang was reluctantly persuaded to choose the name "The Christian Tabernacle", or "Christian Assembly Hall". This first building seating 450 people was completed in the same month as the notorious Japanese "Marco Polo Bridge Incident", July, 1937. On 28 July, the Chinese Army withdrew from Peking and the Japanese entered the city on 8 August. This meant that Wang's preaching tours were now restricted because of the fighting in the northern provinces, and kept him preaching in Peking.

When the Japanese declared war on Britain and America in December 1941 they ordered all places of worship, both foreign missionary and Chinese, to be closed. The Christian representatives got together to form "The Peking Christian Preservation Committee" to talk with the Japanese officials, to see if some compromise could be reached. Wang refused to join them, and continued with his services in his Christian Tabernacle – without being stopped by the Japanese.

The following year a "North China Federation Promotion Committee" was set up, and again Wang was approached to join. This time considerable pressure was applied, the representative pointing out to Wang that if he failed to participate then his own and other churches would suffer. Further, the Japanese authorities had insisted that participation was compulsory for all churches.

Three months later Wang received an official letter from

"the North China Christian Federation Committee" peremptorily ordering him to attend a meeting to discuss setting up a Branch office in Peking, and demanding a formal reply in writing. He replied:

"I acknowledge the receipt of your letter directing me to join the North China Christian Federation Promotion Committee. On examining your statement with its reference to Western Missions and to the objective of becoming self-supporting, self-governing and self-propagating, I conclude that it is not necessary for us to join your group. In addition to that your Federation is made up of churches of different faith from ours, and in order to preserve an unadulterated faith it would be difficult for us to affiliate with churches of different faith. Consequently we are unable to follow your directions and to send a representative to your meeting. I hope that you will understand our position."

After the meeting Wang was told that the Japanese military officer had pocketed Wang's letter without comment, and had gone straight to the Japanese headquarters.

In August-September the name of the Christian Federation was changed once more, to "The North China Christian Federation", to reflect Japanese practices in Japan, and the Ministry of Home Affairs called a meeting of church leaders to formally launch the new organisation. The meeting lasted for three days, and no attempt was made to contact Wang. On the evening of 9 October a Japanese and a Chinese interpreter came to the Christian Tabernacle to inform Wang that the Investigating Officer of the official North China Cultural Bureau wanted to meet Wang the next morning at his office. Wang gives an account of the discussion:

Wang: "Mr Takeda, there are two things I would like you to know. The first is that personally I will on no account join any group or organisation. The second is that the church for which I am responsible will on no account join any group or organisation."

Takeda: "You have strong views, but the government has decided that all the churches will unite and it is essential that this policy is carried out."

Wang: "In order that I may obey God whom I serve, in order that I may hold firmly the truth that I believe, I will on no account obey any instruction that cuts across God's will. I have prepared myself to pay any price, to make any sacrifice, and nothing will make me change these principles. It is out of the question for me or for my church to join the Association".

After an hour of discussion and argument Wang was allowed to leave without signing any agreement. Four days later the North China Christian Association convened a large inaugural meeting in a Government department, with Japanese military and civilian officers in attendance, to "honour war dead" and "new citizens". Five weeks later Wang was summoned to a meeting at the Military Police headquarters where he found pastors from other churches in the city. They had been summoned to hand over their property to the Japanese authorities. Wang protested vehemently and after discussion it was "discovered" that he had been summoned "in error". He heard no more, and the meetings continued.

Over the next few years Wang Ming-dao went on to build up the largest church in Peking, and to reach the whole Christian community nationwide through his writings.

In his book, *Christian Missions and the Judgement of God*, the Anglican missionary David Paton wrote:

"The result (of professional clericalism exported to the mission field) at all events is evident; it is sterility. Immense energies are occupied, as they are in England, by simply keeping things going; if the ecclesiastical organisation in England is out of date and irrelevant, how much more so in China ...

"A sacramental system that is exalted but practically

unusable falls into contempt. The indigenous sects already referred to spread their influence. If your own Church cannot provide you with an effective ministry and frequent sacraments, and is not organised, whatever its formal theology, in such a way that you feel you are a member of a spiritual fellowship, you will (if you mean business) more often than not join some other which can provide these blessings, whatever its other failings. One of the most widely spread of these sects has, in the manner of the Plymouth Brethren, a breaking of bread for believers each Sunday and is both a real and expanding fellowship..."

The group that Paton had in mind here was, presumably, the so-called "Little Flock" but it was also a description of some of the other movements. The indigenous groups placed varying emphasis on different aspects of Christian doctrine but, generally speaking, there was minimal difference. They would meet several times a week for prayer, teaching, Bible study, "breaking of bread" or communion, and fellowship. At these gatherings either a pastor – unordained, chosen from among themselves – or, more often, one of the male members gifted with preaching or teaching ability would be responsible for expounding the Scriptures. They would meet in private houses, or simply designed halls, or rented buildings; and the congregations would vary from thirty to a hundred or a thousand or several thousands. The money to pay for the buildings, or to sustain the communities and the many activities, was obtained from the members by "tithing" – giving a percentage of one's income, usually ten per cent – or by voluntary contributions.

Authority and discipline was exercised among the indigenous groups on a Scriptural basis. The leaders were rarely selected or appointed; they "emerged" and were publicly recognised by "the laying on of hands" by the elders and, often, the whole church. According to the New Testament the churches were to be ruled by elders (*presby-*

teroi) and deacons, who could be equally called overseers, or bishops *(episkopoi)*. Some made a distinction between bishops and elders, but it was generally agreed that this was a distinction of function and not of status; that is, all bishops were elders, though not all elders functioned as bishops. A bishop, in the words of the New Testament they affirmed, "must be blameless, the husband of one wife, vigilant, sober, of good behaviour, given to hospitality, apt to teach; not given to wine, no striker, not greedy of filthy lucre, but patient, not a brawler, not covetous". There was no *single* elder or bishop in a church, but always several.

The function of the elders or bishops was to be "shepherds of the flock", pastors responsible for the spiritual conduct of the members of the church and the church's activities. In addition, there were those who were recognised as "teachers" and "evangelists". The latter were responsible for the preaching to non-Christians and making converts; and the former for building up of the Christian believers in the community. All of them were recognised for the spiritual qualities which they possessed and demonstrated; when that spiritual quality disappeared for any reason – complacency, pride, apathy, sin – their authority in the church was also suspended.

Each local church was completely autonomous. In addition to the local church in any town or village, or section of a city, there were also "household churches". The local church would be the meeting place for the formal services, while the "households" would reflect some aspect of the activities for the street or neighbourhood – prayer meetings, Bible studies, Christian fellowship, community help.

The most distinctive indigenous group practising all or most of the aforementioned activities was the "Little Flock" founded by Nee To-sheng, or "Watchman" Nee as he came to be known, in the Fukien Province of East China.

Among the first foreign missionaries to arrive in Foochow, capital of Fukien province, were Congregationalists of the

American Board in 1847, followed by the American Episcopal Methodists, and, in 1850, by the English Church Missionary Society. They opened a school in Foochow in 1853 offering western-style education and, in 1857, Watchman Nee's grandfather who went to this school was baptised as a Christian. Later he trained as an evangelist and was ordained as a pastor, the first Chinese to be so honoured in the three north Fukien missions.

Watchman Nee's father also had a mission school education, and he went on to become a State Customs official. In 1900 he married the gifted adopted daughter of a wealthy businessman, and went to live in Swatow, a Treaty Port some 250 miles from Foochow. There they had three children, two girls and a boy, Watchman, born on 4 November, 1903. Eventually there were nine children altogether.

Watchman's father only earned a small salary, half of which he sent to his widowed mother. But his mother was a woman of considerable intelligence and drive – she had been among the first Chinese women to leave home to study medicine, which she gave up to get married at her parents' insistence – and she set up a small clothing export business which rapidly became very profitable. This had to be suspended when her husband was transferred back to Foochow. There she devoted herself to supervising her growing family's education, employing classical Chinese scholars, music teachers, and western-style schooling.

Watchman Nee grew up in the period of revolutionary turmoil in the country, especially in the schools and universities – the "intellectual revolution". His father was quiet and scholarly, but his mother was a forceful and eloquent feminist, fund-raising and politicising for the new Nationalist Party of Dr Sun Yat Sen. She formed a "Women's Patriotic Society", with herself as General Secretary, and enrolled several prominent figures as leaders of the movement. When Dr Sun Yat Sen arrived in Foochow in 1915 she was given an official role in his Presidential reception.

Through this she discovered that a former classmate of hers was Dr Sun's private secretary and this gave her more prominence.

Watchman's western-style education was obtained at the Church Missionary Society's Middle School and St. Mark's High School, where he was usually top of the class. He was sixteen when the new revolutionary impetus swept the universities following on the "May Fourth Movement" in Peking in 1919. His mother had become increasingly involved with the Nationalists, and had been awarded the promotion to "The Order of the Second Class for Patriotism" by the Peking Government.

Then, suddenly, through a friend, she became a Christian in February 1920. With the same zeal she had shown for commerce and politics she now threw herself into her new spiritual life. First, she confessed her previous wrongs to her long-suffering but admiring family; and from this unexpected demonstration of a transformed life Watchman Nee was convinced of the reality of the gospel of Jesus Christ and he, too, became a Christian. He was eighteen years of age.

His fellow-students were deeply involved in the right- and left-wing politics of the Nationalist Party, the increasing debates regarding the new Marxist theories, and the anti-Japanese demonstrations. Ironically, his poorest subject in his studies was "Scripture Knowledge", in which he often cheated in order to get a pass mark. Now, as a practising Christian, he felt he had to confess this misdemeanour to the Principal; and then to take several months leave from school to go, privately, to a Bible School in Shanghai for extra teaching. At the same time, he studied the Bible for himself at every opportunity.

Soon he found several others who joined him in the Bible studies, and they began meeting together regularly. Also, they began to go out publicly to distribute Scripture leaflets, and while doing this they carried placards with Bible texts. They also began attending the meetings being held by a Christian woman, Miss Margaret Barber, a former Anglican missionary but now working independently. She baptised Nee and his mother, and afterwards he said: "Lord, I leave my world behind. Your cross separates it from me forever, and I have entered another. I stand where you have placed me in Christ!"

Towards the end of 1922 another woman influenced Nee, a Miss Ruth Lee. She had been a convinced atheist and avid follower of the early Chinese Marxists, especially of Chen Tu-hsiu's *New Youth Review.* But recently, after reading a Bible, she had become a Christian, left her government post, and become a full-time Christian worker. Her fiery preaching greatly appealed to Nee and his growing group of Christian colleagues, who were themselves helping to transform schools, colleges and university classes with their preaching and teaching of the Bible.

When he graduated at 21 Nee felt there was only one thing he could do: "I had a lust to preach", he said. "It was impossible for me to keep silent. It was as though there was something moving within me, that drove me forward and I had to keep going. Preaching had become my very life".

But he also had to find some means of financial support. Here the influence of Margaret Barber was paramount. Nee had read accounts of the life of faith of Christians like George Muller of Bristol, and Hudson Taylor of the China Inland Mission, but he had personal experience of knowing that Margaret Barber was often down to her last dollar; and, after praying about it, she had been miraculously supplied. He had heard her ask God for a ten-room extension to house her work, and had been astonished to see a twenty-room industrial school offered to her. So he, too, began to pray to God alone to meet his needs. He went to a nearby village called Ma-hsien and rented a hut, and made this a base for his preaching ministry, with visits into the surrounding villages, for the next two years. He also began writing for the first time.

In 1924 he went to hold meetings in Hangchow in Chekiang Province to the north of Fukien, and from there he went on to Nanking, the capital of Kiangsu Province, a centre of government and missionary activity. There he gained experience of publishing, working for several months with the Spiritual Light Publishing Society of the Presbyterian Mission, where his friend Ruth Lee was on the editorial staff. Unknown to each other at the time, it was only one year before Wang Ming-dao made the same journey to Nanking from Peking for the same purpose in 1925.

On his return to his little hut in Ma-hsien he brought with him some books by the famous Plymouth Brethren writer and teacher, John Nelson Darby. Darby had been an Anglican minister in Ireland but had resigned the Anglican orders, as had two others, Govett and Panton, whose writings Nee now read avidly. From them he learned of the simple New Testament principles of worship, simple obedience to God through Scripture, and, above all, a high spiritual quality of life.

About two years previously, at the National Christian Conference held in Shanghai, the "National Christian Council" was created at which the standing of the Chinese representatives was made identical with that of the foreign missionary delegates. Its main function was to coordinate the activities of the various churches and denominations, and to promote cooperation wherever possible. Unfortunately, it was estimated that about two-fifths of the Western churches' Chinese Christians were not represented on this body, primarily because it did not have a credal statement or basis acceptable to them; that is, so framed to exclude the liberals and modernists. Nor did it even recognise the existence of the emerging and proliferating Chinese indigenous groups, whose numbers were beginning to exceed "the official Christians".

The nature of the challenge to Christian workers was

demonstrated in an exhaustive survey published at the time, entitled, "The Christian Occupation of China", which showed that in 333 counties, with 166,500 towns and villages, and a population of over 38 million, there was no Christian evangelistic church, of any kind, and not a single Christian witness. To try to meet this need, in 1924, almost ten million copies of portions of the Bible were printed.

It signalled a switch in emphasis from evangelisation to education by the Western missionary organisations, and the indigenous groups set out to meet the challenge. Also, on 30 May, 1925, following on an incident in Shanghai when the police of the International Settlement fired on some students demonstrating outside a police station, there was begun a nationwide agitation for the abolition of the extra-territorial rights of the Western powers, and the abrogation of "the Unequal Treaties". Because the foreign missionaries were in China as part of these Treaties the protests and attacks were also directed against them.

In Foochow and Fukien Province the missionaries swiftly resigned their posts in favour of Chinese nationals in the hope of continuing their work when the disturbances passed. But several buildings were burned, one of them by a known Marxist enthusiast. Nee, meanwhile, had been invited to return to Nanking to help edit a Bible study course, and on the way there he stopped over in Shanghai to meet with the many readers of his increasingly popular magazine, *The Christian*. He felt strongly that he should begin thinking about moving to Shanghai, and discussed this with Ruth Lee when he went on to Nanking.

At this time there was a political crisis in Shanghai which was greatly exacerbated by the growing schism between the Nationalists and the Communists after the death of Dr Sun Yat Sen in 1925. The right-wing faction established its headquarters in Shanghai, and the left-wing faction in Canton. In March, 1926, Chiang Kai Shek emerged victorious from the struggle and, after he had consolidated his position in the southern provinces, he marched his army to Shanghai.

There he was faced for a time with the critical possibility of a showdown with the Western powers who had vast commercial interests in Shanghai and no great confidence in Chiang Kai Shek. The Communists in the city had great influence in the labour unions and secret societies, but Chiang Kai Shek also had his influential supporters among the bankers and wealthy industrialists who had their own associations with the secret societies. Eventually, Chiang Kai Shek expelled the Communists and ordered their leaders – Zhou Enlai among them – to be shot. Zhou Enlai escaped, and Chiang Kai Shek marched northwards to capture Peking in 1928.

It was a time of exciting promise to be in Shanghai, a turbulent centre of national and international events, and Watchman Nee was aware of the tremendous possibilities opening up in the "New China".

However, on his return through Shanghai he fell ill, and after being examined by a doctor he was told that his chest X-ray showed extensive signs of tuberculosis, and that he had a poor chance of recovering, perhaps six months to live in fact. He returned to his village, and as he grew weaker he was nursed by his friends. He recovered slowly, and during his convalescence he began to write of the Christian's spiritual life, and of the strategy of the heavenly conflict on earth, as he saw it. Eventually he completed the first four parts of *The Spiritual Man*, "a work of Bible psychology".

When he had recovered from his long illness Nee returned to Shanghai, partly to complete the book and partly because he was convinced that his work lay there. In Shanghai he became friendly with a foreign missionary in the accounts department of the China Inland Mission, Charles Judd, and the two became close friends. Ruth Lee also came to Shanghai and introduced to Nee her Shanghai friend,

Peace Wang, daughter of a wealthy magistrate who was an evangelist in great demand in the schools of Shanghai.

It was a time of some heart-searching among the various churches and organisations for, following on the anti-missionary attacks in the previous years, several thousand foreign missionaries had left China. The China Inland Mission, however, had decided to alter its missionary policy to one which "provided for immediate self-government of the Chinese Church". At the same time it appealed to 200 new foreign missionaries and, between 1929 and 1931, 203 new China Inland Missionaries sailed from Britain, the Commonwealth and America for China.

However, even an actively evangelical organisation like the China Inland Mission, with its new policy of sinification, was presented with a dilemma. In his book, *China Calling*, the then Director of the C.I.M., Frank Houghton, recounted how, in a certain district, there were 57 Mission-paid workers. When the Society adopted the policy of an annually diminishing grant as part of its "self-support" programme for a "Chinese Church", only four or five of the 57 continued – and the majority were not even engaged in active Christian work a few years later.

Nee, with the help of Charles Judd, Ruth Lee and Peace Wang, set up a "house church" in Peace Wang's home "to worship God in the breaking of bread"; or, hold communion as described in the Scriptures and in the Brethren books he had read. Then, in 1928 he found premises in a lane off Hardoon Road in the International Settlement, Wen Teh Li, three miles west of the famous Shanghai Bund, as the first meeting hall. In June, 1928, the year after Mao Zedung completed his *Report of an Investigation into the Peasant Revolution in Hunar*, and the same month as Chiang Kai Shek's Nationalist Party victoriously occupied Peking, Nee completed his book, *The Spiritual Man*. It was his first and last book; all other publications under his name were transcriptions of his preaching and teaching.

Nee had sent to England for more publications by Brethren writers, and was deeply influenced by them. The combination of profound insights into the teachings of the Scriptures, and the simplicity of gatherings and practices appealed to him and he introduced them into his own work. He now had his Bible addresses published in leaflet and booklet form, in addition to his magazine *The Christian*, and another periodical, *The Bible Record*, and these contributed to a rapid expansion of his work and church outreach. He had also made a collection of favourite hymns and these he published as *The Little Flock Hymns* (in English translation), some taken from a Brethren hymn-book, *Hymns for the Little Flock*. This became so popular that the Nee groups became known as "the Little Flock", as they had no other designation.

At this time a British engineer, Charles Barlow, a member of the Exclusive Brethren in England, visited Shanghai and became very friendly with Nee, and when he returned to England he worked enthusiastically to have Nee invited to Britain to conduct meetings. Before he left for England, Nee went to Peking to preach, and there, for the first time, he met and became friendly with Pastor Wang Ming-dao, whose preaching and writings were also influencing many tens of thousands in the eastern provinces of China.

Nee arrived in England in June, 1933, and stayed with Charles Barlow in Peterborough. From there he visited many Exclusive Brethren churches in Scotland and England. His comment to Barlow when he left the country however, was: "Your people have wonderful light, but oh so little faith". During his stay in England, on an unaccompanied visit to London, he met with another Brethren- type group, less strict than the Exclusive Brethren, known as "the Christian Fellowship Centre in Honor Oak", whose leader was T. Austin Sparks, a former Baptist minister. This visit, and its doctrinal consequences, precipitated a breach between the rigidly doctrinaire Exclusive Brethren and Watchman Nee which greatly depressed him, but which resulted in a widening of his own spiritual horizons.

On his return to China he joined with a Christian business friend, Ma Muh, during 1934, to go on a preaching tour by car to the remote south-west Provinces of Kweichow and Yunnan. They travelled through Hunan, the province made famous so recently by the Hunanese Communist Mao, now occupied on his historical "Long March" to the West and north-west of China. Wherever the car stopped for ferries, petrol, meals or lodgings, Nee preached fervently to individuals and crowds. Through the driving rains of Kweichow they travelled to the high winds and icy snows of Yunnan; and their own "Long Drive" to the west gained them a considerable reputation. For some years Nee had wanted to preach to Tibetans and they went on to the north-west of Kunming until they reached camps of Tibetan traders. Ahead of Mao's Communist Army the two Christian preachers covered a similar six thousand miles carrying the gospel of peace and forgiveness through Jesus Christ.

When Nee returned to Shanghai his work expanded rapidly through the evangelistic preaching of the gifted but independent John Sung, of whom it was said, "when he preached the sheep woke up and were hungry, and because there was no-one to feed them Watchman Nee's teaching ministry was timely to fill the gap".

By 1938 the work of Watchman Nee had so expanded that there were 128 "apostles" (church- commended teachers responsible for setting up new churches) who established these churches in villages, towns and cities on a locally autonomous basis. If there was already a local church in existence these apostles subjected themselves to the local elders. Many of these local churches showed a high preponderance of the educated elite of the universities. One report stated:

"Among the students who in Peking in 1936 composed

almost entirely the regular congregation of the Christians' Meeting Place in that educational centre, there were 'top honour students' of Yenching, Ching Hua, Peking Union Medical College, Peking University, and nurses in training in the Methodist and Presbyterian Hospitals."

Nee returned to England to speak at the annual Keswick Convention held in Cumberland, England in 1938, the year following the Japanese invasion of China. He led the gathering in prayer for the Far East in memorable terms:

"The Lord reigns: we affirm it boldly. Our Lord Jesus Christ *is* reigning, and He *is* Lord of all; nothing can touch His authority. It is spiritual forces that are out to destroy His interests in China and Japan. Therefore we do not pray for China, nor do we pray for Japan, but we pray for the interests of Thy Son in China and Japan. We do not blame any man, for they are only tools in the hands of Thine enemy. We stand for Thy will. Shatter, O Lord, the kingdom of the darkness, for the persecutions of Thy Church are wounding Thee. Amen."

He travelled from England to Denmark, where he gave a series of ten addresses at the International School at Helsingfor on Romans chapters 5-8, entitled, "The Normal Christian Life" which, supplemented, later became a worldwide appreciated book. He also agreed to a translation and re-publication of his *Rethinking the Work,* which appeared in England as *Concerning Our Mission* and, later, as *The Normal Christian Church Life.* He explained its title: "*The title of the book explains its nature.* It is not a treatise on missionary methods, but a *review* of our past work in the light of God's will as we have discovered it in His Word". (his italics).

Some time after his return to China his brother George, a research chemist with his own laboratories, invited Watchman to join him in expanding the family business, the China Biological and Chemical (CBC) Laboratories. Later, Nee confessed to friends that he agreed to do this "out of temporary boredom". His mind, he felt, was not being stretched enough, and he needed a new and big challenge. He used his brilliant and analytical mind, and his acquired expertise in writing and teaching, to great effect in business and the company expanded rapidly. Because of the war with Japan there were huge demands for anti-bacterials, the sulpha-drugs, and vitamins. He also used the commercial and financial contacts to expand his own spiritual work, and that of churches in his care. He flew to Chungking, where Chiang Kai Shek had retreated before the advancing Japanese, and there he met with government and university and business leaders, obtaining new contracts and contacts.

The Japanese military advance and occupation had destroyed and closed down many of the "Little Flock" meeting-places, including the first one in Shanghai, but with the signing of the Armistice with China on 9 September, 1945, in Nanking, Nee returned once again to Shanghai to rebuild the Christian work there. He occupied himself less and less with the affairs of the CBC Laboratories, except for Directors' meetings; at which a proportion of the profits was set aside for gifts to full-time Christian workers, and the expansion of the company into new areas was used to introduce the Christian workers into those areas to build new churches.

He also purchased a property in Fukien and set it up as a "training centre", where he could conduct teaching sessions for Christian workers. With the ending of the war, and the availability of his book, *Concerning Our Mission*, there was tremendous interest among both foreign missionaries and Chinese Christians in his work. Huge crowds gathered to hear him teach, and large numbers of foreign missionaries left their denominations and missionary societies to join the "Little Flock" churches. The "Little Flock" elders, in response to the post-war circumstances and challenges in a chaotic China, out of their experience of setting up and caring for self-supporting, self-governing and self-propagating churches without the help of foreign missionaries or foreign funds, now proposed "mass migrations" of Christians from the east coast provinces to settle in unevangelised areas to the west.

By the middle of June, 1948, over a hundred young and enthusiastic workers met together to discuss a programme to carry the gospel of Jesus Christ into every major town and city within the next ten years. Some sympathetic foreign missionary friends of Watchman Nee were invited to participate in this challenge to evangelise the whole of China. I was one of them, but I was in Chengtu in West China on my way to Tibet.

The "Little Flock" kept no records of numbers of converts or members or churches, but they were widely recognised in the late 1940s as being the most numerous of all the indigenous groups. In a nation of some 600 million in 1947 the total membership of these indigenous groups was proportionately very small – probably around 500,000 – but their influence was out of all proportion to their actual numbers in the areas in which they were represented. Unlike the majority of Chinese associated with the churches and missionary organisations they were conspicuously *not* "rice Christians" – those who were Christians only for the benefits to be derived from or through the foreign missionaries. Their exemplary manner of life in the family, employment and community surpassed that of the Communists, and their non-coercive motivation of love was more attractive than the imposed beneficence of the Communists' "for the good of all". The Communists could not ignore their influence and zeal, and, above all, their allegiance to God above the State which the leaders, especially Wang Mingdao, taught so vociferously. So long as such indigenous Christians existed the Marxists could not claim to speak for them as "people's representatives", for they were a publicly distinctive cross-section of all classes – peasants, workers, doctors, professors, armed services, government officials of all levels. It was said that even the mother of the top

Communist leader Zhou Enlai, attended "Little Flock" meetings.

All of these factors, and several more were sources of strength to the indigenous groups when the mounting pressures from the victorious Communists were being put on them in occupied areas before 1949 and when they gained power after takeover. Religion in China, especially Christianity, had fitted into such a standard pattern that the formulas and slogans of Marxism borrowed from Europe and Soviet Russia seemed to be tailor-made to fit the situation in China. So it was easy to ignore an apparently unorganised, heterodox, non-political agglomeration of unworldly Christian sects and steam-roller them into submission to a State authority reflecting "the will of the people".

As the 1940s ended Christian missionaries in China were claiming that there were evidences of a greater interest in "spiritual things" than ever had existed in the country. They quoted three million copies of the Bible being distributed in one year, and that it was the best-selling Chinese book. Work among universities and High School students was successful and increasing – although there was admitted confusion among honest observers as to whether the true cause was interest in religion or in acquiring free English lessons. The China Inter-Varsity Fellowship had its most successful summer conference in 1947 in Nanking with over 200 delegates from all over China. The big city churches were well attended, some of them packed with one to three thousand people. More young people than ever before were preparing for the ministry, it was claimed, and for the first time many of these included a good number of university graduates.

In the second (1948) edition of *China Calling*, the Director of the China Inland Mission wrote complacently:

"It is therefore gratifying...that there is a strong and growing tendency towards union. Anglicans have long since united to form the *Chung Hwa Sheng Kung Hui* (literally, the China Holy Universal Church) with about 35,000 communicants. Ten Lutheran bodies are merged in the Lutheran Church of China, with 24,000 communicants. The three British Methodist bodies, numbering over 21,000, have, of course, followed the parent organisation in England and joined forces. In the Church of Christ in China no less than fourteen former Church affiliations with communicants totalling 125,000 are united. These include churches founded by Baptist, Congregational, Methodist, Methodist Episcopal, Presbyterian, Reformed, and United Brethren Churches, and while these churches have reached unity on basic principles, no parent society is asked to renounce anything in its historical heritage. Outside these union bodies, the largest organisation is the China Inland Mission, and the churches connected with it include 90,000 communicants..."

But the close association of both Protestants and Catholic churches and missionary societies with their Western governments, and with the Nationalist Party of Chiang Kai Shek, was to provide a rude awakening for, and a catastrophic decline in, these Christian denominational enterprises because of their misjudgements and compromises. The unfortunate policy of identifying too closely with the claimed "Christian" regime of Chiang Kai Shek was especially disastrous because of the vast corruption at all levels of the Nationalist Party. The lack of moral fibre was apparent to everyone, it seemed, except to the denominational Christians; or, if they did see it, they thought they could do little about it. If anything, when indigenous Christians such as Wang Ming-dao or Watchman Nee opposed corruption and other practices, the denominational representatives were vocal enough in their public denunciations of the two indigenous leaders. Most of the leaders of the Churches and Missions went out of their way to thank God on public occasions for the "Christian leadership" of the Nationalist

Party.

C.P. Fitzgerald, the noted historian on China, has written: "The Catholics, however, under the general opposition to Communism which the Vatican had endorsed, tended to support the Nationalist cause. The leading members of the Chinese Hierarchy were openly on the side of the *Kuomintang*. The foreign missionaries who, as among the Protestants, were also strongly anti-Communist, and, although not great admirers of the *Kuomintang*, still felt that from the point of view of religion, it was the cause to back. Not all foreign Catholics agreed with this attitude; many would have preferred neutrality, but the church as a whole came to be regarded as one of the few non- governmental organisations which supported the *Kuomintang*. This did it great harm in the years that followed."

The religio-political situation in China, therefore, as the Communists took over power in 1949, presented problems for both traditional Marxists and institutional Christians. This was summed up admirably at the time by the Anglican missionary, David Paton, in his book *Christian Missions and the Judgement of God:*

"...We are faced with the debris of one dead doctrine, and the competition of two extremely alive ones. The dead doctrine of progress sustained by our fathers in the carrying of capitalist democratic culture to most parts of the globe. Its core was the conviction that in thus extending the range of western liberal culture and developing its assumptions, they were in effect establishing on earth that which would grow into the kingdom of God...The whole view exists today only as debris, for it has foundered on the rock not so much of human sin, as of the complexities and contradictions of the very western culture which was the substance of its belief.

"It is otherwise with Marxism...The Marxist at all events believes that in history there is a movement, dialectical, stormy, checked here and there, but finally and certainly advancing, to the goal of a classless society which may be postponed but cannot fail of achievement, and in which all human strivings and yearnings will be fulfilled...He understands the drift of history, and sets himself scientifically to advance it. The day may not dawn in his time, but that it will dawn he knows, and knows also that its dawning is hastened by his labours...

"On the other side of conventional Christianity are the Adventist sects. *They also see in the events of our time a revolutionary situation, and set themselves to take advantage of it. But it is a revolution of another sort altogether;* it is the End of which the New Testament speaks, and the wars and civil wars, the famines, riots and disturbances are the signs of the End, the harbingers of Armageddon, as the explosions of atomic energy are the fulfilment of II Peter 3.10. *These men also have hope in history; and their preaching takes on a renewed and practical urgency as they seek by their witness to discover the elect and to save them from the wrath to come..."*

CHAPTER 7

The Christian-Marxist Battle For The Soul Of China

My Experience of China's Christian-Marxist Struggle: 1946-60

I arrived in China in 1946, just after World War II ended. At the end of the war I had been accepted as a missionary to Tibet by my Plymouth Brethren group of churches in Scotland, and had decided to go to Tibet via China rather than India. Through friends I had arranged to spend some time in the Brethren mission stations in Kiangsi Province, Central China, to learn some Chinese before proceeding further west.

A few years before I had experienced a period of spiritual rebellion against the sterility and irrelevance of all denominational and sectarian Christianity, including "Brethrenism". During that time I had become interested in Marxism as a comprehensive and satisfactory philosophy. But after an intellectual and spiritual struggle I concluded that Jesus Christ had far more answers to the multifarious problems of life than Karl Marx, and that the sterility of Christianity lay in its institutional structures and its apathetic exponents in the twentieth century. When Brethren emerged as a movement of protest against the apathy and doctrinal disobediences of the nineteenth century it had been a dynamic force in Church and society in several countries; but, like several similar movements throughout history, it chose to follow idiosyncratic teachers with verbal expertise in Scripture but little vision of the majesty of God and His purpose in the world. The spiritual giants Irvine, Darby, Kelly, Newman, Muller, Tregelles, Mackintosh, were followed by lesser men, and these in turn by nonentities, until the movement lost impetus and identity in a multifarious collection of sects tenaciously propagating their particular system of doctrine.

The missionary work of the Brethren started with the work of Anthony Norris Groves and expanded rapidly until there were over a thousand Brethren missionaries in the late 1940s. The early missionaries from the time of Groves and Lang had literally gone abroad to preach the gospel as Jesus taught, with no organisational backing, no guaranteed financial support, and depending on God alone for guidance as to the places visited, the time spent, the type of churches established. But this, too, had become corrupted into developing a "forwarding agency" (strenuously denied as a form of "organisation" like the denominations), with authoritative powers at home and abroad regarding candidates and practices, a company to register mission field property, a "prayer-list" of approved people for financial support, and regular financial support for those "approved" missionaries.

In Scotland it was widely known that I disapproved of this system; and I had chosen to give away all my money without saying anything to anyone, including my parents, for eighteen months before leaving for China, in order to test whether the words and promises of Jesus Christ were applicable to a follower in the twentieth century. If I was going half-way round the world, to travel to the forbidden and closed land of Tibet across a chaotic and war-ravaged China, with no known banks, post-offices, or viable organisational back-up system, then it was imperative that I find out if it worked in Britain before I tried it in China and Tibet. My journey to Tibet, therefore, was not so much a vocation to preach the gospel – although I was doing that wherever I went – or an intellectual exercise as to the relative merits of Christianity and Marxism in the twentieth century, or even a vindication of unadulterated Brethrenism and New Testament principles; it was what Christopher Fry called "an exploration into God". Where was He in the turmoil of the twentieth century, and how did He work through His servants in the complexities of the modern world?

I arrived in Shanghai to find the missionary community full of optimism for the future in China. Chiang Kai Shek was a Christian, as were his brothers-in-law and their influential wives, and such well-known leaders as C.T. Wang, Wang Chung- hui and Feng Yu-hsiang. There was an atmosphere of heady excitement, both among the missionaries on our ship returning to their mission stations and the old-hand missionaries already in Shanghai planning to return to their allocated mission areas.

The local Brethren missionary had arranged accommodation in a former Methodist Mission Home which had been converted into a block of flats and then re-converted into a series of dormitories to meet the demand of post-war over-crowding. There were nine people in my dormitory, sleeping on camp beds, washing in cold water, and living out of suitcases. The poorly cooked food cost 33,000 dollars a day; it cost 40,000 dollars for a coolie to carry luggage a few hundred yards; 1500 dollars for a cup of tea.

The railway between Shanghai and Nanking was not completed, the roads were in a desperate condition and travel dangerous, the little transport available travelled in convoys with whatever armed guards could be obtained. The only way to get from Shanghai to Nanchang in Kiangsi was to take a boat from Shanghai upriver to Kiukiang, a four days' trip, and there find a truck going the hundred miles or so to Nanchang. At Shanghai the mouth of the River Yangtze was wide as from Hull to Chatham, in England, and navigable as far as Constantinople by the same reckoning. Beyond Chungking it stretched for a further several hundred miles to its source in Tibet. The Chinese Communist armies were said to be only about a hundred miles to the north of the Yangtze in their widening sweep to the south.

Millions of refugees had poured into Shanghai and at night and in the early mornings they could be found sleeping on the pavements, while the dead, young and old, were left in the gutters to be picked up by the garbage trucks. But the shops and restaurants were crowded with well-dressed people, the streets were busy with vehicles of all kinds, and there seemed to be plenty of food.

The ship fare from Shanghai to Kiukiang was extortionate because so few ships were prepared to risk the journey upriver. Those that risked the trip were crowded below and on top, with passengers packed into cabins and sleeping on their baggage on deck. When we reached Kiukiang it cost 275,000 dollars for a seat in the back of a truck, plus baggage, to go to Nanchang. It took us 28 hours to travel the 120 miles; primarily because of the fear of bandits and undisciplined soldiery, but also because of breakdowns.

Nanchang was the capital of Kiangsi in central China, and it still showed signs of the heavy fighting that had taken place there over the past decade. It was not a particularly attractive city; mainly one long, wide main street, the surface of which was split and pot-holed, with other unsurfaced, uncared-for streets tapering off into lanes and slums on the city's outskirts.

The homes and "compound" of the Brethren missionaries were situated quite near to the centre of the city, surrounded by the low, one-storied quarters of the servants. To the side was the church, or, as it was known among Brethren, "the Gospel Hall".

It was my first experience of the "compound", or "paternalist" system practised by missionaries. Several times during missionary talks back home a tenuous doubt had crept into my mind regarding discrepancies between what was being said and what was being practised; but this was usually dismissed because it seemed inconceivable that such dedicated individuals could possibly misrepresent a spiritual vocation.

But now I was faced with cold, factual evidence that what was believed and taught in Britain was certainly not being practised or taught abroad – or in China, at any rate. It was even suggested to me that I ought not to take photographs of the missionaries' large houses, because "people at home would not understand and might get the wrong impression". Here were foreign missionaries only paying lip-service to fraternal relationships while overtly practising the most blatant paternalism – anticipating permanent residence, registering houses and land in a foreign company based in England, imposing Western life-styles and values and cultural practices on an ancient and powerfully chauvinistic population. All this with a militant Marxism only a few hundred miles away and advancing rapidly. It was just over ten years before in this same Province that the Russian Marxists had to learn through bitter defeats that an imposed Soviet-style traditionalist Marxism-Leninism would not be accepted by the Chinese people. How much less a traditionalist Western-style Christianity?

It was not just that old-style missionaries were unable to change; they were unwilling to consider change in the lives of other, younger missionaries who arrived with burning zeal and vision for a more dynamic form of Christian witness. They came with a vision of a nation informed of a God and a gospel for the nations, and saw this remorselessly whittled down to a God of Western nations and European culture to be taught to a small section of Chinese society, in restricted districts drawn up by denominational representatives, under the control of supervising "senior Western missionaries" who had gained authority through submission to Foreign Mission practices. The foreign missionary was an essential lynchpin in all denominational groups to hold them together in some semblance of conformity to a contradictory and diverse Scriptural pattern.

There was no way out of the impasse, for the established missionaries could not envisage leaving their allotted areas, and violating the terms of 'comity' by entering areas which had been allocated to other missions. They could not contemplate the possibility of leaving the large, roomy, western-style house and settled living, for the dubious Chinese inns or rented Chinese houses on a temporary basis. How could they leave the whole carefully thought-out, meticulously planned system for a simple dependence on God alone? It would mean the end of missions, the end of family life, the end of secure, ordered existence, the end of an assured life-job. They could not see that it would be only the beginning of a mighty work of God.

The only alternative would be to fight to preserve it, to resist any attempt to destroy it, and to adhere quite consistently to the principles on which they were operating, justifying the strange practices by using the accepted phraseology and platitudes in their own minds – a sort of spiritualized 'double-think' and 'double-talk', and getting by on a reputation for vocational sacrifice and a sound knowledge of the Scriptures.

Many of them had come out filled with enthusiasm to evangelize and build like the early apostles, but they were met by the solid and formidable weight of opinion and tradition of senior missionaries; and finally, faced with certain unpopularity and all that that could involve, they succumbed to the futility and bewilderment of it all. Some of the senior missionaries with reputations as 'sincere, godly men' were bound to pass on this traditional point of view to the novice. And, quite apart from this, his own practical sense would suggest to the novice that he would have no place to live in if he did not agree to live in a 'compound' house, and take over the responsibility of running and perpetuating the very system with which he might disagree in principle.

There was also the risk that he would have no one to help him with the important primary arrangements regarding language lessons, or even, in the last analysis, that he might find himself isolated by the very force of his own convictions. Nobody who had come out to take part in this work would care to find himself in a minority of one. He would begin to ask himself whether the position he was getting himself into was not due to his inability to work in harmony with his fellows, his dogmatic scriptural ideas and his general all-round unsuitability for the work of a missionary. This last doubt was the most deadly of all, of course; for the young missionary, full of new zeal and vision, might not greatly care whether or not he lived in a mud hut, nor in his early faith trouble much about the lack of sympathetic helpers in a foreign land, but the thought that he might have to forfeit his calling because of unsuitability would be too terrible to bear.

Then again who at home would understand *him* – a fresh young recruit – if he set himself up against reputable men, who had 'spent a lifetime in the field', who could be heard expounding the Scriptures ably from conference platforms when they were at home, and who were acclaimed as missionary 'statesmen' for their glowing accounts of their missionary work? And so many such bowed before the inevitable, and the paternalist-compound system and other incongruities were perpetuated.

When I spoke out against a state of affairs with which I could not agree, my passionate denunciations and 'revolutionary' suggestions were met by complacent assurance that I would eventually change my mind and come to see how mistaken I was, in the same way as others who had held like beliefs. But I held two advantages that were virtually unassailable. One was the obvious utter ruin of the traditionalist Christian work in Kiangsi following on the Maoist revolution, then the Japanese and Second World

Wars; and one was the fact that I had the confidence of some of the churches at home with which I had come into contact before coming to China.

The argument that the old school, the paternalist-compound school of missionaries, had something to show for their efforts could not be substantiated in Kiangsi at least, for the whole area was an empty shambles as far as a living Christian testimony was concerned, even at that time. The missionaries returning after the war found not only empty mission houses, but also empty mission halls, the so-called believers having melted away when the source of their employment, the missionaries, went home, and the very missionaries who were now arguing the advantages of the paternalist-compound system were those who had had to go out week by week on their return to China to look for the erstwhile Christians who had formed the local 'assemblies'. Here and there a family might be found standing steadfast, but of one virile, functioning New Testament assembly – never a trace. The situation was farcical in the extreme, but tragic in the context of lives spent, money wasted, and imminent judgement at the hands of the Communists. A meagre handful to show for the labour of a century when the support of the missionary was removed. Almost any theory would be better than the evidence produced in support of that one.

Yet all the preparations were going ahead to rebuild houses, rebuild halls, look for the former 'Christians' and carry on as before, and the methods used to ensure the continuance were the old, old ones of: 'You'll do as we think best'. These methods had fallen down as far as I was concerned, for I would not accept any theories of this kind, and even if I had to withdraw from the field, I warned, I would declare from every platform and to every church back home how strongly I disapproved of the paternalist-compound system. I had been well enough known in Central and Eastern Scotland before I left for the believers there to be aware that I knew what constituted a New Testament church, so that I felt I would have their support, and this encouraged me to believe in myself and to feel that I was not unfitted for the work of a missionary.

There could be no doubt about the issue between a vitiated Christianity and a dynamic Communism, whether in China or elsewhere. The top-heavy structure that went by the name of Christianity must collapse, and only equally dynamic, Christ-centred Christians remain. They were the true Church as God had expressed it, the fellowship of Holy Spirit-indwelt believers, the true Christians, the real Christianity, in communion with God and each other, through the work of Christ and the Spirit, requiring no organization, no ordination of clergy, to ensure its existence and continuance, but maintained virile and unconquerable by the Holy Spirit as the result of Spirit-bestowed gifts, which incomparably exceeded the forces of materialism. Soviet Communism could no more harm this than could Roman Imperialism in the first century of its manifestation.

The last known figures for foreign missionary involvement in China were those of 1936, before the Japanese invasion disrupted all communications. These figures showed that there were some 500,000 Chinese Protestant communicants, 5,875 foreign missionaries connected with 138 societies, and some 2,000 ordained Chinese workers, with an unknown number of unordained evangelists, and male and female Bible distributors, both paid and voluntary. A Christian education was being given to about 150,000 students in Mission schools and colleges, while an estimated 100,000 more attended Sunday schools.

The Roman Catholics had some 2.6 million communicants, 4,534 foreign missionaries, 5,496 Chinese bishops, priests, "brothers" and nuns, and seminarians. They, too, had about 150,000 in ordinary schools and colleges, and over 200,000 in their catechetical schools.

My first "evangelistic" work in China was done in the schools, colleges and university classes. There was an insatiable demand for English language teaching, and it was possible to get almost any number of students together for lessons and discussions on any subject which involved the use of English. I was even in great demand, when it was known that I came from Scotland, to give readings of Robert Burns' poetry in the original Lallans Scots vernacular! I discovered then and later that Burns was a favourite in China because his "peasant" imagery was understood and appreciated.

But what I found most fascinating and useful were the debates on Marxism and Christianity which ensued from any English lesson based on extracts from the Bible. From these it was evident that Dr Sun Yat Sen's and Chiang Kai Shek's "Three Principles of the People" democracy was being defeated; that Marxism was attracting the young intellectuals; that traditional Christianity of the denominations was despised; and indigenous Christianity was too little known as yet to be significant.

With some Brethren missionary colleagues we conducted English language Bible Study classes, for those interested, in our own home.

A very gifted Chinese preacher had begun attending the local Brethren church, and he asked if he might attend the English Bible study class. He was a valuable acquisition for he was teaching in the nearby Bible school of another mission. A striking feature about him, setting him apart from other Chinese "Christian" workers, was that he would accept no payment for his service in the Bible school, maintaining that he was God's servant, and not the servant of a mission, and that he wished to depend on God alone to supply his needs. He could then be free to move elsewhere whenever God should so dictate.

For the first time light began to shine for me in the dark testimony of Christian activity in China. Here was a man who was the living antithesis to all that the missionaries maintained and practised, for he had no 'system' behind him to supply his needs. A lonely apostle in China. It appeared that he was in Nanchang with another friend who had not been too happy about associating himself with the local church, because there was unconfessed sin amongst the Chinese members. The light in the darkness began to blaze! A Chinese believer, depending on God alone miraculously to supply his needs, while he preached and built up the groups of converts into New Testament churches, was a miracle enough in itself, in view of all that the senior missionaries had maintained about their shortcomings; but that the Chinese believer should also point out that his fellow-countrymen were living in sin and therefore endangering the testimony to the glory of God, and that he should refuse to take part in it until the offenders were suitably disciplined, swept away for ever the intolerable theories of the paternalist-compound school, and gloriously vindicated the power of God and His Word.

"But why didn't your friend go to the missionary and tell him the position?" I asked the Chinese preacher, "and then the matter could have been brought before the church. After all, the matter must be made known before it can be judged."

"But he did go to the missionary," he replied, "and the missionary did not think that anything could be done."

And so the church was deprived of the teaching of men who could have revivified it, and that was maintained which John Nelson Darby described in a translation of Ephesians chapter 4 – "that teaching which is in the sleight of men, in unprincipled cunning, with a view to systematized error". The Chinese, who, according to the old school, could not grasp the fundamental principles of Scripture, could sit with us and discuss the Scriptures from the Hebrew and Greek originals, talking familiarly of the return to New Testament principles in the early days of the Brethren in Britain, debating the difference of opinion between the leaders of that period, and could select a book from my bookcase by one of the ablest expositors from the West and point out a grave weakness in the argument submitted.

It was my first introduction to those who were known as 'the Little Flock' in China and to their leader, Watchman Nee. I had heard of the phenomenal rise of this movement in the Eastern Provinces of China from other missionaries, but they usually dismissed it with disapproval, and often with contempt, for many and varied reasons. The "Little Flock" were holy rollers – they went into trances – they prayed for the gift of tongues – they believed in permitting women to pray and speak – they believed that not all Christians would go to heaven when Christ returned – they were "exclusive", very rigid in deciding whom they would receive into their fellowship and communion – they insisted on baptism by immersion – they believed that Christians should not save money as the Lord's return was imminent – they were anti-foreigner – they were divisive – and so on. The list was impressive if only for its contradictions and possibilities. Only one missionary of those whom I had met had a good word to say for the Little Flock, the same missionary who had been denounced by his colleagues for "thirty years of wandering with nothing to show for it"!

Yet here were two Chinese believers who could have competently occupied any conference platform in Britain with the leading expositors there, and in 80 per cent of the cases would have shown up more creditably. There was an oddly familiar ring about the accusations, a faint echo from the apostolic times, the disapproval of reactionary conservatism throughout the centuries, the frightened complaint of hierarchical sectarianism which sensed a threat to its own security.

As far as I was concerned the die was cast. This was to be the sphere of my Christian associations in China. These groups, whose excesses in many places were admitted but were due merely to ignorance and lack of teaching, were products of the Spirit of God working in simple believers. It was the responsibility of those who were more enlightened in the Scriptures to teach these others until they were brought into a more deeply instructed conformity to the Scriptures. They were open and willing to receive any servant of God who would teach them, hungry for teaching, but it would have to be the Word of God that was taught and not men's opinions.

They were spreading out of the eastern provinces of China, where they had begun, across the country to the far north and west in organised groups of "mass migrations". This they derived from the *Acts of the Apostles* where it declared: "There arose on that day a great persecution against the church which was in Jerusalem; and they were all scattered abroad throughout the regions of Judea and Samaria except the apostles. They therefore...went about preaching the word". And again: "They that were scattered abroad travelled as far as Phoenicia and Cyprus and Antioch...speaking the word and preaching the Lord Jesus".

The plan was conceived by Witness Lee, a colleague of Watchman Nee, who worked out the details. Groups of families, selected as to types of personnel and representing an appropriate cross-section of trades and professions – gardeners, shoemakers, teachers, nurses, barbers, carpenters, watch-makers and -repairers – were chosen and carefully prepared for their great evangelistic venture. Their home church supplied travel expenses and three months' living costs for use whey they arrived at their destination. After that they were expected to support themselves in the chosen base of operations.

In 1943 one group of 30 families went northward into Manchuria, another of 70 families went westward to Shansi and beyond. The Japanese were highly suspicious of their activities and even imprisoned and tortured Witness Lee.

They had variable success, but in several areas churches sprang up where there had been none previously.

To me they represented a provision of God, for it meant that there were groups of Chinese Christians whose beliefs were compatible with my own in Chengtu and Chungking and other places in West China, where previously I had expected only incompatible Mission stations.

When I finally left Kiangsi for the journey west across China to Tibet it was the "Little Flock" groups which provided practical as well as spiritual help. One of the most difficult decisions I had to make was to turn down Watchman Nee's invitation to participate in the programme to evangelise all of China's major cities and towns within the next ten years. But I was in Chengtu, in West China at the time, and about to enter Tibet for my longest and fullest journey of exploration. It was Watchman Nee's family firm, China Biochemical Laboratories, which made my journey to Tibet possible, for I had all my British cheques paid to their office in Hong Kong and was provided in exchange with a large variety of medical equipment and supplies; as well as supplies of brick tea and other goods to serve as barter inside Tibet. So, without banks or post-offices, without a back-up organisation, I was able to survive for the next few years inside Tibet.

It was also through my ability to help Tibetans medically that I became close friends with the leading Tibetan war-lord and his influential family. While still learning the language I was brought by him into confidential political discussions in which he was involved. During the recent war with Japan, Generalissimo Chiang Kai Shek had appointed the Tibetan leader, called Topgyay Pangdatshang, an honorary General of the fighting Kham tribesmen of East Tibet, with responsibility to cover his rearguard west of Chungking and south to the Burma Road. However, Topgyay Pangdatshang had already been planning to lead a revolt of his Khambas against the feudal government in the Tibetan capital of Lhasa in Central Tibet. During the war with Japan he used his China-recognised authority to acquire large supplies of military equipment with a view to leading a revolt when the war finished.

But ten years before he and other Tibetan leaders had been contacted by the Chinese Communist leaders as they retreated through East Tibet on their famous "Long March". The Chinese Communists also made attractive offers to the Tibetans, whom they regarded as popular "leaders of the people" against "an oppressive feudal and aristocratic regime" in Lhasa. As the Communists now swept southwards and westwards from their base in Yenan in northwest China, the large and influential western provinces of Tsinghai, Szechuan and Yunnan, and the smaller province of Sikang, fell to them in 1949.

Before then Pangdatshang had withdrawn deep inside Tibet, with several Tibetan leaders, taking me with them to Litang, Batang, Derge, and Bo, where we finally made our headquarters on the upper reaches of the River Mekong, to the south of Chamdo. Here strings of hard-riding Tibetan couriers arrived with news from the Chinese Communists to the east, and from the Central Tibetan Government to the west, while Pangdatshang tried to decide whether (i) to launch the Khamba revolt against the Central Government as planned; (ii) to come to an arrangement with the Central Government of Tibet, in which he would have greater powers in East Tibet but still be under the Central Government's control; or (iii) to agree with the Chinese Communists who were offering to help him overthrow the Central Government in Lhasa, but as a representative of the Chinese Communists. The fall of Peking to them in late 1949 critically sharpened his dilemma. His major objection to the Chinese Communists – other than the historic racial antagonism – as with all Tibetans, was their militant atheism, while the Tibetans were ardent Buddhists.

My own dilemma was equally acute. My medical supplies were low and I was unable to renew them as we were cut off from the C.B.C. Laboratories by the Chinese Communist advance southwards in China. I was now speaking reasonably fluent Tibetan and able to understand the political crisis facing the Tibetan leaders. I was also able to understand, and to sympathise with, their spiritual quandary. Their lives revolved around their religion, as did the many millions of Muslim Chinese and Tibetans to the north, but it was obvious to Pangdatshang and to me that while the Chinese Communists were passionately committed to fighting for their atheistic ideology it was not apparent that Buddhists and Muslims would be any more enthusiastic than the bulk of professing Christians to defend their beliefs.

Pangdatshang resolved his dilemma by deciding to throw in his support for the Central Government of Tibet against the Chinese Communists, but that threw up two other major crises for him: one, he needed large and immediate supplies of arms to fight what might be a long and would be a bloody war with the advancing Chinese Communists; and, two, he needed an English-speaking messenger who could travel quickly across hitherto unexplored South-East Tibet on a direct route to India in order to inform the Indian, British, and whichever Tibetan leaders might be in the Indo-Tibetan border towns, of the critical situation in East Tibet. I was asked to be that messenger.

The physical hazards of such a journey were monumental, as there was no Tibetan who had ever made the journey to India by this route; and I would have to complete it in three months in order to give me sufficient time to complete my tasks and return as the Chinese Communists were expected to invade East Tibet within the next six to nine months. The political involvement for me was mind-boggling as I, an unknown missionary from an obscure Christian group and a small village in Scotland, had to make myself and my information credible to a just-liberated

Indian (1947) administration and a post-imperial British diplomatic corps, and highly suspicious Tibetan aristocrats. But it was the spiritual implications which presented me with the greatest obstacle and greatest challenge in the whole enterprise.

For I had gone to Tibet on a personal spiritual odyssey. I had there a rendezvous with God. Nor had I been disappointed in this, despite the disastrous paternalist missionary experience in China en route; and I had emerged after three years' profound spiritual experience in Tibet with a greatly expanded knowledge of God and His ways. I had come to terms with the fact that I had no place in the institutional Christian system. I had accepted, albeit regretfully, that I probably had no place in the much more attractive Brethren system. But I had had a new vision of something exciting through the "Little Flock" in China to which I could commit myself, a divinely provided, spontaneously expanding, household-based and community-orientated, movement to transform disappointing and disillusioned people into confident children in the kingdom of God.

Yet it now appeared as if the "Little Flock" would be swept away with all the other churches, societies, sects and groups, in the post-war Marxist holocaust facing China. I had been disappointed, and eventually disillusioned, with Christian missionaries in China professing the paradox of an all-powerful God while at the same time making panic-stricken arrangements to flee back to the safety of the godless West from an advancing atheistic Marxism. Now I was facing the same decision myself.

Yet – not quite. I was being asked to leave Tibet temporarily – but in order to return with renewed supplies. The Tibetan leaders wanted me to go back and be with them in their struggle against godless Communists. But it was right there that the crux of my dilemma lay. For, if I was successful in reaching India safely; if I did manage to alert and persuade the Indian, British and Tibetan authorities of the dangerous situation inside Tibet vis-a-vis Communist China; and if I did manage to return with adequate medical supplies to East Tibet before the Chinese Communists attacked – it would be as a political and not as a spiritual messenger. And so I had to first sort out my spiritual responsibilities in the real world of the twentieth century as a servant of God and follower of Jesus Christ. In effect, I would have to do spiritually what I was about to do physically: launch myself out on a journey across the worst terrain in the world, with no guide, no maps, and depend on God alone to show the way and tell me what to do and say. Was it John Osborne, the well-known playwright, who said that there were no great causes left?

I crossed Tibet into India in three months. I spoke with all the authorities requested by the Tibetans. I bought and transhipped medical supplies by yak caravan into Tibet. But I never left India to go back to Tibet – not for many, many years, anyway. First, the monsoons isolated me in the Himalayan border town of Kalimpong; then, the great Assam earthquake cut my return route through South-East Tibet; and, finally, I went down with a sudden onset of thrombo-phlebitis which kept me bedfast for several months. The Chinese Communists invaded East Tibet towards the end of 1950, capturing the Kham Tibetan leaders.

My dramatic journey across Tibet to India, my knowledge of Tibet and the Tibetans, and the exodus of Tibetan refugees into India precipitated me into a new dimension of literary and political involvements. I was asked to write books about my experiences, to act as a stringer for Indian, British, Commonwealth and American newspapers and journals, and to be an interpreter for newspapermen, diplomats and scholars interested in the Tibetan situation. I was also brought into close involvement with Communists of similar interests – and with intelligence agents of all ideologies. All of them wanted to obtain, or impart, information to or about the Tibetans and Chinese – and I was the only person able to talk the language or with appropriate and trusted contacts.

Kalimpong, on the Indo-Tibetan border, in the early 1950s was called by Indian Prime Minister Nehru, with considerable justification as well as irritation, "a nest of spies". The invasion of Tibet by a rampaging Chinese Communist Party had opened up exciting new possibilities for Marxists of all kinds, and their espionage counterparts. The New China was pushing back the frontiers of Old China encroached on by the imperialists to the north, west and south, and the New Chinese Communist leaders in Peking were making it very clear that China would claim those many areas annexed under "the unequal treaties" – and that a dynamic Marxism would conquer Asia, and the world.

Lenin was supposed to have said (although no-one has ever discovered the source of the much used apocryphal quotation): "The way to Paris lies through Peking and Calcutta". And Mao Zedung added his own revised version: "The way to world conquest lies through Havana, Accra and Calcutta". Significantly, both had agreed on Calcutta – and Kalimpong was on the direct route from Peking to Calcutta.

Mao had already served notice to the Western imperial powers who had plundered China:

"In defeating China in war the imperialists have taken away many Chinese dependent states and a part of her territories. Japan took Korea, Taiwan and the Ryukyu Islands, the Pescadores Islands, Port Arthur; England seized Burma, Bhutan, Nepal and Hong Kong; France occupied Annam, and even an insignificant country like Portugal...took Macao..."

Taiwan, Tibet, Korea, Burma, Nepal, Hong Kong, Annam: The Maoist-Marxist foreign policy of Communist China was already being clearly outlined – the "liberation" of all former Chinese territories, no matter who held them. To make it more explicit the Chinese Communist General Chu Teh, addressing a mammoth gathering in Peking in 1950 had stated that "the great People's Liberation Army would march to further victories until the liberation of all Asia was completed".

There was no doubt that this included India as well, for Mao Zedung, in a letter to the Communist Party of India, published in *The Communist*, Bombay, in January, 1950, expressed the hope that "relying on the brave Communist Party of India and the unity and struggle of all Indian patriots, India certainly will not remain long under the yoke of imperialism and emerge in the socialist and People's Democratic family..."

On my arrival in Kalimpong on the Indo-Tibetan border I had quickly established a line of communication with my Tibetan friends in East Tibet through the Paugdatshaug family and its trading headquarters in that border town. They had mule and yak caravans travelling regularly between Kalimpong on the Indian border and Kangting on the Chinese border some 1500 miles to the east. From them I discovered that a written ultimatum finally had been delivered to Topgyay Pangdatshang stating the Chinese Communists' intention to "liberate" Tibet, and after that the neighbouring Himalayan states.

On 5 August, 1950, General (subsequently Marshall) Liu Po-ch'eng, Chairman of the South-West China Military Affairs Commission said that "the People's Army would soon enter Tibet with the object of wiping out British and American influence there. When the country had been liberated Tibetans would be given regional autonomy and religious freedom. Lamas would be protected. The Communists would protect existing customs..." and so on.

On 25 October, 1950, Peking Radio broadcast that the process of liberating Tibet had begun. The Kham Tibetan leaders did not actively resist and were mostly confined to their immediate residences or areas. But in 1952 they were sufficiently confident and organised for the individual tribal leaders to revolt against the occupying Chinese army. They sent word to me pleading with me to get military and political support from the Indian, British or American authorities to help them in their struggle.

When the Dalai Lama travelled to China in 1954 several influential members of his entourage made contact with the Kham Tibetan leaders as they travelled through their territories in East Tibet and laid plans for a full-scale revolt against Communist China. In March 1955 the Communist authorities in Peking announced the formation of a committee to prepare for regional autonomy for Tibet; and in September administrative offices were set up in Lhasa in Tibet to bring Tibet more closely within the Chinese administrative structure. This move was accompanied in East Tibet by ruthless plundering of monasteries by the Chinese Communists, the removal of the priests into forced labour camps for indoctrination, and the levying of crippling taxes. This was the signal for widening what until then had been a tribal revolt by the Khambas into a provincial, then a national, revolt against the Chinese by all Tibetans. By mid-1958 20,000 East Tibetans had fallen back on Central Tibet, and there they found fresh supplies of arms and ammunition to extend their rebellion against China. On 17 March, 1959 the capital of Tibet, Lhasa, revolted against the Chinese, the Dalai Lama fled, thereby precipitating a political crisis between China and India.*

The Chinese radio and newspapers accused the Indian border town of Kalimpong of being "the commanding centre of the revolt" and alleged that the Dalai Lama was abducted from Tibet by rebels at the instigation of certain

* See REQUIEM FOR TIBET, by George N. Patterson: published by Aurum Press, 33 Museum Street, London WC1A 1LD (March 1990)

Indian elements and was being held against his will. Chinese propaganda claimed that India had the help of British and American imperialists, reproducing an article which the official organ of the Communist Party of India, the *New Age*, published on 5 April, 1959, alleging that Mr George Patterson (myself) had an active role in the rebellion and was on the friendliest terms with Mr Apa Pant, the Indian Political Officer in Sikkim, as well as other leading Tibetan officials.

Actually, I had been actively involved in the whole Tibetan situation from 1950 onwards, particularly with the leaders in Kham in East Tibet who kept me informed of developments by courier. Since 1950 I had written for newspapers, the *Statesman* of India, the *Manchester Guardian*, and the *Daily Telegraph*, as well as American newspapers and journals. I had also published five books: *God's Fool*, *Tibetan Journey*, *Up and Down Asia*, *Tragic Destiny*, and *Tibet in Revolt*. I had also become well-known internationally because of my journalistic differences of opinion over Indian and Chinese policies in Asia, especially in Tibet, and had been on the verge of expulsion as "irresponsible and alarmist" – alleged by Prime Minister Nehru – until my articles were dramatically vindicated by the arrival of the Dalai Lama in India with personal news of the Tibetan revolt and its genocidal consequences for the Tibetan people.

But in my ten years in India I had also become involved with the Indian Christian indigenous movement. The largest group was very like the "Little Flock" in China in its principles and practices, and was led by a friend of Watchman Nee, a Sikh called Bakht Singh. He was a civil engineer who had become converted to Christianity in the West, had returned to India to preach the gospel of Jesus Christ without any association or support from Western denominations, and had been responsible for the growth and spread of these churches in India. Bakht Singh had asked me to join him and I had been glad to do this on many occasions, preaching and establishing churches, particularly in South India. He wanted me to do this work full-time, and I would gladly have done this but for my strong conviction that God's purpose for me was to be His servant in the political jungle of the world, articulating the lessons I learned there.

Individuals and groups of these Indian believers were spreading beyond the cities and towns and villages of India into the remote border areas of Sikkim, Bhutan, Nepal and Kashmir to the north east; and to the frontier tribes of Nagas, Kachins, Karens and others on the Indo-Burmese borders, who had become Christians in large numbers in the past century. The Christian leaders of these tribes were being drawn into revolt against India and Burma because of the increasing Hindu-ising and Buddha-ising of these countries; and the disinterest of the West in coming to their aid in any way was leading them into considering the blandishments of Marxism from the Chinese Communists to the north.

From 1960 onwards I became as deeply embroiled in "the Naga question" with the *Observer* as I had been with "the Tibet question" for the *Daily Telegraph* in the previous five years, with the militant opposition of the Burmese government in much the same manner as with the Chinese and Indian governments over Tibet. At the request of the Tibetan, Naga and Shan revolutionary leaders I returned to Asia after a short spell of three years in Britain, during which I worked for the *Observer* and the *B.B.C.*, writing and broadcasting on Asian affairs and publishing two books, *Peking Versus Delhi* and *Asia Handbook.* I went back to Asia with a Granada Television unit, comprising the distinguished TV documentary makers Adrian Cowell and Chris Menges, to do a series of special documentaries on the revolts in Tibet, Nagaland and the Shan States of North-east Burma.

We went over the Himalayas in Nepal into Tibet in company with the Kham guerillas who were marauding

Chinese Army convoys on the strategic China-Tibet road inside Tibet, and produced an award-winning documentary, "Raid Into Tibet" on the subject. We dropped the Naga film because the Indian government for the first time made serious overtures for peace with the Naga revolutionaries and we did not want to create any problems by our presence. Filming the "Christian" Shan revolt against the dictatorial regime of the Buddhist Ne Win, Adrian and Chris also secretly filmed the opium-growing activities of what is now widely known as "the Golden Triangle", and made the first ever film of the cultivating and trafficking process from the Shan States through Burma, through Bangkok in Thailand to Hong Kong, "The Opium Trail".

I arrived in Hong Kong in late 1964, en route to Taiwan where I was doing research for the next film and completing the research for "The Opium Trail" ahead of the film crew. While I waited for them to arrive I made enquiries regarding the "Little Flock" groups in Taiwan and Hong Kong and through them became acquainted with another newspaper correspondent, Jack Chow, who was with the *Hong Kong Standard* and was also a Christian with the "Little Flock". Through them I was able to pick up directly once again my contacts with the religious as well as political situation inside Communist China.

From the time I had left them in West China I had developed a deep interest in the work and future of the "Little Flock" under a totalitarian and atheistic Marxist regime in China, and I made a special study of discovering everything I could from whatever sources regarding individuals and groups over the years. As China had become more and more closed to foreigners this had been increasingly difficult in many ways, but as a political correspondent I had fairly high connections among diplomats and other correspondents from countries friendly to China – such as Canada, for example – who were able to pass along interesting information. Also, the Indian Christian preachers with Bakht Singh, such as Jordan Khan, and some Western associates, in Taiwan, Philippines, Indonesia and Singapore, who knew of my preaching activities in China and India were glad to pass on information, so I had a fairly broad if not too detailed picture of what had been happening between 1950 and 1964, when I arrived in Hong Kong to become yet another "China-watching" correspondent.

CHAPTER 8

The Christian-Marxist Battle For The Soul Of China

A Marxist's View of the Destruction of Institutional Christianity: 1950-66

1966 was the year in which the Chinese Communist government claimed that the institutional Christian churches had ceased to exist in China.

In 1950, at a meeting of church leaders, the Chinese Communist Prime Minister Zhou Enlai, had affirmed:

"We are going to let you go on teaching, go on trying to convert people; provided you also continue with your social services. After all, we both believe that truth will prevail; we think your beliefs untrue and false, therefore, if we are right, the people will reject them and your church will decay. If you are right, then the people will believe you; but as we are sure that you are wrong, we are prepared for that risk".

But just to make sure that the people chose Marxism and not Christianity the Chinese Communist Party leaders devised a programme of extermination which they thought would leave the Chinese people with little choice other than Marxism. Writing in his authoritative book, *Religion in Chinese Society*, in 1961, the Chinese scholar, C.K. Yang, declared:

"In the first ten years of the Communist rule, there was little serious difficulty in China proper in executing this policy of permitting continued restricted existence for theistic religion under the condition of political submission. The traditionally weak institutional religion could offer little effective organized resistance to Communist pressure, a situation substantially different from Communist countries where there are large and organized churches. *The only organized religion by which the Communists feel threatened is Christianity*, particularly the Catholic Church, because of its long association with Western powers, but the numerical size of the Christian group is not so large as to present difficulties to the Communists." (My italics).

When the Communists took over in 1949 there were an estimated 11,470 Christian churches, 70 Christian hospitals, 18 Christian universities, 21 Bible institutes, 48 seminaries, and 7,500 "gospel centres". This was the Christian institutional threat to the Marxist regime's ambitions in China. It took them several years to comprehend the threat of indigenous Christianity in China, and by then it was beyond their control. The official organ of information – Government and Party statements, reports in the media, church announcements – provided a framework to follow and understand the anti-religion policy of the new Chinese Marxist government in Peking; but the essentially integrated and committed spiritual nature of the evangelical indigenous Chinese movement, giving little importance to keeping statistics of membership, provided little scope to the Communist authorities for their standard practices of infiltration, accusation and control that they used with the institutional organisations.

However, by an unusual combination of circumstances, while I was in Hong Kong I was introduced to a high-ranking Chinese refugee who had been closely involved with the structure and work of the notorious Religious Affairs Bureau. Because of his importance he was being kept under strict surveillance in Hong Kong by the British authorities, but as he wished to have asylum in the United States he was being de-briefed by American officials and my friend, Jack Chow, who was the official interpreter. Jack Chow knew that I was working on a book about the Sino-Soviet border conflict at the time, *The Unquiet Frontier*, and he suggested that I get permission to sit in on the de-briefing sessions to obtain the very interesting information being provided by the refugee official. I was able to do this, and made copious notes of his direct personal experience of how the Communist authorities destroyed the institutional churches in China from within.

Hsiao Feng – a pseudonym to hide his true identity at the time – was the son of a Chinese Nationalist Army colonel who had been a graduate of the famous Whampoa Military Academy in Canton and, later, a regimental commander fighting the Japanese and Communists. When Canton fell in 1949 he fled with his family to Hong Kong, and it was in Hong Kong that Hsiao Feng first openly associated with Marxist groups. Through a Communist relative he was given an introduction to the chief of personnel in the newly established Municipal People's Government in Canton, in the Civil Affairs Bureau, in 1950, as a registrar dealing with religious bodies, civil, relief and welfare organisations. In November, 1951, he was transferred to the Propaganda Department of the Canton Party Committee, with a special assignment to help prepare for the establishment of a separate Religious Affairs Department, with himself as section chief.

The outbreak of the Korean War in June, 1950, had provided the new Chinese Communist government with an opportunity to get control of the Christian churches and organisations. They did this by producing a series of "Manifestoes" and "Declarations" calling for "the unification of all churches" and "dissociating from imperialist structures by the disposal of American subsidized missionary institutions and groups". The authorities also published a document in 1951 outlining "Foreign Preachers' Intrusion into the Interior and Intervention of Domestic Affairs" which, among other things, declared that the Christian Bible translator, Robert Morrison, had also drawn up the infamous Nanking Treaty and the Reverend Gutzlaff had prepared the draft of the text.

The Communist authorities then stated that the Christian churches would enjoy "constitutional freedom" but they must "sweep their houses clean" and "accept the leadership of the Party". This meant accepting three things:

1. Policy determination and financial administration must be passed over to Chinese leadership.
2. The missionary's future contribution must lie in special service projects only.
3. Mission funds without strings attached would be permitted to enter China temporarily, but from henceforth the Chinese churches would have to be responsible for their own support.

A Manifesto was issued which demanded obedience to a list of stated principles:

1. Christian churches and organisations must give throughgoing support to the "Common Political Programme", opposing imperialism, feudalism, etc., etc.
2. They must participate in the movement opposing war, upholding peace, government activities, agrarian reform, etc.
3. They must cultivate a democratic and patriotic spirit, self-reliance, self-respect, self-criticism, and achieve the goals of a reformation of the churches.

These principles and practices were enshrined in long passages of Marxist slogans and political euphemisms, but they were sufficient to indicate radical changes in the churches and organisations, widespread interference by the Communist authorities in their activities, and serious punishments for any violation.

Divested of jargon, what this meant in practice was that every professing Christian in China would have to recognise, by persuasion or force, the importance of the Communist Party line on every subject. Then, when its importance was admitted, the individual was responsible for persuading others.

In order to enforce this the Religious Affairs Bureau of the Peking Municipal Government and the United Front Work Department of the Chinese Communist Party set up the "Three Self Reform Movement" in July, 1951, for "Learning Meetings" for all Christian churches in the Peking Municipality. About 300 ministers and church members attended every morning for a month. Discussion groups were set up, and every member had to say something regarding the topics on the agenda. Every sentence spoken was recorded. The Communist chairman of the group "guided" the discussions, and drew up the "agreed" contributions of the participants at the close.

This "Three Self Learning Meeting" held in Peking was the pilot project for similar movements covering the rest of the country, including Canton, which came within Hsiao Feng's jurisdiction. All churches which had "foreign" connections were forced by one means or another to attend, but it was noticeable that several of the indigenous groups did not take part. These included the "Christian Tabernacle" of Pastor Wang Ming-dao, the "Little Flock" groups of Watchman Nee, the "Christian Assembly" of Wang Chen, and several other smaller groupings. These groups claimed that their churches were already governed by Chinese Christians, they had no connection with foreign churches, they were already self-supporting, self-governing, self-propagating as required by the law, and so the "Three Self Reform Movement" did not apply to them.

There was an official move to counter this legitimate but unacceptable argument after a time, by local officials imposing a regulation that any group of more than six people meeting together for any purpose would be assumed to be "a counter-revolutionary cell", and therefore subject to severe punishment. This was found to be ludicrously unenforceable, for almost every Chinese family meeting with relatives added up to more than six people. It was then changed by the fanatical Communist local officials to "thirty people" constituting a "counter-revolutionary cell"; but this had the opposite effect to that intended, for the indigenous groups then began splitting up as soon as their members reached thirty into two or more smaller groups and the movement increased in impetus.

Because the indigenous groups had had many years experience of meeting together in small groups for communion, Bible study and prayer, without the need of a foreign missionary, pastor or priest, they were also the recipients of large numbers of members from the institutional churches who were no longer happy with the increasing Marxist domination of their respective churches. So the Communist Party officials found that the most committed and active members moved away from their control to the Christian indigenous movement which, theoretically, under the official provisions of the Religious Affairs Bureau and Three Self Movement, were not authorised to do anything about them, officially at least.

The leading initiator of the Three Self Movement was Wu Yao-tsung of the Y.M.C.A. Wu, and the Secretary-General of the China Buddhist Association, Chao Pu-ch'u, were both actually secret members of the Chinese Communist Party assigned to special tasks, according to Hsiao Feng. Chao, on his return from a visit to Japan, represented the Communist Party in a secret investigation in Hsiao Feng's area to check what the Municipal Party Committee was doing with regard to certain Buddhist problems. Hsiao Feng was ordered to report to him. Before initiating the Three Self Movement Wu Yao-tsung received a directive from the Director of the Propaganda Department of the Communist Party Central Committee, Li Ting-yi. He was instructed to approach the Christian leaders of Peking, Tientsin, Shanghai and Kwangchow for signatures to the statement that launched the Three Self Movement.

In Shanghai, where the Roman Catholics were strongly concentrated, Bishop Kung Ping-mei and his priests openly refused to participate in the Three Self Movement. Bishop Ch'en Yi-hsiu in Kwangchow, after initially agreeing to join the parallel Catholic Three Self Movement which was officially dissociated from the Vatican, later withdrew. This was also true of the whole South China Diocese which included Kwangchow, Kwanghsi, Hupeh, and Kiangsi.

Hsiao Feng and his colleagues interpreted their function largely for themselves. They ordered every religious organisation or unit, such as a church or monastery, to compile a report about its history, table of organisation, membership, assets and property, and numbers of daily attendances by members. They also demanded the proceedings of all administrative meetings, and sent cadres to attend them on a random basis. Every pastor and priest had to submit their sermons to his Bureau, which censored what it considered contrary to the Party's interests.

Hsiao Feng enforced the central policy regarding religion at all times: (i) People who believe in a religion have freedom; (ii) People who do not believe in a religion also have freedom, including the freedom to oppose religion (but religious believers usually did not get to hear this clause); (iii) People have freedom to change their religious belief.

In practice, what this meant was, for example, (ii) could conduct their activity only in places of worship; namely, Christians in their church, Buddhists in their monastery or nunnery, Taoists in their temple, etc. The reason given for this restriction was that "it would protect the activities of the religious from being disturbed by the non-religious, and at the same time protect the non-religious from being disturbed by the religious". It also meant that Christians could not conduct open-air meetings, sing outside carols and hymns, distribute Christian Bibles or literature.

These conditions served to exacerbate old conflicts and foster new ones between different denominations, church groups, and sects. They also caused arguments and divisions between the clergy, and between the clergy and laypersons. The Communist cadre responsible would then use the conflict to manoeuvre the opposing parties or individuals into confessions of error or accusation, and from this bring the church or group under greater control of the Communist Party.

Ironically, Hsiao Feng claimed that he was often pressed into solving internal problems in Protestant churches – even after he had expressed a reluctance to do so. Sometimes he would be asked to appoint a pastor, or help a pastor examine a candidate for baptism.

But the chief method used by the Communists in "secularising" the Christian churches was by "hidden strength" operatives with "single string connections". These operatives were specially selected "underground" Communist Party members recruited from capitalist organisations, democratic parties, minority nationalities and religious groups, who could use their Party accepted status and connection with the respective group to infiltrate them: hence "hidden strength". They were directly under the control of the Party, attached only to the director of the local United Front Work Department, and had no contact with any other department or person: hence "single string connection".

The work of these special operatives was to subvert their particular organisation from within by opposing any measure, or supporting any person, which would further the interests of the Party. They were not to reveal their Party affiliation, but to get themselves appointed to key positions and delegations, to where they could manage a church or group of churches as a secret Communist.

Through these various measures detailed reports on individuals and practices were compiled, which were then used in the "accusation meetings" of public self-criticism. These Communist "accusation meetings", at which individuals were intimidated into confessing crimes that almost everybody present knew they did not commit, were impossible for Western observers to comprehend – unless, perhaps, they had read the book, DARKNESS AT NOON, by the late former Communist Arthur Koestler. To those who have not read his book the blatantly stage-managed spectacles conducted by Communist regimes would strain the credulity of any school- child. The French philosophy professor, Raymond Aron, compared the "ceremonies of self-accusation" to:

"...religious rites, rather than instruments of a rational method...the goal is to manifest the absolute nature of the supreme power by forcing millions of men and women to act as if they took absurdities to be the truth... All religions tend to impose upon the faithful the image of a world that is more true than the world of the senses. In Stalinism, that world is simply the interpretation which the Party gives to events, an interpretation which is never definitely fixed. By confessing crimes which they have not committed, disgraced officials help create this super-reality, of which the Party is supreme master...The faith which the trials are intended to spread has for its object neither the testimony of its victims nor the doctrine of the masters, but the omnipotence of a Party which must (be made to) seem stronger than truth itself".

Nation-wide in China, the accumulated reports obtained from these public "accusation meetings" were compiled in a set of documents entitled "Reference Materials On The Crimes Of Imperialists Using Religion To Commit Aggression Against China". These were then used in three ways:

(i) to provide clues for the investigation of any foreign spy cases by the Public Security officials;

(ii) as reference for the Religious Affairs Bureau in every city, to be used as a means of control of the churches and other "subversive" groups;

(iii) as a "Handbook" of instruction for the Party Propaganda Department.

All these activities were not accomplished without a considerable amount of suffering, and even terror. In 1952, a "Five-Anti" movement was initiated, theoretically to punish those guilty of bribery, tax-evasion, stealing state property, theft of state economic secrets, and embezzlement in carrying out state contracts. In fact, it was a ruthless campaign intended to cripple the money power of the merchants and manufacturers, and to coerce them into submitting to the new centralised Marxist political system. It was also used as a means to discredit Christians through the politically biassed interrogations of the publicly conducted accusation meetings. In a high-profile campaign conducted over many months it struck terror into the hearts of the whole nation because of its ruthlessness and severity.

Increasing the terror was the associated campaign against those designated as "counter-revolutionaries", during which at least hundreds of thousands were put to death as "enemies of the State", while millions of others were sentenced to enforced "reform through labour". The campaigns were a deliberate policy of the ruling Marxist regime to instil fear of authority on the politically apathetic people of China as a whole, while emphasising the power of the new Marxist rulers after previous decades of political impotence.

Following on the first wave of pressure and persecution of the foreign missionaries, which ended with their departure from China by the end of 1952, this second wave of national public exposure of all forms of internal subversion was used to remove the majority of Western-approved Chinese pastors, priests and indigenous Christian activists from the mainstream institutional churches and organisations.

In 1951, Isaac Wei, son of the founder of the "True Jesus Church", was arrested, together with several other leaders of their group. In 1952, Ching Tien-ying, the founder of the "Jesus Family", and Watchman Nee, founder of the "Little Flock", were arrested on trumped-up charges and imprisoned. It seemed as if it would only be a matter of a short time until the outspoken Peking pastor, Wang Ming-dao, would be arrested in a similar fashion.

It was during this turbulent period that Hsiao Feng became aware of the counter-productive effects of the measures being used by the Communist Party leaders. He had made a statistical survey of the number of churches and their membership in Canton in 1952, including a record of their monthly increases and decreases. At the time there were some 52 churches, with about seven thousand members; a considerable drop, it was estimated, from the previous year.

But he noticed in late 1952 onwards that the graphs of Christian groups and memberships were climbing again for some reason. On investigation, he found that groups of Christians visited the city and province from other places in small numbers; then, within a short time after the visit, a new small group would emerge and expand until it numbered two hundred or more. They could not all meet together in one place at one time, under the existing regulation, so they broke up into small, inter-related groups for their "fellowship meetings". Hsiao Feng was disturbed to note the quality of membership, which included university lecturers, school-teachers, government officials, and even military personnel.

This was confirmed for me by an anonymous Christian who sent a letter secretly to a friend living in Hong Kong, which read:

"...They (the Communist authorities) proceeded to attack the genuine self-governing, self-supporting, self-propagating churches, which they regarded as "nails in the eyes" to be removed. These church organisations were organised by Chinese Christians, were entirely supported by them, and had no relationships with foreign churches. They were well-organised, had good fellowship, were well-supported by members who were faithful in attendance and ardent in their piety...They adhered unanimously to one principle: the worship of God is the only purpose in religion, not participation in politics...Elder Yen Chia-lee, a leader of the Little Flock, surrendered to the Three Self Movement under the most difficult circumstances, but Wang Ming-dao, Wang Chen, etcetera, never failed..."

In 1954, the first National Christian Conference was permitted by the Communist authorities to be held in Peking, from 22 July to 6 August. It was attended by 232 Protestant delegates from 62 different missions and groups. A new national committee of 139 members was elected, among whom were well-known Chinese "Christian" leaders such as Y.T. Wu of the YMCA, Bishop Robin T.S. Chen, the Reverend Z.T. Kaung, Wu Yi-fang, and H.H. Tsui. Addressing the delegates, Y.T. Wu declared that the Chinese churches "had basically cut off imperialist control", and that the Christian Manifesto had been signed by 1,527 leaders and members of Christian churches representing over 400,000 members. A "message of respect" to Chairman Mao was drafted and sent, reading:

"During the past four years, through the self-governing, self-supporting and self-propagating movement, the Christian churches of China have basically severed their relations, both administratively and economically, with imperialism, begun to rid themselves of the influence of imperialism, and started to govern, support and preach themselves. All these successes are inseparable from your wise leadership and deep concern, as well as the brilliant achievements of the New China for the past several years. We are, therefore, offering our deepest gratitude on behalf of the entire Christians (sic)".

The National Conference marked the beginning of a new stage in the activities of the official Three Self Movement, including giving it a new name. The former name was dropped and substituted by "The Chinese Christian Three Self Patriotic Movement". The reason given for this was:

"...The purpose of the Three Self Patriotic Movement is to unite the Christian Church in China in the Three Self Campaign, in positive participation in opposing imperialism and in furthering patriotic movements and world peace. We know that the purpose of 'self-government' is not to unify or modify the organisation of the various churches, but to get the churches to cut off all relations with imperialism, so that the churches will be ruled by Chinese Christians; the purpose of 'self-support' is not to interfere in the finances of any church, but to cut off all connections with imperialistic funds, so that the responsibility will be on Chinese shoulders; the purpose of 'self-propagating' is not to unify or modify our creeds, but to wipe out the influence of imperialist thought, and bring the preaching of the church into harmony with the true gospel of Jesus Christ..."

Despite the glowing propagandist expectations of the Marxist-approved Three Self Patriotic Movement the effect on the churches was to decrease attendance in the officially recognised churches at an even greater rate of decline than before. A report in the officially approved Church of China periodical *Hsien Feng* stated:

"The required socialistic propaganda in the ministers' sermons was distasteful to the congregations. Any breach of the socialistic line in a sermon could quickly lead to purge so preachers were extremely cautious. Their sermons were weak, perfunctory and ineffective. So the more devoted Christians turned away and attended Wang Ming-dao's services or those of the Little Flock. Superficial members just stopped going to church. The attendance at Wang Ming-dao's Tabernacle increased greatly; on many occasions there was not even standing room in the yard.

This not only aroused Government resentment, but also aroused hatred from the churches which deserters left. This mounting opposition from several sectors led to Wang Ming-dao's arrest.

"Communist authorities tolerated Wang Ming-dao for several years, although the Government wanted to utilise him from the beginning. His courage, independent spirit and commitment to the truth were admired by people in all walks of life, so the Communists had to be careful in dealing with him in order to avoid unfavourable reactions in China and abroad. He was well-known internationally. It was said that when (Britain's) Labour Party ex-Premier Attlee visited Peking he wanted to see Wang Ming-dao as soon as he arrived".

Ironically, it was interesting to remember in the contemporary circumstances of China that the English word "propaganda" was derived from a religious practice – although it has become refined and developed for use almost exclusively by politicians, and especially by the irreligious Marxists. Originally, according to the Oxford Dictionary, "propaganda" was a committee of cardinals in the Roman curia in charge of foreign missions, established by Pope Gregory XV in 1623; which then came to mean "the spreading of ideas, information, or rumours designed to promote or change an institution, movement, person, etc.". Under Chairman Mao in China every government action, nationally and internationally, was determined by and infused with Marxist propaganda importance; and any opposition, especially religious in emphasis, had to be ruthlessly eliminated lest it threatened the domination of Maoist-Marxism.

It was the visit of Clement Attlee which was among the causes leading to Hsiao Feng's disaffection with the Communist Party in China, and his subsequent flight to Hong Kong. In 1954 Hsiao Feng had toured the whole of Guantong Province, investigating the reports of spreading "underground Christian congregations" then multiplying in many areas. These Christian activities were creating conflicts in various Party departments, and he was being held responsible.

About the same time he wrote a favourable review of a book – *Battle of the Marshland*, by Lu Ling – which was not approved by the Party critics. Then, after a visit to Canton by Clement Attlee, Hsiao Feng was accused of not having "properly prepared" Bishop Mu Jun-hsien to answer Attlee's penetrating questions.

In August, 1955, Hsiao was suspended from his post on full pay, accused of "sentimentalism towards religious people", "discontented with the Party", and "speaking with a strange tongue". He was subjected to daily and nightly "struggle meetings" to reform his "bourgeois thinking", and in December he was sent to a "thought reform" camp pending further investigation. On 20 July, 1956, through a change in official policy made known at a public meeting at which he received an apology from Party members, he was cleared of all charges and reinstated immediately. But from that time he began planning to leave Canton and China.

During the 1956 "Hundred Flowers Blooming, Hundred Schools of Thought Contending" period many of the Three Self Patriotic Movement leaders publicly denounced some of the previous policies of the Peking authorities. When the leaders of the Party became worried at the mounting criticism they ended the official leniency and imposed a rigorous clamp-down on all religious as well as political protests. By this time there were only four churches left open in Peking, from the previous sixty-five. These, with the YMCA and YWCA, were allowed to continue as Christian institutions in Peking to demonstrate "Marxist tolerance" of the Christian religion to visiting foreigners; but it was rarely, if at all, permitted in other parts of China.

A Three Self resolution of total loyalty to government was imposed on all Christian groups, one of which was reproduced in *Tien Feng*, entitled "Five Don'ts, Five Musts, Five Loves and Five Excellencies":

"Five Don'ts are: not to break the law; not to preach reactionary doctrine; not to get people to become Christians on the plea that Christ could heal the sick; not to invite freelance evangelists to preach in their churches; not to attend or preach in underground services in their homes.

"Five Musts are: to cooperate in the Government's religious policies; to expose freelance evangelists and underground home services; to be economical; to discipline their bodies; to take part in every socialist campaign.

"Five Loves are: to love country, Party, socialism, the Three Self Patriotic Movement, and labour.

"Five Excellencies are: to improve through self-criticism, to improve through self-reform; to improve in mutual respect; to improve in street activities and relations with neighbours; to improve in political studies".

Through these and other officially imposed Marxist propaganda exercises the Three Self Patriotic Movement became increasingly like any other secular branch of the Marxist Government. By 1958 the emphasis of the Three Self Patriotic Movement was no longer on the "three selfs". These were considered "political issues" and, as such, already settled by the Government. The main purpose of the Movement was to organise all pastors and priests into acquiring "political and current affairs learning"; and to have every church activity "completely fulfil the demands of the government and law".

By 1960, with the exception of a very few courageous individuals, Catholic and Protestant, the politicising and secularising of the Christian churches was considered successfully completed. The Christian Peking Union Theological Seminary was said to be free of government control, but in fact was run by influential Communist Party members, and most of the students were government-approved and selected. There was a smaller proportion of Party members in the Nanking Theological Seminary, but the restrictive policy was the same, and the consequences could be seen in the fewer numbers of applicants to the University. The Canton Theological Seminary was closed down in 1960 because of the shortage of personnel.

With the enforced union of churches, and the closing down of most church buildings, many pastors were put out of work. Older pastors and priests were "persuaded" to retire; and younger, Party-approved, ones took over. Pastors and priests of any kind had to have some secular work in order to conform with the Marxist slogan: "No labour, no meal". In Peking, the young men were sent to work at the State Farm in Han Yuan; the middle-aged were sent to the "Peking Husbandry Ranch"; and the elderly were sent to work in a former Methodist church building which had been made into an envelope-making factory.

Eventually, even the courageous pastor Wang Ming-dao was imprisoned and broken by sustained interrogation and Marxist propagandistic brain-washing. He was confined with two Communist guards as constant companions, and out of this period of imprisonment he was "persuaded" to write a blatantly ludicrous "confession":

"I am a counter-revolutionary offender...As a result of the patient attitude shown by the government, and the re-education given me, I have come to realise my errors. I have been accorded generous treatment by the government, and have been saved from the abyss of crime. For this my heart is full of gratitude".

For this cooperation he was released in September, 1956. But as his physical, mental and spiritual health improved he was deeply distressed by this "betrayal" of his Lord, which he likened to the Apostle Peter but not to Judas, and eventually he repudiated the extorted confession and was returned to prison by the Marxist authorities.

A second "National Conference of Chinese Christians" was held in Shanghai in November, 1960. A total of 319 delegates attended from 25 different provinces, autonomous areas, or enlarged city representations. The constitution was revised, a six-year revision was delivered, 34 speeches were given, and a national committee of 145 members was elected.

The six-year report of important developments since the previous National Conference in 1954 declared that "reactionary forces had still not been purged from the church". In 1955, as part of the "anti-revolutionary campaign" the People's Government "on the initiative of the people and of Christians broke up the counter-revolutionary rings headed by Wang Ming-dao and Watchman Nee". At the enlarged committee meetings of 1956 and 1957 the members had come to realise "they must accept the leadership of the Party and walk the road of socialism". In 1958 "the Christian community made a great advance...in our understanding of socialism". Since that time, preachers from all over the country had enrolled in the study programme to gain an increased recognition of the problems facing the country; and in the past two years the preachers and laymen had been "thoroughly united with all Chinese in upholding the leadership of the Communist Party, and to love the enlightened standpoint of socialism..."

The Director of the Chinese Church Research Center in Hong Kong, Dr. Jonathan Chao, has written:

"By 1958, all the institutional churches in China were brought under the control of the State...(but) in less than ten years, under the strong hand of the Party, all these institutional churches were brought under control and destroyed...Church boards were dissolved; contact with and support from the outside world was cut off; sacraments were suspended; and open evangelism was forbidden. The people of God at that time faced the challenge: Can the life and ministry of the Church continue when all these forms (sic) of the Church were removed? Is there anything left when the buildings were gone, when the money was gone, when the pastors were gone, when foreign friends were gone, when Bibles were no longer available, when the seminaries were closed?..."

What was evident following on the National Conference of Chinese Christians in 1960 was that the only representative official body of institutional Christianity in China – the Three Self Patriotic Movement – had compromised and connived with the Chinese Communist Party to its own destruction. Worse, the representative institutional Christianity had traitorously embraced the empty, cynical slogans of Maoist Marxism as of greater importance than the teachings of Jesus Christ. They were not Christians, obedient disciples of Christ; they were "Christers", disobedient imitators of Christ.

Yet, on the perimeters of the Three Self Patriotic Movement – or, strictly speaking, beyond its confines – there was an unknown number of true Christians faithfully worshipping and following their Lord in "underground house services", who refused to bow the knee in any way to the cynical Marxist regime, and whose continued existence continued to greatly trouble the Marxist leaders. In that same year of 1960 the Roman Catholic Bishop, Ignatius Gong Ping-mei, the Vatican-recognised head of the Shanghai See, was sentenced to life imprisonment as "a counter-revolutionary leader camouflaged in religious clothes" because of his refusal to accept the authority of the atheistic Marxist regime in Church affairs.

All the Marxist slogans, threats, mass indoctrinations, accusation meetings, arrests of Christian leaders, and persecution of church members, discrimination in education and employment, over a period of ten years since taking power over China, had only resulted in "cleansing" the true Church of Jesus Christ of its pew-filling weak membership and stimulating the faith of true believers.

These were subject neither to imported Western-type missionary organisations, nor to Three Self Patriotic Movement administrative mechanisms, nor to suspect association with any foreign elements, nor to cultural adulteration of Western denominationalism (and Jesus was demonstrably more "Oriental" than Marx). At the same time they conformed in all matters of civil and social demands of government like good citizens; as their Master commanded, "rendering to Caesar the things that are Caesar's, and to God the things that are God's". As such they could not be attacked officially by the Marxist regime in Peking without the Party being exposed to the legitimate allegation of "persecution of religion", "violating freedom of religion", "breach of constitution", etcetera – a course which, officially, they were reluctant to pursue, but which, unofficially, they did implacably and unscrupulously by pretending that such actions were for "political reasons" and therefore legitimate.

But, to all intents and purposes, within some fifteen years since taking over power in China, it appeared that the Marxist regime had been able to destroy all institutional religion in China. In his comprehensive survey, *Religious Policy and Practice in Communist China*, Donald MacInnis has stated:

"Institutional activities were also curtailed so that by the mid-1960s even the handful of religious journals that had survived ceased publication. In 1965 only one Protestant theological seminary with fewer than 100 students remained open, while there was none for the Roman Catholics. Even this closed in 1966, along with the remaining institutes of the Moslems and Buddhists..."

CHAPTER 9

The Christian-Marxist Battle For The Soul Of China

A Dynamic Christianity and a Dying Marxism: 1966-1989

"A moribund society," said Arthur Koestler, "produces moribund gravediggers". This is an appropriate epitaph for Marxism in China as its fifth decade of rule in China draws to a close.

The years between 1960 and 1964 were critical for Marxism as a claimed universal philosophy – or, more specifically, as an alternative belief system to the previously practised Westernised Christianity. During those years the differences between the Chinese and Soviet Union views of Marxism became acute, and then ended in total disruption, with each going its own way*. The China scholar Ross Terrill, in his biography, *MAO*, states:

"In late 1962 Mao took a step that was fatal to the worldwide Marxist church. He announced that power in the USSR 'has been usurped by the revisionists'. That clinched the schism. Party to Party relations dried up. Nineteen sixty-three brought a stream of letters about ideological betrayal between Mao and the Russians".

In the communications Mao denounced the Soviet Union as "a dictatorship of the bourgeoisie", a "fascist German dictatorship", and a "Hitlerite dictatorship", "worse than

*See *The Unquiet Frontier*, by George N. Patterson.

de Gaulle", "worse than the United States". When, later, Krushchev was overthrown and replaced, Mao suggested sarcastically that Moscow should "send him to China to study Marxism in Chinese universities".

But, despite Mao's confidence, within China itself the hitherto triumphant Maoist-Marxism was in critical decline. The economic failure of "the Great Leap Forward" campaign led by Mao, following on the collapse of the political "Hundred Flowers Bloom, Hundred Thoughts Content" campaign, had seriously affected Mao's popularity and undermined his authority in the higher levels of the Chinese Communist Party, although his popularity among the ordinary Chinese people was still immense.

During "the Great Leap Forward" he had swept the nation into the mass-collective of 24,000 people's communes, and had tried to double the pace of economic developments by simplistic methods. He was impatient with the bureaucracy around him, and scathing about theoretical economic solutions. He was convinced that it was the intellectuals who were responsible for the failure of the "Hundred Flower" campaign.

In mobilising the "Great Leap Forward" Mao had to create a religious fervour, a sense of evangelical commitment among the idolising Chinese masses, especially the youth, that would inspire the whole nation as his earlier visionary Marxist maxims had done. The slogans reflected this spiritual emphasis: WE SHALL TEACH THE SUN AND MOON TO CHANGE PLACES; WE SHALL CREATE A NEW HEAVEN AND EARTH FOR MAN. He wrote a poem in which he prayed for the help of heaven in his earthly efforts:

> "Only in the wind and thunder can the country show its vigour.
> Alas, the ten thousand horses are all muted.
> O Heaven, bestir yourself, I beseech you,
> And send down men of many talents".

Ross Terrill, in his book, *MAO*, records of this period of Mao's "magic power":

"Was even Marx, now, one of the superstitions to be fought against?

"Mao did begin to put Marx gently in his place. 'Marx was also a human being with two eyes, two hands and one brain', he reminded a Party session. 'Not much different from us – except that he had a lot of Marxism in his mind'.

"Had not Marx failed to make revolution? Did not Lenin surpass him in this respect? 'Marx never undertook China's great revolution', he said to clinch this point. 'Therefore our actions have also surpassed Marx'.

"The Great Leap Forward did not do away with magic power. It substituted Mao's magic power for that of all rival ways of thought, including part of Marx's". (my italics).

Between 1961 and 1966 Mao, as Chairman of the Chinese Communist Party, only convened one meeting of the Central Committee. In the Politburo he was increasingly pushed aside by the other, less visionary and more pragmatic, leaders. It was during this period that the diminutive Communist leader, Deng Xiaoping – even less Marxist than Mao – emerged to contest the leadership with Mao when, it was said, he "met on equal terms and treated (Mao) without ceremony". Deng was at the opposite end of the economic spectrum of the visionary Communist purist, Mao. The economic pragmatist Deng, in what has become a famous phrase, believed "what does it matter whether a cat is black or white so long as it catches mice".

Ross Terrill records of Mao at this time: " 'They treated me like a dead ancestor', Mao later complained of Liu and the blunt Deng. They nodded at him with eyes glazed. They applauded his words and then did nothing to implement them. They 'forgot' to report to him. At a conference they would steer to the opposite side of the room from him to avoid an unsettling query or acidic interruption".

To Mao, his Marxist opponents in the leadership of the

Party were "capitalist roaders", corrupted by "economism". "There are at least two factions in our Party," he declared at the time. "The socialist faction and the capitalist faction". Liu Shao-chi and Deng Xiaoping were offering temptingly "a capitalist production incentive of five per cent bonus to workers and peasants". Mao was offering a vision of a new society of transformed people. Liu and Deng were preaching a "a revisionist line like the Soviet Marxists". Mao was preaching his distinctive "revolutionary line".

Whatever his decline in the leadership of the Party Mao was still the idol of the Army and of the Chinese people. He now courted the People's Liberation Army and the Defence Minister, Lin Biao, in seeking to defeat the opposing Liu/Deng faction. The PLA became "the great school of Mao Zedung's Thought". Their ideal was "the Four Firsts": put men first above weapons; political work first above other work; ideological work first above routine political work; and practical ideology first above book knowledge". Army officers formed choirs to sing hymns praising Mao-Thought. The *Liberation Army Daily* printed Mao-Thoughts in bold type, boxed print, on page one. The PLA was the first to publish selections of Mao-Thoughts in the famous booklet, *Quotations From Chairman Mao.*

At a Conference in Chengtu in West China in 1958 Mao had deprecated excessive adulation, and had himself provided a definition of the deplorable "cult of the individual":

"There are two kinds of cult of the individual. One is correct, such as that of Marx, Engels, Lenin and the correct side of Stalin. These we ought to revere and continue to revere for ever. As they held truth in their hands, why should we not revere them? We believe in truth: truth is the reflection of objective existence. A squad should revere its squad leader; it would be quite wrong not to. Then there is the incorrect kind of cult of the individual in which there is no analysis, simply blind obedience. This is not right...The question at issue is not whether or not there should be a cult of the individual, but rather whether or not the individual concerned represents the truth. If he does, then he should be revered..."

The "definition" of Mao had begun officially at the Seventh Congress in April, 1945, when the new Party Constitution contained a preamble in which "The Thought of Mao Zedung" was officially enshrined as necessary to "guide the entire work of the Party". At that time Liu Shao-chi, the Party's "organisation man" had praised Mao as "not only the greatest revolutionary and statesman in Chinese history, but also its greatest theoretician and scientist". And despite Mao's radical fall from grace among the Party leaders – now practising economic pragmatists – from the mid-1950s to the mid-1960s, his popular deification by the Chinese masses was tolerated by the Party and allowed to continue. Edgar Snow, in *The Other Side Of The River,* written in 1962, said:

"Today's image of Mao among the masses is hardly that of an executioner. What makes him formidable is that he is not just a Party boss, but by many millions of Chinese is quite genuinely regarded as a teacher, poet laureate, national hero, head of the family, and greatest liberator in history. He is to them Confucius plus Lao-tzu plus Rousseau plus Marx plus Buddha...Mao has now become an Institution of such prestige and authority that no one in the Party could raze it without sacrificing a collected vested interest of first importance. Probably no one knows that better than Mao himself..."

The most important song in China at the time proclaimed:

"The east is red,
The sun rises,
On the horizon of China
Appears the great hero Mao Zedung:
He is the great Saviour of the people".

It was inevitable, therefore, that the "economic pragmatism" of Deng and Liu which came to the fore during the decade 1955-65 would clash with the "ideological evangelism" of Mao when he tired of his imposed isolation and began his come-back. To those who still listened to him Mao complained that the priority being given to economic theories must destroy the visionary convictions which had inspired the greatest victories of the past three decades in China. People, he argued, were more important than the machines they operated. What they believed was of greater significance than how much money they made. He declaimed against the materialism and corruption that was emerging from the "capitalist-road line" of Deng and Liu.

Mao was aware of the Chinese national disposition to materialism, and even avarice, with their attendant corruption; and it was this which had inspired his greatest slogan: "Fight Self: Serve the People". This, he taught, was not easy, but it was necessary. People could not be made to change their nature simply with economic incentives, but with fiery convictions. So it was this central political issue, and not the spiritually challenging and threatening spread of the "underground churches" – significant though this was at the time – which made Mao decide to reach once again for national power and domination in the spiritualised "Cultural Revolution".

When I arrived in Hong Kong in 1964, and became personally and professionally closely associated with Jack Chow – the news editor of the *Hong Kong Standard*, and also a "responsible brother" in the leading Little Flock church in Hong Kong – I quickly discovered how extensive and numerous the "underground churches" were becoming inside mainland China. Two years previously, in 1962, Jack had already reported in the *Hong Kong Standard* from his first-hand sources:

"Although the visible and formal churches are dying out on the mainland, the invisible, formless, non- political and true ones are growing in number in Shanghai, Nanking,

Peking and other towns and cities...'"

He went on to give an example:

"One of the arrivals (in Hong Kong), the wife of a former professor at Peking University, belonged to a small prayer group of four Christian women prior to her departure from Shanghai. She says that there are many such small groups, formed by people whose churches have either been shut down or taken over by the Communists. They meet irregularly but not infrequently at different homes for prayer-meetings, Bible study and fellowship. They have won many souls who have found God a great help in time of trouble. When they pray together they do not kneel: and their meetings, which have no form of any sort, are usually short because they do not wish to invite any trouble. The Communists forbid religious meetings in private homes. If more than two people are found praying together at home, they are liable to prosecution on 'counter-revolutionary' charges, and to imprisonment".

This emergence of "underground home churches", or, as some Chinese officials called them, "Roman Empire Christianity", was the main cause behind the "great debate" on religion in the Chinese media in the 1960s, despite the closure of all the churches. It was not serious enough to be part of the Party leadership crisis being fought out in ideologically political and economic terms, but it was serious enough for it to be given top-level official clearance for major public debate.

The Marxists were aware from their own recent experience that it only took a small number of enthusiastically committed people to alter the course of China's history. After all, it was Mao himself who had declared in a similar context: "A small flame can cause a prairie fire". And the nucleus of committed Christians who had been forged in the fires of the persecutions of the 1950s, and who had survived, were formidably equipped to be an important instrument of change in the country if any national figure emerged to lead them – such as the imprisoned Watchman Nee or Pastor Wang Ming-dao. All it would require was for one of them to articulate a political instead of a non-political Christian message.

In March, 1965, a report in the officially-approved *Tien Feng*, beneath an editorial headed: "What Are Our Risks As Christians In The Present Situation?", outlined a five-point reply:

"...(2) to continue to practise the principle of arranging religious activities with the primary aim of obeying the laws of the government – *religious activities should take place in church*, and should not interfere with production; (3) *to beware of admitting reactionary elements into the church*, and of using Christianity for reactionary and subversive activities. We must help the government stop all illegal activities, using the cover of Christianity..." (my italics).

This was only one of a spate of articles on the subject of religion which began to appear in 1963, and from then until 1970 at least fifteen major articles on religion, and scores of lesser ones, were published in the national press, followed by innumerable contributions of letters to the editors. The official stance on religion was defined:

"Religion and superstition have their similarities. They also have their differences. All religious activities are superstitious activities. This is their similarity. But not all superstitious activities are religious. This is their difference".

True Chinese Communists, it was stated, had to be atheists and to work for the elimination of religion and superstition, because "religious belief was one of the greatest dangers to socialism":

"Religious superstitious thoughts constitute a serious threat to socialist revolution and its construction. Socialist revolution aims to exclude the old social systems of exploitation and oppression and to destroy classes. On the other hand, religion teaches people to seek happiness, solve the problems of life and reach the happiness of the after-life through prayer. Therefore, belief in religion must make revolutionary ardour fade..."

In September of 1964, as this debate was developing on the mainland of China, I left Hong Kong for Taiwan in company with Jack Chow to see if I could arrange an interview with Generalissimo Chiang Kai Shek. Our television team's next proposed assignment was to persuade the Chinese Nationalist government-in-exile in Taiwan to permit us to accompany their army guerilla raiding parties which they claimed were landing regularly on the Chinese mainland.

I was not successful, partly because Chiang Kai Shek was indisposed at the time and was not giving interviews to anyone, and partly because I would not agree to the official alternative proposed, namely, that we film the Nationalist guerilla groups leaving Taiwan and then use their official film of their landings.

However, without seeking it, I was offered an interview with Madame Chiang Kai Shek. I was about to turn down the offer, seeing no immediate advantage, when I had a sudden thought: I could question Madame Chiang regarding her widely publicised "Christian" beliefs in the light of the claimed "historic defeat of Christianity in China by Marxism", and the current debates on religion in China.

I was surprised to receive permission to do this in an interview, but was told by the Director of Information, Jimmy Chen (former journalist colleague of Jack Chow and later Ambassador to the United States) that the interview would have to be confidential and not for immediate publication. I agreed, and Jack Chow went with me.

For a good two hours Madame Chiang answered my questions without reservation, describing personal and historical incidents that neither Jimmy Chen nor Jack Chow had known about previously. The main thrust of my questions was directed towards finding out if the Christian belief of Madame Chiang and her husband was simply a nominal acceptance of an inherited family tradition which, in the national circumstances of the time, was a useful political instrument in the country's relations with Western "Christian" nations; or, were their respective beliefs of a deeply held personal kind which the current catastrophic Marxist circumstances in China had now destroyed?

She replied by describing two incidents which were of profound significance to both herself and her husband: one, just before the final collapse in China which led to their decision to retreat to Taiwan; and one in 1952, on Taiwan, in which her own personal faith was "restored" after a time of agonising doubt. She concluded that whatever mistakes had been made in the past, her husband's and her own conviction was that the present circumstances of apparent Marxist triumph in China would pass, and that the Christian vision they shared for China eventually would be fulfilled. They might not live to see it, but that was the assurance they had been given by God, and which lay behind their policy of an eventual "return to the mainland".

On returning to Hong Kong and "China-watching" I found that in China Mao Zedung was once again successfully stirring up revolutionary fervour among the Chinese masses, in opposition to the "economic pragmatists" who had been in the ascendant for the past several years. He even refused to read the official *People's Daily*, it was reported, and would only read the *Liberation Army Daily*. He denounced all contemporary literary, artistic, cultural and scientific associations and journals, comparing them with the reprehensible effete Russian intellectual elite. What was needed, Mao declared, was "determined people who are young, have little education, a firm attitude, and the political experience to take over the work...When we started to make revolution we were mere 23-year-old boys. While the rulers of that time were old and inexperienced. They had more learning, but we had more truth..." This call to renewed struggle appealed to the nation's youth, and the "Red Guards" were born.

Mao launched his second – "Cultural" – revolution, this time with the notorious youthful "Red Guards" in the vanguard. He summed up his view of Marxism in the words: "Marxism consists of a thousand truths, but they all boil down to one sentence: It is right to rebel".

Mao left Peking for Shanghai in the autumn of 1965, conscious that, after sixteen years in power, Marxism as practised by the Chinese leadership was still only acceptable to one per cent of the Chinese people – and most of these were now only nominal and reluctant members. He was aware that unless some radical, new measures were taken to enthuse the masses this figure was likely to drop catastrophically, because each year more than twenty million Chinese were being added to the soaring total of the nation's inhabitants. In the Soviet Union, after fifty years of Marxism, it was well known that there were still more Christians than there were Marxists. The Soviet official figures were published as: 26.2 per cent "firm believers", and a further 21.1 per cent "waverers"; as against 11 million Communist Party members in a population of around 200 million.*

At a meeting with France's Minister of Culture, André Malraux, in 1965, Mao said to him: "Revolution is a drama of passion; we did not win the people over by appealing to reason but by developing hope, trust and fraternity. In the face of famine, the will to equality takes on religious force...Men do not like to bear the burden of Revolution throughout their lives. When I said 'Chinese Marxism is the religion of the people' I meant – but do you know how many Communists there are in the countryside? 1 per cent! – I meant that the Communists express (sic) the Chinese people in a real way if they remain faithful to the work upon which the whole of China has embarked as if on another Long

*Towards A Society Free of Religion: pub. 1970.

March".

Mao launched his new revolution from Shanghai – after displaying his own "renewed youth" by reportedly swimming fifteen kilometers of the mighty Yangtze River in sixty-five minutes without showing signs of fatigue! He called on China's youth to "knock down the old"; and they responded in their millions by taking to the streets in an orgy of adulation and destruction. They smashed temples and church buildings, burned books other than Marxist, raided the homes of intellectuals and paraded them through the streets in large dunce-caps in public mockery. Everything from dark sun-glasses to chess was denounced as "revisionist". Tens of millions of these rampaging "Red Guards" stormed across the country on a licensed holocaust of destruction in the name of Maoist-Marxism.

Mao himself mobilised the communication machinery to better serve his "revolutionary line". He put his wife, Chiang Ching, in charge of "culture"; one daughter, Li Na, was made editor of the *Liberation Army Daily;* another daughter, Li Min, was appointed to the Science and Technology Commission, responsible for the development of nuclear weapons in the Ministry of Defence. During a period of five months in 1967 over 35 million copies of Mao's "Selected Works" were printed, and in two years over two billion copies of his writings were issued. Every shouting Red Guard in the country waved a copy of "the Little Red Book" of a selection of "The Thoughts of Chairman Mao", as did every Party official – including the suave statesman Zhou Enlai!

Mao was Prophet (inspired revelation, plus charisma), Priest (official interpreter of the true doctrine, and representative of the people before the Supreme Marx), and King (the enthroned and acclaimed ruler of the people), fit to take his rightful place in the Marxist trinity with Marx and Lenin. Every day throughout China a great paean of worship and love flowed upwards to the god-like Mao –

Great Teacher, Great Leader, Great Helmsman, Great Commander – for the revelation he had brought; not just revolution, but revelation which inspired it. He was the Marxist Word made flesh.

The "Thoughts of Chairman Mao" now effected miracle cures, made the blind see and the deaf hear, the lame walk, peasants grow better crops, scientists discover better secrets, doctors perform more successful operations. Women fed lambs at their breasts before their own babies in order to increase production for Chairman Mao. Juvenile delinquents gave up their bad habits after reading "the Little Red Book", and wept bitter tears at their belated repentance. Artists signed their paintings with the sycophantic eulogy "Ten Thousand years to Chairman Mao" rather than their own names.

Mao began to act even more god-like. Whereas previously he had made lengthy speeches, written books and poems and pamphlets, he now rarely spoke, remaining mute on the towering dais with his arm raised, and with a fixed smile. He watched in silence and approbation the millions of worshippers chanting slogans, weeping from emotion, mindlessly jumping and waving their copies of "the Little Red Book". Over ten million of them on one occasion gathered at Tien An Men Square – "the Gate of Heavenly Peace" – for ten sunrise rallies.

But, instead of lifting these besotted followers to a higher level of spiritual performance, and to become more compassionate people caring for their neighbours more than themselves according to Mao's premier slogan "Fight Self: Serve The People", their new- found commitment to revolution fuelled resentment and hatreds, destroying social and family relationships. Children denounced parents, wives betrayed husbands, husbands abandoned wives, parents blackmailed children, families reported neighbours. Then Mao further incited them to attack the official Politburo itself by "knocking power from half of them".

Fear lay over the whole country like some poisonous miasma. When challenged by his colleagues about his actions and their fearful consequences, Mao replied: "You should replace the word 'fear' by the word 'dare' ".

One Western scholar, James T. Myers, wrote: "The Thought of Mao Zedung has been expanded to make room for *fa-pao*, supernatural or magic weapons..."

The huge rallies of the Mao-worshipping Cultural Revolutionaries resembled Billy Graham-like Crusades in conception and presentation. Eleven million or so revolutionary Red Guards from all parts of China "shed tears of joy" as they participated in rituals of "mass intoxication and conversion", and were admonished to "convert the masses" and "transform society". Smaller rallies were held in local areas, more like standard Christian church services; with a processional, reading of "Mao-Scriptures", sermon, recessional and benediction. One such, held in Heilunkiang, was described:

"After (i) opening ceremonies to the strains of "The East Is Red" and (ii) a recital of quotations from Mao Zedung, (iii) a directive to hold high the great banner of Mao Zedung's Thought, vigorously grasp class struggle, and do a good job on the production of summer-ripening crops...was read...the rally (iv) ended with the song 'Sailing the Seas Depends on the Helmsman' ".

In an article in the American journal, *Saturday Review*, entitled "The Deification of Mao", Professor Homes Welch described in detail a family ritual performed in one home in front of a table "on which were placed four volumes of Mao's collected works, and above which hung his portrait", and continued:

"The first service of the day was called 'asking for instructions in the morning'. The noon service was conducted before lunch, for which it served as a kind of grace since it was called 'thanking Mao for his kindness'. The evening service was called 'reporting back at night' ".

Ross Terrill, in his biography, *MAO*, tells of a Red Guard reporting his conversation with a woman speaking reverently of Mao: "I asked her what was in heaven. She said Mao Zadung was in heaven, constantly watching over everybody. He would know whoever was not working hard and have him punished". Terrill concluded: "If the Red Guards at times seemed like religious zealots, Mao had handed them an apt doctrine. His line of thought was reminiscent of the maxim 'Love God and do what you like', which some Christians down the ages have believed in".

In the Cultural Revolution Mao had not only transformed orthodox Marxism; he came to epitomise it, and then transcend it. He took the mediocre Marxist pseudo-religious faith, gave it a wider "spiritual" dimension than simple class struggle and class victory. He sought to make the Party a Church, a distinctive Body of born-again believers only. Liu Shao-chi, contemptuously, would have nothing to do with it; and Deng Xiaoping reluctantly played only a minor role – until he was exiled to the countryside by Mao to be "reformed".

At the Ninth Congress of the Chinese Communist Party in 1969 (the Eighth had been held in 1956) it was said that "Mao behaved like a Buddha – and was treated like one". The sessions were conducted in secret, and consisted of ritual rather than debate. Only eleven out of the 1,512 delegates spoke from the rostrum, and over half of the delegates were in PLA uniforms.

But Mao began to fear the consequences of the cult-like adulation, suspecting that the status of a God might mean the remoteness of one in which anything might happen. He was aware his sycophantic Defence Minister Lin Piao was advocating that "The Thoughts of Chairman Mao" would outlive Mao, and that in themselves they contained superior "magic power". In 1970 the media gushed daily: "The Thought of Mao is the Brightest, Brightest Red Sun".

What all this meant for Christians in Mao's new China

was described in an article in TIME magazine:

"In 1966 Red Guards burned Bibles in the streets of Shanghai for several afternoons. When boredom set in the surviving stock was sent off to a pulping plant. In Ziamin (Amoy) a similar burning took place but with a sinister twist: YMCA and YWCA workers were forced to kneel by the books until their hands and cheeks were blistered from the fire. All over China church buildings were pillaged, closed down or turned into warehouses. Chinese Christians were often tortured or killed if they did not repudiate their beliefs. At the height of the 1966-69 Cultural Revolution the last eight Western Christian workers in China, Roman Catholic nuns from a school for diplomats' children in Peking, were hounded across the border into Hong Kong by jeering Red Guards. Their cruel expulsion seemed to symbolise Communist China's last judgement on four centuries of Western missionary endeavour..."

Many years before Mao had declared: "...a revolution is not a dinner party...a revolution is an act of violence by which one class overthrows another...to put it bluntly, it is necessary to create terror in every rural area...proper limits have to be exceeded in order to right a wrong..."

The sacrificial price for China's Marxist revolution was high. From the time of the first casualties arising from the early 1950s' "accusation meetings" the figures of death had soared well beyond the million mark. A Report to the U.S. Sub-Committee on Internal Security by Professor Richard Walker estimated "Communism in China, from the time of the first civil war (1927-36) until today (1971) has cost a minimum of 34 million lives". The same report included an estimate from Moscow that "in the course of ten years, more than 25 million people in China were exterminated".

While it is common knowledge how important the "Little Red Book" of "The Thoughts of Chairman Mao" played in Mao's "Cultural Revolution", it is not so well-known how the real inspiration of the revolution was a much smaller booklet entitled "The Three Greats", or "The Three Constantly Read Stories of Chairman Mao". These stories were not new in the sense of Mao creating them, or even recounting them throughout that period; but at least two of them had been in existence for some thirty years. It was only during the Cultural Revolution that they were resurrected, and made their unique "miraculous" impact in the "spiritual transformation" of the nation.

The "Three Constantly Read Stories of Chairman Mao" were not much in themselves, and the foreign correspondents and scholars who read and re-read them seeking an explanation of their influence were baffled, and had a similar reaction to that of the Pharisees and Scribes trying to make sense of the impact of the parables of Jesus. In fact, the "Three Greats" of Mao were remarkably similar to the stories told by Jesus, as were the effects on the lives of those who "heard and believed".

The stories illustrated themes of sacrifice, self-abnegation and service to others; or, put another way, demonstrated aspects of faith, hope and love. The stories were entitled *Serve the People*, *In Memory of Norman Bethune*, and *The Foolish Old Man Who Removed Mountains*. These stories formed the third major element in Mao Zedung's unique spiritual Maoist-Marxist "revolutionary line" for the transformation of human beings: "Mao-Vision", "Mao-Thought", and now "Mao-Parables".

Serve the People was part of a funeral oration delivered by Mao on the death of a comrade, Chang Szu-teh, in 1944, the key part of which read:

"...We hail from all corners of the country and have joined together for a common revolutionary objective. And we need the vast majority of the people with us on the road to this objective...In times of difficulty we must not lose sight of our achievements, we must see the bright future and pluck up our courage. The Chinese people are suffering; it is our duty to save them and we must exert ourselves in struggle. Wherever there is struggle there is sacrifice, and death is a common occurrence. But we have the interests of the people and the suffering of the great majority at heart, and when we die for the people it is a worthy death..."

It was only a short peroration of some five hundred words altogether. Jesus said more in fewer words to greater effect when he said "Love the Lord your God with all your heart, with all your soul, with all your strength and with all your mind; and your neighbour as yourself...Do that, and you shall live". The majority of the Chinese Communist Party preferred Mao's version.

The second story was entitled *In Memory of Norman Bethune*. One of the largest mausoleums in Communist China has been dedicated to this Canadian socialist doctor. In 1926, when he was 36 years of age, Norman Bethune was an acclaimed socialite surgeon, but secretly dying of tuberculosis. Out of his then fatal condition he developed the revolutionary technique of artificial pneumo-thorocoplasty (or deflation of the infected lung), which became the standard practice for saving all tuberculosis sufferers. But to cure this scourge he became involved in seeking to cure the associated social ills of poor food, poor housing and poor health which caused it, and his conservative colleagues dubbed him a socialist and communist.

When a Canadian medical unit was sent to Spain to help in the civil war, Norman Bethune, now one of the most famous thoracic surgeons in the world, sold off all he owned and went to Spain in December, 1936. There he organised the first mobile blood transfusion unit to be used anywhere.

In 1938, ostracised by the Canadian medical profession for his radical beliefs, he went to China and joined the Communists. There, under conditions that would have killed an ordinary man, he set up a guerilla medical service, writing nursing and medical textbooks, inventing and making surgical instruments, training all his own staff wherever he went, operating night and day without respite, until he died of septicaemia due to operating without gloves. He was passionately loved and respected by millions of Chinese who had only known him for a year. At his death Mao declared: "We mourn more than the passing of a man", and continued:

"Comrade Bethune's spirit, his utter devotion to others without any thought of self, was shown in his boundless sense of responsibility in his work and his boundless warm-heartedness towards all comrades and people. Every Communist must learn from him...I am profoundly grieved by his death. Now we are all commemorating him, which shows how profoundly his spirit inspired everyone...We must all learn the spirit of absolute selflessness from him..."

Again there were echoes of Jesus and his passionate soliloquy on hearing of the death of John the Baptist.

The third of the "Three Greats" was the story of *The Foolish Old Man*. Mao had told this story on several critical occasions when the Party was facing possible defeat:

"There is an ancient Chinese fable of an old man who lived in northern China...His house faced south, and beyond his doorway stood two great peaks, Taihang and Wangwu, obstructing the way. With great determination he led his sons in digging up these mountains, hoe in hand. Another greybeard, known as the Wise Old Man, saw them and said derisively, 'How silly of you to do this. It is quite impossible for you to dig up these two huge mountains'. The Foolish Old Man replied: 'When I die, my sons will carry on; when they die there will be my grandsons, and so on to infinity. High as they are, the mountains cannot grow any higher, and with every bit we dig they will be that much lower. Why can't we clear them away?' Having refuted the Wise old man's wrong view, he went on digging every day, unshaken in his conviction. God was moved by this, and He sent down two angels, who carried the mountains away on their backs".

"Today, two big mountains lie like dead weight on the Chinese people. One is imperialism, the other is feudalism. The Chinese Communist Party has long made up its mind to dig them up. We must persevere and work unceasingly and we, too, will touch God's heart. Our God is none other than the Chinese people. If they stand up and dig together with us, why can't these two mountains be cleared away?".

Some two thousand years earlier Jesus said to his followers: "If you have faith as small as a mustard-seed you can say to this mountain, 'Move from here to there' and it will move. Nothing will be impossible for you". In the second half of the twentieth century in China the followers of Marx with their belief that "the people is our God", and the followers of Jesus with their belief that "Jesus is God", were engaged in a gigantic struggle for the allegiance of the Chinese people.

Lenin's and Stalin's faith in the human will being able to conquer the social and political world has been raised to a new dimension by Mao, with the possibility of "the subjective creating the objective" and thereby making new men and new women. This was demonstrated in the communiqué of the Eleventh Plenum of the English Central Committee in August, 1966, when it celebrated Mao's unique role in history:

"Comrade Mao Zedung is the greatest Marxist-Leninist of our era. Comrade Mao has inherited, defended and developed Marxism-Leninism with genius and creativity in an all-round way *and has raised Marxism-Leninism to a new stage...*" (my italics).

The China scholar, James Chieh Hsiung, summarised "Mao's Revolution" in its uniqueness in his book, *Ideology and Practice:*

"...(i) the restructuring of Chinese society to create a new system of authority, new institutions, new roles, and a new hierarchy of relationships most conductive to social-political reintegration as conceived by the CCP leaders; (ii) the reorientation of social values and patterns of behaviour through a ceaseless process of indoctrination, re-education and acculturation to create a Marxist ethos... (v) the formation of a new identity, both national and personal, forged in the 'proletarian' spirit..."

Another scholar, Robert J. Lifton, in his book, *Revolutionary Immortality: Mao Tse-tung and the Cultural Revolution*, analysed Mao's distinctive "spiritual" revolutionary techniques:

"Western students of Mao's thoughts have some difficulty explaining the sources of its power. While often disagreeing on the question of whether Mao has demonstrated originality as a Marxist, most have rightly stressed his persistent preoccupation with the themes of 'struggle' and 'contradiction' and 'rectification and reform'. But what has not been adequately recognised, I believe, is a characteristic quality of tone and content that, more than any other, shaped the psychic contours of the Cultural Revolution. I refer to *a kind of existential absolute, an insistence upon all or now confrontation with death.* Mao always further insists that the confrontation be rendered meaningful, that it be associated with a form of transcendence. One must risk all, not only because one has little to lose but because even in death one has much to gain...

"The Thought of Mao becomes, not so much an abstract blueprint for the future, as a 'way', *a call to a particular mode of being on behalf of a transcendent purpose.* Behind this way are two psychological assumptions long prominent in Mao's Thought but never so overtly insisted upon as during the Cultural Revolution. The first is an image of the human mind as being infinitely malleable, capable of being reformed, transformed, and rectified without limit. The second is a related vision of the will as all-powerful, even to the extent that (in his own words) 'the subjective creates the objective'...

"The Maoist corpus is elevated to an all-consuming prophecy, it nurtures men, predicts their future, and changes the world to accomplish its own predictions; it sets in motion spiritual forces against which nothing can stand..." (my italics).

It was this fiery evangelical Maoist vision which first enthused, then inflamed, the Red Guards; but which was eventually corrupted by Mao's wife and her close associates – later designated "the Gang of Four" – taking advantage of the ailing Mao and Zhou Enlai, and turning it into a destructive, pseudo-Marxist, rabble-rousing farce. It became, like all such fanatical existential movements, manipulated with the greatest malevolence against what they saw as their main philosophical threat – a highly principled and value-centred Christianity. It was reckoned that almost a third of the elders and responsible leaders of the "Little Flock" churches were either killed, imprisoned or apostacised during this period.

This paranoid fear of Christian leaders was evident in the attitude of the Communist leadership towards Watchman Nee, who was due for release from his fifteen years' imprisonment in April, 1967. He had been charged with posting "under-cover agents" to "Christian meeting-places in many cities, to expand his counter-revolutionary influence under the guise of gospel migration and preaching of the Word of God". Through such means, it was alleged, he had "hurried into action his conquer-China-with-the Gospel plan whereby evangelism became an effective cloak for political propaganda...madly he had announced his aim within fifteen years to cover China with the Good News that would be better than a Communist revolution". This deception, the charge stated, had spread like wildfire through the nation's nearly five hundred Little Flock "Christian meeting-places", netting an estimated $500,000 in cash and sale of goods. Finally, Nee was charged with being "a dissolute vagabond of corrupt and indulgent living, who frequented brothel neighbourhoods and had always been a shameless and indiscriminate womaniser".

But in April, 1967, at the end of Nee's fifteen years' imprisonment, the Communist leadership were faced with a dilemma. They had always taken a special pride in their system of "justice" – when compared, for example, with the exile and psychological hell imposed by their Soviet counterparts – and when any convicted person had served their full sentence he or she was usually freed with an appropriate warning against renewing their activities.

When Nee was due to be released they applied pressure on him to give assurances that he would not return to his preaching and teaching; an assurance which Nee flatly refused to provide. He was threatened that if he did not agree to the conditions he would be given another five or seven years' imprisonment. Nee still refused to agree.

He was under great pressure from his family and friends to give way, if only because his wife, Charity, was in poor health; and two sisters in Hong Kong and Shanghai were concerned that his own health, never robust, might be worsened under the new strains.

This was the same year, 1967, in which two billion copies of Mao's writings were being distributed to spiritually transform the Chinese people – yet they were afraid of a single Christian who had only ever written one book! Thirteen times in as many months the rampaging Red Guards raided Charity Nee's small home, scattering her few possessions, mocking her personal treasures and simple Christian faith.

From this time all church services throughout the country were officially forbidden, and any itinerant preachers were ordered to return to their native villages. Even the hitherto-approved *Tien Feng* publication was closed down.

Then, in September, 1967, the elders in the Little Flock church in Hong Kong – where I was in fellowship, as was Jack Chow – received word from a high official source in Peking to the effect that Watchman Nee and his wife might be ransomed out of China if a large enough sum of money in U.S. dollars were deposited in the Hong Kong branch of a bank of China. A similar incident had recently occurred when this had been done with a political prisoner, and his release was followed by a great deal of propaganda inside China about his defection to the West for "monetary reasons". It appeared, therefore, that the Peking authorities wanted to be rid of Nee by discrediting him as being "a tool of Western imperialists". Writing of this incident in his biography of Watchman Nee, Angus Kinnear states:

"Assuming that the offer was real and that it reached Watchman, he was certainly fit to form a decision on it one way or another, since a September letter in his handwriting which found its way to Hong Kong with a refugee affirmed that he was in very good spirits and reasonable health. It is therefore held by young fellow-workers who had been close to him that, like those earlier men of faith who 'disdained release' (Hebrews 11 v 35) he himself turned down the proposal...By staying firm to his principle of cooperation with the State in things neutral – study, labour, translation work – he would do least damage to the image of Christians 'subject to governing authorities'. His model behaviour might even ease the lot of others, whereas for him to 'defect to the West' would certainly involve them all in an appearance of compromise".

On 1 June, 1972, after twenty years in prison, in his sixty-ninth year, Watchman Nee died. Later reports indicated that, two years earlier, he had been moved from his Shanghai jail to an open prison or work camp in the country. It is not known whether the conditions there to "labour and reform his thinking" were too much for his frail condition. His wife died, and nine months later Watchman Nee followed her. In Hong Kong, both Western and Chinese friends assiduously compiled a collection of all the sermons he had ever preached over the years from notes taken by those who had listened to him preach, and these were printed and distributed to be read by millions throughout the world.

The other leading Christian feared by the Chinese Marxists was Pastor Wang Ming-dao and, like Watchman Nee, the Chinese authorities were reluctant to release him to continue his former preaching, despite his advanced years and poor health. Many other Christian leaders, women as well as men, were detained in prison well beyond their times of sentencing in a futile attempt to restrain the spreading influence of the Christian gospel. What was stopped in the cities and towns through the detention of Christians was scattered like wildfire in the "labour reform camps" where the Christians were incarcerated. Enforced exile to remote places like Sinkiang, West China and Tibet only resulted in these "Gulag Archipelago" places being actively evangelised by the dedicated Christian believers.

Following on U.S. President Nixon's historic visit to China in 1972 there was a "thaw" in the Chinese Communist anti-Christian persecutions, and the *Los Angeles Times* carried an article headlined "Rebirth of Christianity Seen Possible In China", based on an interview with the reputable former China missionary-scholar Dr. Francis P. Jones.

Summing up the situation in 1972 in his book, *Religious Policy and Practice in Communist China,* Donald MacInnis concluded:

"Where provocation and alienation of friends, neutrals and foes alike characterised China's foreign relations at the height of the Cultural Revolution, she now actively seeks friends on the world scene and is moving rapidly toward normalised relations in her dealings with the nations of the world...There have already been reports of complaints to Chinese authorities by visitors of such nations who could not find a place of worship while travelling in China..."

With the opening up of China in late 1972 overseas Chinese as well as foreigners began flooding into the country; and what had been previously a trickle of news gained with difficulty from isolated sources now became a flood of information, both official and unofficial.

In November of 1973 the Prime Minister of Australia, Gough Whitlam, visited China and met with Chairman Mao Zedung and Premier Zhou Enlai. Both Chinese Communists were nearing eighty years of age and showing it, physically and mentally. During the discussions Gough Whitlam asked if the future of China's revolution was safe in the hands of the young. Mao replied: "Neither Zhou nor I will be around for the conclusions of the Cultural Revolution. My body is riddled with diseases. I have an appointment with God".

Over the next several months the two close comrades and architects of China's Marxist Revolution saw each other less and less, as Zhou especially became critically ill. Mao's wife Chiang Ching, chose this time of Mao's declining health to use her position to take more control of the government – until even Mao complained about her interference. Deng Xiaoping, who had continued to be outspokenly contemptuous of Mao's actions during the Cultural Revolution, was provoked into filling the vacuum left by the ailing Mao and Zhou.

In January, 1976, Zhou died of cancer, at 78 years of age. He had been China's Prime Minister for twenty-six years. In the struggle for power that followed, especially between Mao's wife and Deng Xiaoping, Mao made his antagonism towards Deng clear when he declared, "He has never been a Marxist...he is a capitalist roader".

Three months after the death of Zhou, on the day following a great public tribute to him in Tienanmen Square in Peking, there was a massive protest by the crowds when they discovered that someone had ordered their floral tributes to Zhou to be removed from public display. The protests rapidly escalated into public demonstrations denouncing Mao; and the Party leadership responded by dismissing Deng from office as they suspected him of organising the incident. Then, on 9 September, 1976, Chairman Mao died. Less than a month later a relative nobody, Hua Guofeng, was appointed the new Chairman of China's Communist Party.

With the death of Mao the historic attempt to convert China to Mao's evangelical Marxism ended. Mao had gambled – and lost. He learned in the hardest of ways the incontrovertable truth that only a heavenly Creator can eternally transform earthly creatures.

Mao's self-chosen successor, Hua Guofeng, mediocre and without support in the Party, quickly passed from the scene; to be followed, dramatically but with equal importance, by Mao's wife and her close cabal, "the Gang of Four". With their contrived and expedited dismissal Deng Xiaoping once again returned to centre-stage – tough, cynical and unprincipled – and he proceeded to open up China even more to foreigners, especially businessmen who could help push forward his theories of "economic pragmatism".

With the more relaxed atmosphere inside China, and the huge numbers of visitors and tourists, it was easier to obtain information from almost all parts of the country. The most prolific source of Christian news was obtained from the province of Fujing in south-east China – the former stronghold of Watchman Nee's Little Flock churches.

In his book, *God Reigns in China,* the former missionary Leslie T. Lyall, described how in 1974 an overseas Chinese Christian woman visited her native village and found "eighty rejoicing believers with a strong, pure faith, for which some had been sent to prison...In Fushan, the provincial capital of Fujiang Province, by 1973 a Christian community of over a thousand had grown up...The authorities, alarmed by the large number of Christians, then ordered the meetings to cease. In 1974 five leaders were arrested, paraded in dunce's caps and imprisoned. On their release, these men and women bravely continued their pastoral visiting and the number of believers multiplied dramatically..."

Lyall also quotes a visitor to Hong Kong, a member of the "True Jesus Church", who claimed that in her area of mainland China from fifty to a hundred groups were meeting regularly, without any prohibition from the authorities. Another report given by Lyall stated:

"...We have greater freedom and are meeting quite openly now. Everything is so convenient compared to the past. Every week we have great meetings – very crowded and warm in the spirit. Many people have turned from their old superstitious ways and from their old beliefs. Also, quite a number are coming back to us who were previously with us but who left us because of the difficulties. Therefore we are adding new members very rapidly. Great miracles and strange events with powerful manifestations are happening frequently. Not only are they more in quantity but also greater in quality. In the past few decades we have seen such wonderful things. Comparing now with the past we can expect even greater things from (God)..."

The Christian Far Eastern Broadcasting Corporation based in Manila and Hong Kong, under its able director Gordon Bell, had earlier launched a broadcast series of Bible instruction studies and readings delivered at dictation speed. They were now informed from their widespread sources inside China that these were being copied into exercise books where there was a shortage of Bibles.

As former missionaries were allowed to return to China for short visits – among them David Adeney of the China Inland Mission, Ruth Bell Graham the wife of Dr. Billy Graham, who was born of missionary parents in China, and later Billy Graham himself – reports of spreading Christian activities emerged from Mongolia and Tibet as well as other more populated regions. Attendances at churches ranged from the hundreds to the thousands. In one former China Inland Mission area, in a population of 400,000, Christians were said to number tens of thousands.

By 1980, according to Leslie Lyall, when Bishop Peter Hsieh of Fuzhou – whose predecessor had been tortured to death – completed a pastoral journey, he found "7,000 new Christians in seven remote mountain villages being taught by two elderly workers", and Christians throughout the whole province were known to number 600,000". In one area alone 6,000 new believers were baptised.

It was not only the Christian visitors and media who reported the extensive Christian presence in China. My sceptical journalist colleague in Hong Kong, Richard Hughes of the London *Times*, (3 July, 1980) wrote:

"China is having a 'religious revolution – Christians and non-Christians' in the opinion of Professor Audrey Donnithorne, a member of the Economics Department of the Australian National University in Canberra and former director of the University's China centre, who has just completed a seven weeks' tour of the country...

"The almighty Mao is dead (she said), the Marxist supremacy of materialism has proved hollow, and the masses are searching for a spiritual outlet beyond the realms of politics and state'...

"For thirty years everything has been interpreted to the people in the temporal. Now there is a hunger for faith in the absolute beyond the grasp of the state..."

And TIME magazine, in an article entitled "Let A Hundred Churches Bloom", reported:

"Reports of Christianity's renewal are coming in from every province of China...Pastors and nuns freed from 'labour reform' camps, where many had been held for twenty years, are returning to their parishes...

"On the basis of 180 taped, in-depth interviews in China, Hong Kong's Chinese Church Research Center told TIME correspondent Bing Wang that there are five million Protestants in the more than 50,000 'house churches' that kept functioning during the Cultural Revolution and became the mainstream of Chinese Christianity...The underground services fostered a truly indigenous form of religion that has finally freed Chinese Christianity from the control of foreign missionaries and this has strengthened its appeal to xenophobic Chinese".

Shortly afterwards a booklet entitled *Households of God on China's Soil* was published by the World Council of Churches, Geneva. In the Preface the well-informed Raymond W.M. Fung described the conclusions gathered in Hong Kong from the representatives of 14 Christian communities in China:

"By October 1980 our pilgrimage had taken us to encounters with 42 grassroots Christian communities in China, spread over eleven provinces...(and)...we discovered that one of the 42 cases we studied considers itself to be part of a huge fellowship of some 400 Christian communities in three southern provinces...

"Perhaps the single most obvious conclusion about Christianity in China today is that it is Chinese. People in the streets and communes no longer see Christianity in China as a foreign religion...Now, after some 25 years of isolation and eight years of acute suffering, with zero visibility, the church is seen to have survived and grown. *For the first time in its history, the church has now won its right to exist in China as a Chinese church. For the first time in its existence it has its roots in Chinese soil*...and this is how Chinese people look at Christianity today...Confessional and denominational claims have lost their binding power in China..." (my italics).

To the north of Fujiang Province, in Zhejiang, another stronghold of the "Little Flock", it was claimed that in many outlying regions one in three of the population had become Christians. On one occasion 500 church leaders attended a retreat to compile a discipleship manual to help instruct the huge numbers of new converts. In some rural areas over 90 per cent of the population were Christian. Leslie Lyall writes: "...One semi-official estimate is that in

Zhejiang alone there may be as many as five million Christians".

Shanghai is said to have over one million Christians, and during the Christmas period in 1982 over 4,000 house groups gathered for special meetings, in addition to those being held in "open churches" (that is, those associated with the Government-approved Three Self Patriotic Movement).

Similar reports emerged from Henan Province in the interior. With a population of over 70 million it is claimed that in recent years some 3,000 baptisms took place *every day of the year,* most of these young people, and that there could be as many as ten million Christians in the province.

A China-watching colleague of mine in Hong Kong received a letter from a Chinese friend in Henan who spent all his time travelling and preaching throughout Henan. He stated:

"...In (place-name deleted) there are over 100,000 believers in just a few counties. In the whole province there are dozens of Christians on the run who cannot return home. They live a peripatetic life constantly on the move...I myself was in prison doing reform through labour for 23 years, but I never wept. But when I saw the old mothers, the wives, and the children whose sons and husbands had been imprisoned for the Lord's sake, I could not control my emotions...During the day I travelled. In the evening I held meetings...In the whole province there are many people who wish to serve God full-time, more than ten thousand people. But I only saw about a twentieth of the Christians..."*

Another Hong Kong based, China-watching missionary, Paul Kauffman, founder-director of *Asian Outreach,* reports many interviews with Christians from mainland China and

* Published in *Research Paper: No. 3,* by Christian Communications, PO Box 95364, Hong Kong.

refugees in Hong Kong. He states that there are literally innumerable gatherings of Christians from small household meetings to "50,000 Christians meeting regularly in a city of 400,000 people".

Obviously the Marxists authorities in Peking were in a quandary. They could not afford to have a dynamic Christianity expanding on such a scale outside of their control. For a time they tried to deny its existence by quoting only The Three Self Patriotic Movement churches' statistics as their countering propaganda.

For example, when Mother Theresa visited China she met with the Government-approved Chairman of the Patriotic Catholic Association, Bishop Zong Huade. He informed her that there were over 3 million Catholics in China, 44 Bishops, 1,200 priests, 600 large and more than 1,000 small churches, and seven seminaries.

These figures, and the ones quoted by all officially approved Chinese church representatives, were all ridiculously inadequate, compiled by accredited Party members to satisfy Party propaganda purposes. The Party leaders themselves did not believe the sycophantic Christian leaders.

The political leadership in Peking had little confidence in the doctored statistics and limited knowledge of the Three Self Patriotic Movement. This was evident in one remarkable incident involving their favourite religious puppet, Bishop K.H. Ting, head of the China Christian Council and the Three Self Patriotic Movement. He led a delegation of Chinese Christians on "a fraternal visit to Europe and Africa in the autumn of 1982 as a sign of the new 'religious open doors' policy" He represented the official Party line as:

"There has been a return to the policy of religious freedom. The work of the church is developing at a good pace. At least 1,600 churches are open to Protestants meeting in houses for worship. 1,300,000 Bibles have been printed and distributed..."

He went on to point out that the Church in China had increased from 700,000 in 1949 to about 3 million at the present time, and that new seminaries were being opened in several provinces to accommodate the increased demand. He refuted reports of Christians being imprisoned as "base propaganda", and claimed that anybody in prison was there for a "criminal offence".

While in Europe Bishop Ting was questioned regarding an ambitious evangelical Christian project., launched by a Hong Kong Chinese Christian businessman, Heile Lee. Mr Lee had set up a Christian organisation in Hong Kong called the "Jin Hua Foundation" devoted to the advancement of education, science, health, and social welfare in mainland China, and to "the promotion of cultural exchanges between China and other countries". On 21 December, 1981, an agreement for the construction of a US$10 million, 5-10,000 square feet International Cultural Exchange Centre of China, located in the embassy district of Peking, was signed in the Great Hall of the People, with the Minister of Culture, and former ambassador to the USA, Mr Huang Zhen, presiding.

During his visit to Europe Bishop Ting was asked about this intriguing evangelical Christian project, apparently blessed by the leading Communist authorities, and he unexpectedly exploded into an intemperate denunciation. He claimed that the Jin Hua Foundation project and claims were fraudulent and untrue, and that he would see that they were officially repudiated when he returned to China. The quisling Bishop had had time enough to do this since his return but has been conspicuously silent and supposedly unsuccessful. Significantly, the Peking authorities have not supported him, or the Three Self Patriotic Movement, in the matter; and, to the contrary, gave considerable encouragement to Heile Lee and his associates in the Christian venture.

In 1982 a new Constitution was launched, in which Article 35 was directed towards religion, Clauses 2-4 declaring:

"Citizens of the Republic of China enjoy freedom of religious belief.

"No organs of state public organisations or individuals shall compel citizens to believe in religion or disbelieve in religion, nor shall they discriminate against citizens who believe or disbelieve in religion and to propagate atheism.

"The State protects legitimate religious activities. No-one may use religion to carry out counter-revolutionary activities, or activities that disrupt public order, harm the health of citizens, or obstruct the educational system of the State.

"No religious affairs, may be dominated by any foreign country".

About the same time the Central Committee distributed a supporting explanatory document entitled "Concerning Our Country's Basic Standpoint and Policy on Religious Questions During The Socialist Period". Clause 5 declared:

"In the whole country there are now about 59,000 religious workers of every kind. These include about 27,000 or more Buddhist monks, nuns and lamas; 2,600 or more Taoist monks and nuns; 20,000 or more Muslim professional religious workers; 3,400 or more professional Catholic workers; and about 5,900 or more Protestant pastoral workers. Through many years of natural wastage, the present number of professional religious workers is much less than at Liberation...At Liberation, across the country there was a total of over 100,000 places of religious activity. Now, if one adds together churches, temples, simple meeting-places, set up by the believers themselves, there are more than 30,000..."

It was unmitigated propagandistic rubbish, of course, and was only a political cover for the real fear of the spreading Christian influence affecting their own Party members. This was evident from the document itself, which went on to warn Communist Party members that *"the policy of freedom of religious belief is only for ordinary citizens, and not for Party members. A Party member differs from an ordinary citizen and is a member of a Marxist political Party"*. (my italics). It also emphasised: "We should maintain a high vigilance, and a close look-out, on the underground churches and other illegal organisations...We should resolutely crack down on them..."

It was not just Christians who came under hard-line Marxist pressure but also the intellectuals, or "bourgeois intellectuals" as Mao scathingly called them because of their "liberalist ideologies". Following the "Hundred Flowers Bloom" fiasco, Mao had put Deng Xiaoping on to the task of eliminating their influence throughout the country. In Deng's campaign one million intellectuals – a category that included not only social scientists, humanities workers, writers and artists, but hard-core scientists as well – were publicly humiliated and then consigned to oblivion for the next two decades.

In 1983 Deng launched a clamp-down on crime, which he concluded was caused by his policy of opening up China to Western economic interests. He called on neighbourhood committees to assist him in his policies by searching out culprits. One deputy director of Public Security in Shanghai was reported as saying that 35,000 people, including neighbourhood committees and relatives of offenders, had formed more than one thousand groups to persuade young people away from a life of crime. According to the Public Security Ministry, over 70,000 offenders were handed over to their neighbours in the first year of the campaign. Some foreign observers estimated that, in the first two years of the campaign, as many as 10,000 criminals were executed, usually by the standard method of a bullet in the back of the head. Amnesty International reported five thousand dead in the first year.

While the official statistics of Catholic and Protestant

religious activities were ludicrously low by reported Chinese Christian estimate, they were still a surprising official admission of the widening spread of Christian beliefs and practices over the previous decade. The figure of "more than 30,000 meeting-places set up by the believers themselves" (in view of the omnipresent snooping neighbourhood committees) indicated a very high proliferation of what were known as "official" house-churches, because all others not registered with the Three Self Patriotic Movement were categorised as "unofficial".

In April, 1984, an "Open Letter to Brothers and Sisters Overseas" from "The Suffering Mainland House-Churches" was smuggled into Hong Kong for world-wide distribution. The Foreword stated:

"Two years ago, several Christians wrote an open letter to Christians abroad with the aim of explaining to overseas churches why for 30 years the Mainland house-churches have resolutely refused to attend the Three Self Patriotic Movement (TSPM)...We have discovered that in the last two years, with the increased activity overseas of the TSPM that there has begun to be a split in the attitude of the overseas Christians towards the mainland Church. Some still adhere to the principles of Biblical Truth and are not deceived by the TSPM propaganda and soft words, but still believe that the millions of suffering and oppressed house-church Christians are the main force for the gospel in China and are genuinely the church revealing the glory of Christ. But others cannot withstand the sugar-coated bullets of the TSPM and are unwilling to see through to the TSPM's real nature and its propaganda. For the future of the organisations, or for other personal reasons, they knowingly utter lies in accordance with TSPM's views, and say there is no longer any house-church movement in China, and only the church led by the TSPM is the true church of China, etc..."

As 1984 drew to a close the Chinese Communist Party

exploded a political bombshell. The official *People's Daily* of 8 December, in a front-page leading article, declared to an astounded world that many of the ideas of Marx and Lenin were out-dated, and accused the ideological specialists in the Communist leadership of "delaying progress": It continued:

"There were many things that Marx, Engels and Lenin did not experience or come into contact with. One cannot take a dogmatic attitude towards Marxism...to take some theories out of Marx's works in order to limit the richness of contemporary life can only impede the development of history".

The pronouncement raised a storm of debate inside and outside China, and the subsequent "clarification" only made matters worse. On 1 January, 1985, *Red Flag*, Communist China's leading theoretical journal, exhorted the Chinese people to stop seeking a magic remedy in the works of Mao and Marx, and to look instead at the "present realities". Both Mao and Marx were beacons of socialism, it continued, but Mao Zedung sometimes got it wrong and Karl Marx did not have all the answers. Marxism was a science, it declared, not a religion, and could not provide magic remedies. It concluded with a strong denunciation of the Mao slogan with which he justified his Cultural Revolution: "There can be no construction without destruction".

It was a long and humiliating retreat from the arrogance of the previous Marxist and Maoist slogans, with their confident assertions of changing human beings as well as social conditions. Analysing the spate of negative Marxist announcements from Peking, the China scholar, John Gittings, in an article in the *Guardian*, wrote:

"Post revolutionary countries like China, Vietnam and Cuba have followed the same pattern, painfully casting aside illusions about the possibilities of transformation...

"The real casualty has been the loss of confidence in the ability of human beings to transcend material limitations. It was natural at first to transpose the revolutionary ethic – where man was more important than weapons – to the new society, and to seek to infuse it with new Socialist ideals...

"Responsibility for the death of Mao's new Socialist person is a subject deserving much more attention than it has so far attracted. Was it just that Marxian theory was inadequate?...Or was it caused by the dictatorship of the Party masquerading as the dictatorship of the proletariat – for which we should blame Lenin?"

Deng Xiaoping's new open door policy of co-existing "two systems" – socialism and capitalism – in the economic interests of China meant embracing capitalism with great fervour, and for rapidly jettisoning former Marxist ideals. This quickly resulted in both civilian and military Party leaders indulging in blatant instances of corrupt and fraudulent practices on a large scale. On 4 March, 1985, NEWSWEEK magazine's Peking correspondent reported:

"Peking's recent burst of economic reform has unleashed a rash of white collar crimes that officials say is reaching 'epidemic proportions'.

"Corruption is hardly what Deng Xiaoping had in mind when he exhorted the masses to go out and get rich. But most of all his capitalist-style innovations have been followed inexorably by capitalist-style abuses. Since credit cards hit China in 1981 fraud has become so rampant that four card companies have requested temporary restrictions on their use. A new corporate income tax, levied last October, has given rise to widespread evasion. Blackmarketeers in foreign currency are flourishing from Peking to Canton. And the licensing of private businesses has fostered a cottage industry in under-the-table bribes..."

The worst offenders were mostly Party and Government officials, and even the former incorruptible People's Liberation Army indulged in large-scale illegal operations. In the Fushou Military region – the south-east coastal area so responsive to the sweeping Christian movement – the military units organised a huge multi-million dollar fraudulent scheme of some 180 companies illicitly trading in vehicles, television sets, cassette recorders, and other scarce items, in order to raise money for the livelihood and welfare of cadres and soldiers.

Writing in the London *Times* (21 January, 1985) Jonathan Mirsky concluded:

"Despite Deng's assurances that 'our ultimate goal is Communism' (no date offered) many Chinese must feel that Marxist-Leninist ideals, always uncertain as the Party veered about, have been jettisoned in favour of anything goes, or what Deng calls 'unhealthy tendencies'.

"A country of increasingly rich entrepreneurs bent on buying everything they have ever imagined, who ignore 100 million illiterate, badly clothed unfortunates existing on 1,500 calories a day, was not the vision of the young Deng Xiaoping in 1934 when he set out on the Long March..."

While Marxism in China was demonstrating its inherent inabilities to change either social conditions or human nature, the Christian spiritual revolution continued to make steady and even spectacular advances.

In mid-1988 a Chinese Christian evangelist, John Ting, visited the United States for a six months' preaching tour. I knew John Ting very well, whom I met when I first arrived in China and who joined up with my former missionary colleague, Geoff Bull, and me in the Tibetan border town of Kangting for a series of evangelistic meetings in 1947. I was already in Kangting at that time when John travelled up from Chengtu in West China, a trip of ten days over rugged, bandit-infested mountains. At a certain time of the year, just when John was travelling, the trail became impassable because of rains and snow, and John was anxious to reach Kangting before we were shut off.

One part of the trail crossed a dry river-bed and passed through marshlands which, in the autumn, became a raging torrent and a deadly quagmire. When John, and the other non-Christian Chinese members of the group travelling with him, reached the river, it was rising rapidly and already uncrossable. The local guides, whose job was to take travellers safely across the marshlands, refused to escort the group because it was too dangerous.

John calmly told his fellow-travellers that God had sent him to preach in Kangting and that he was going to ask God to hold back the river, like Moses with the Red Sea, and then guide them safely through the quagmire. He prayed, took a baby from one of the women travellers, and stepped forward. The river dramatically dropped in front of them and they all walked forward. At the other side John stepped forward confidently on to the sodden expanse of unmarked quagmire, with the fearful companions walking in single file behind him, and he took them safely through and on into Kangting. In the evangelistic meetings which followed in the notoriously wicked border town hundreds were converted through John's preaching, several of them his fellow-travellers.

The Communists, when they came to power, put John Ting in prison for over twenty years, subjecting him to horrendous treatment by hard labour as they tried to break his Christian faith. He was made to carry a daily load of bricks and cement weighing seventy pounds, and when for any reason his quota in any single day was not fulfilled it was carried forward to the next day. When he fell from the roof on one occasion, he was seriously injured with a broken neck among other injuries. He was not taken to hospital, and he was left to recover as best as he could. Miraculously, he did survive, but with a permanent weakness of the neck leaving him unable to hold his head upright.

John was eventually released in the open period in early 1980. Since his release from imprisonment John had been instrumental in establishing a group of over 800 churches in West China.

In April 1988 Billy Graham visited China, and a great deal of publicity was given to his visit. But what was not publicised was the restriction placed on Chinese seeking to make known the true conditions of continuing persecution of Christians inside China to the visitors. Dr Jonathan Chao, of the China Christian Research Centre in Hong Kong, issued a press statement regarding one well-known house-church leader in Hunan Province in central China, who in only eight years had expanded his church into over 3,000 churches. Xu Yongze was going to hear Billy Graham preach, but he had also arranged through a mutual friend to speak with Billy Graham privately, in company with several other well-known house-church leaders. Xu was arrested on his arrival in Peking by members of the Ministry of State Security.

Two days after Xu's arrest, one of the seminaries of his church group was raided and taken over by the local Public Security. Six of his students were reportedly taken into police custody. Nothing more was heard of Xu despite attempts to get information regarding his detention.

In December, 1988, in Shanghai, an important conference was convened in which Bishop K. H. Ting, the chairman of both the TSPM and the China Christian Council, unexpectedly and startlingly proposed that the organisation be disbanded. In making this proposal to the delegates he said: "Christians are ill at ease that the position of Christ as Head of the Church has been taken away. The idea that 'the TSPM leads the Church', or 'the Church is a religious organisation run by the Religious Affairs Bureau' is grating to the ears of Christians. From now on we must run the Church in accordance with the Bible and God's will".

Commenting on this radical development Anthony Lambert, the well-informed head of the Christian Communications research centre of the Overseas Missionary Fellowship in Hong Kong (he was formerly a diplomat in the British embassy in Peking before resigning to become a missionary), stated:

"It is unlikely that the TSPM would discuss its own abolition without prompting from higher Party and government leaders. There is documentary evidence that high Party officials have been dissatisfied with the inability of the TSPM to rally all of China's Christians to support Party policies. The TSPM was deeply implicated in the repressive campaigns against Chinese Christian leaders in the nineteen-fifties, and in recent years most evangelical Christians have preferred to worship independently of the TSPM in house-churches...More liberal elements in the government may be pushing for further liberalisation of religious policy, which suffered a set-back when Party general Secretary Yaobang fell from power in January 1987...A Christian source in Beijing warned that the abolition of the TSPM might mean its replacement with something even worse..."

This ambivalence in the religious arena reflected the increasing confusion in political developments as the mounting public pressure for economic and political change was opposed by the hard-line geriatric conservatives in the Communist leadership. But with over half of China's population being under twenty-five years of age it was inevitable that the ageing leaders represented only a temporary immovable block to an increasingly irresistible force.

The inevitable national crisis erupted in 1989. The apparent cause was both the accumulation of pressures due to non-performance of Marxist policies and the blatant nepotism and corruption of the Party leadership – including Deng Xiaoping. From the universities established by Christians – and traditionally the centres of protest and revolution in China – the students launched a series of demonstrations in the spring of 1989, which rapidly escalated into mass public protests, with hundreds of thousands of students and workers of all kinds carrying banners demanding "democracy" and "justice".

But when asked to define what they meant by "democracy" even the most intelligent of the students were inarticulate. Positively, they wanted "equality of opportunity", "rightness of actions", "unprejudiced legal decisions", "better social conditions"; negatively, they wanted "less corruption", "less nepotism among Party and government officials", "fewer empty slogans". Significantly, however, almost all wanted to have more material possessions – to be like Hong Kong, or Taiwan or the United States. It seemed they had been fired by Maoist visions of a utopian society, where spiritual values of concern for neighbours was the supreme goal – but, first, they wanted to be rich like their Marxist leaders.

It still is not known whether there were Christians among the student protest leaders in Tienanmen Square, but it is known that the China Christian Council came out in support of them. During the protests Bishop Ting declared unequivocal TSPM support – for the first time not conforming to the Communist Party line. In Hong Kong Christian circles it was reported that he had asked them to "ask Christians around the world to continue to remember us in their prayers".

There were certainly Christians among the lower-level student demonstrators. One who was deeply involved said: "Last night our group studied Romans chapter 13. We concluded that, since our government is no longer 'a terror to those who do wrong', but the very opposite of what God designed – namely, a terror to those who do right – we no longer owe any allegiance to the present government of China". He claimed that he, and some twenty companions, had taken a vow to "use any possible means short of physical violence to bring down the government",

The Christian Far Eastern Broadcasting Corporation conducted regular ten-minute news bulletins, six times a day, plus a "Student Movement Special" chronicling the students' campaign. Inside China, some twenty thousand foreign Christian professionals in officially permitted posts – doctors, nurses, teachers, engineers, etc – refused to leave the country.

For weeks the elderly leaders were paralysed in the face of such huge peaceful protests, then on Friday, 2 June, the Party's central Advisory Commission met in emergency session. Led by the 84-year old chairman, Chen Yun, the aged veteran of the long March declared:

"We must never make concessions. Not only is there a danger of losing the achievements of ten years of reform, but there is also the danger of losing all the fruits of the revolution and all the achievements of socialist construction".

A few days earlier, on 30 May, the Party leaders had been enraged when, in full sight of the world's television cameras, the students set up a 30-foot-tall white plaster statue, naming her "Goddess of Democracy". The statue was placed on the spot where the father of China's revolution, Sun Yat Sen, had his portrait displayed on national holidays. It also faced the portrait of Mao.

At midnight on Saturday 3 June, the People's Liberation Army was ordered to attack the students and clear Tienanmen Square, and "Bloody Sunday" began. The People's Liberation Army mercilessly put down the demonstrations in a savage display of force while the world watched by live television transmission. Its bloody advance along Changan Avenue leading to Tienanmen Square caused it to be re-named "Blood Boulevard". Hundreds – some said thousands – were brutally massacred by the ruthless soldiers, and thousands more were arrested and imprisoned.

It was the first time in Communist China's forty years that the PLA had turned on the Chinese people – not just with tear gas and clubs, but with tanks and murderous bullets. Following on the PLA massacre the authorities announced the arrest of some 3,000 people across China, and twenty-seven executions since the demonstrations. But independent observers put the figures as nearer 10-30,000 arrests, and over a hundred executions.

In the aftermath of the "Bloody Sunday" massacre, and the subsequent hard-line witch-hunting of the angry and fearful ageing leadership, there is a continuing climate of sullen and simmering resentment in the key university centres of Peking in the north, Canton in the south, and Chengtu in the west. The students are showing a determination to wait for the deaths of the eighty-year-old power-drunk Marxists of the Long March, and have a quiet confidence in their ultimate triumph.

Although they are not against the Communist Party as such there is a demonstrable contempt for its personnel and policies. This is being exacerbated by the current paranoid searches for "wrong thinkers" among the 47 million or so Party members. According to figures published in 1988 by the official Chinese media only a quarter of the Party members were educated to senior high school leavers or above. About 25 million were mostly peasants and low-level functionaries in the countryside, and of these about half had only primary school education, while 3.5 million were illiterate. This is "the vanguard of the proletariat", the representative "Party of the people of China". It is no longer taken seriously by China's students and intellectuals. It is finished.

Against this dramatic background of declining and dying Marxism it is a startling surprise to calculate the figures of a dynamic Christianity. After as close an investigation as it is possible to make in the existing circumstances in China the reputable Christian research groups conclude that *there are now at least 40-50 million Christians in China.* Some other church organisations put the figure much higher.

This figure of some 50 million active Christians exceeds not only in quantity the active membership of the Communist Party, but also in quality. What is beyond dispute is that any breakdown of the Christian church membership shows that they far excel in intelligence and influence the dull and apathetic peasant-based masses of the Communist Party.

So, after forty years of absolute power, total thought control, ruthless persecution, imprisonment, intimidation and death sentences, Marxism is seen to have failed in China and is in its terminal death throes. While the despised and harassed Christians have emerged triumphantly from their living hell of persecution with their Gospel of Jesus Christ more effective and attractive than it has ever been.

They are a first century-type Spiritual Body – a living *ecclesia* of believers such as Paul of Tarsus taught – with Christ alone as head, and spiritual men and leaders. It not only holds immense encouragement for the oppressed and exploited people of China; it demonstrates vast promise and challenge to a world grown weary and disillusioned with the sterile ecclesiastical institutions and their apathetic pew-filling "Christers" rather than discipled Christians.

Their Marxist enemies have taught the Chinese Christians how to analyse, criticise, struggle and organise for transformation of individuals and circumstances. They have been taught to reason logically, to debate in public, to use the well-honed weapons of praxis and dialectic in houses and streets and communes and work places and offices.

The women have learned to throw off the cultural inhibitions of centuries, and to participate in discussions and activities as equals with men.

Above all, the Christians in China have learned from their own Marxist leaders that Marx does not work in China's twentieth century society; and they have learned from their own experience that Jesus Christ does. They are equipped to conquer China. They are equipped to conquer the world.

"This", said the Apostle John, "is the victory that overcomes the world, even our faith".

And the Apostle Paul, who fought a similar solitary, apparently hopeless, battle against a ruthless Roman Empire totalitarian leadership in the first century, said:

"Though we live in the world, we do not wage war as the world does. The weapons we fight with are not the weapons of the world. On the contrary, they have the divine power to demolish strongholds. We demolish arguments and every pretension that sets itself against the knowledge of God. And we take captive every thought to make it obedient to Christ".

THE POWER FACTOR
The key to conquering addiction
George & Meg Patterson

addiction (ədĭk'shən), *n.* the state of being addicted to some habit, practice or substance.

CAN YOU BE SET FREE? IS THERE AN ANSWER?
What you want, what you need, is – POWER. Power to break the habit or practice. Power to deal with the problems that drove you to them in the first place. Power to heal the broken relationships with your family. Power to do something constructive in society. Power to change "the sorry scheme of things entire, and mould it nearer to our hearts desire". Power to know and love the worthy God.

IS THERE SUCH A POWER? WHERE IS IT TO BE FOUND?
HOW CAN IT BE OBTAINED? HOW CAN YOU BE SET FREE?
The answers to these and many more questions are what *THE POWER FACTOR* is all about.

This book is an attempt to make a wider contribution to the solutions necessary in making, *not* just addicts, but a sick society, whole in body, mind *and spirit.*